PSYCHOLOGY RESEARCH PROGRESS

PSYCHOANALYSIS

PERSPECTIVES, TECHNIQUES AND SOCIO-PSYCHOLOGICAL IMPLICATIONS

PSYCHOLOGY RESEARCH PROGRESS

Additional books in this series can be found on Nova's website
under the Series tab.

Additional e-books in this series can be found on Nova's website
under the e-book tab.

PSYCHOLOGY RESEARCH PROGRESS

PSYCHOANALYSIS

PERSPECTIVES, TECHNIQUES AND SOCIO-PSYCHOLOGICAL IMPLICATIONS

ZELDA GILLIAN KNIGHT
EDITOR

nova publishers
New York

Library of Congress Cataloging-in-Publication Data

Names: Knight, Zelda Gillian, editor.
Title: Psychoanalysis : perspectives, techniques and socio-psychological implications / editor, Zelda Gillian Knight.
Other titles: Psychoanalysis (Nova Science Publishers)
Description: Hauppauge, New York : Nova Science Publishers, Inc., [2015] | Series: Psychology research progress | Includes index.
Identifiers: LCCN 2015035124 | ISBN 9781634838580 (hardcover)
Subjects: LCSH: Psychoanalysis.
Classification: LCC BF173 .P77625 2015 | DDC 150.19/5--dc23 LC record available at http://lccn.loc.gov/2015035124

Published by Nova Science Publishers, Inc. † New York

CONTENTS

PREFACE

Psychoanalysis, as an ever increasing conceptual framework that views the world through a specific analytic lens that explores and hermeneutically gives meaning to human motivation and behaviour, has continued to evolve over the past century. Its founder, Sigmund Freud, perhaps one of the greatest European thinkers of the twentieth century, sought to understand his patients' suffering. His remarkable ability to ground his experience as an analyst in developing a theory of mind meant that he was a superb researcher-practitioner and, in a sense, a phenomenologist; his overarching aim was always to grasp the essence of his patients' experience and hermeneutically make some sense of it. His method of meaning-making may have been cause for much criticism later, but his meticulous work with troubled patients is legendary.

At first, Freud's psycho-analysis was conceived of to be a single, unitary theory of the mind, but over the last three decades there has been dramatic theoretical changes in theory, often described as paradigmatic shifts, resulting in a new landscape of contemporary psychoanalysis that now features pluralism of models which have mushrooms into significantly different conceptualisations of human experience. The idea of self, the core unit of analysis in psychoanalysis, emerged to be conceived as existing only in relation to the real other, the inter-play between self-other, and all that lies between.

The sense of self and thus human experience in general has evolved into a dynamic shift towards the notion of intersubjectivity, or 'two person psychology.' This is similar to Heidegger's renowned idea of 'being-in-the-world,' which designates the intertwined connection and reciprocal nature between self and the world. Both self and world/other co-create each other and equally offer meaning to all forms of experience. The Freudian perspective, founded on the ideology of positivism and reductionism, failed to fully grasp the self-other concept as co-constitutive, and with the emergence of postmodernist thought, the understanding of human experience has stretched out its theoretical horizons to view experience as not only embedded in a self-other context, but also embodied. Today, we speak of self-realization, personality strengths, and well-being as much as psychopathology and suffering.

In this book, the chapters explore a wide spectrum of perspectives, techniques and socio-psychological issues. The chapter contents are introduced below.

Chapter One takes a close look at the concept of perversion using a Lacanian framework. The author argues that while Freud's conceptualisation of perversion was free of disapprobation, he argued that human sexuality is essentially founded on a polymorphously perverse disposition. Freud apparently struggled to make a distinction from this notion to a notion of sexual normality. In a climate of increasingly liberal attitudes to certain sexual practices, there is tendency and suspicion of positioning, and thus situating perversion as a clinical category from those with an interest in the creative and dissident potential of transgression. This chapter argues that homosexuality is a case in point: it is no longer criminalized or deemed a perversion. And yet, not all sexual practices can be categorized as either progressively transgressive or 'healthily' normal. This chapter explores and asks that pertinent question of "Can perversion be a category reserved for those who break the law, when the law is so frequently revised and subject to cultural and political revision?" In this chapter, the author addresses some questions about the complexities of the term 'perversion,' with reference to the history of psychoanalysis, the engagement of psychoanalysis and queer theory and published clinical case histories. In so-doing, this chapter will propose that Lacan's nosological framework provides a solution to this problematic concept.

Chapter Two starts with how psychoanalysis has traditionally conceived guilt as the product of superego stricture in response to the desire or intent to violate moral precepts. In this traditional view of guilt, the superego is the main psychic structure involved. While not disputing the importance of this form of guilt, the present paper adds a second form of guilt rooted in the nature of the self. Because self-realization and empathy are mutually dependent, the failure to recognize the other as a source of subjectivity (that is, to treat the other as an object) is reflective of a weakened self and, in turn, weakens the self still further. This objectified treatment of the other results in guilt, although there may be no unethical intent. If the self is derailed in the developmental process, the child cannot see the other as a subject and objectifies the other in an effort to use people as manipulable things. Guilt rooted in the objectification of the other is often mistaken for guilt resulting from destructive intent, because analysts tend to assume that all guilt is due to the desire or intent to violate moral precepts. The clinical importance of understanding guilt due to objectification of the other is demonstrated in the analysis of two cases.

Chapter Three begins by the assertion that psychoanalysis passed its heyday in the seventies and has been usurped by short term cognitive behavioural therapies. However, this chapter involves the countering of this trend, and claims that in the past two decades there has been a small, but significant, growth of psychoanalytic psychotherapy in Aotearoa, New Zealand. This chapter describes the author's experience of using a psychoanalytic sensibility when teaching and supervising intern counselling psychologists in a mental health and university system, which is subtly dominated by a cognitive behavioural worldview. The author outlines the differences between the cognitive behavioural and psychoanalytic therapeutic styles, and presents a few examples to illustrate the systemic foreclosure of potential space, meaningful symbol formation, and the development and understanding of the therapeutic relationship and transference-countertransference matrix. The author describes the implications of using behavioural techniques and homework assignments as being viewed from a psychoanalytic perspective. Supervision vignettes are then presented to illustrate how the author attempted to open the space and introduce psychoanalytic sensibility in supervision. A foray into his supervisory and systemic countertransference is presented, followed by some of his thoughts on supervising different styles of breaks and endings in therapy.

Chapter Four deals with a core question: "What is the precise relationship between loss and trauma?" Access to interviews with survivors of the Holocaust allows the author to argue that traumatic loss has the quality of an intrusion, and in this regard is similar to psychic trauma associated with less dramatic and total losses. The author claims that, unlike those who recover from trauma with the help of therapy, most Holocaust survivors recovered through the process of doubling, a practice originally suggested by one of the founders of trauma theory, Sándor Ferenczi. The author makes the claim that the practice is not without its costs, particularly among older survivors.

Chapter Five pays attention to the problems that arise if the social unconscious is defined as a generalization of parts of the individual dynamic unconscious. In so-doing, the author presents a discussion which results in the insight that the contents of the social unconscious is not mental but social in nature, and that the social unconscious stands in opposition not to a generalized individual consciousness, but to social consciousness. Subsequently, the author argues that the social unconscious appears in social consciousness in mystified form in the same way as the individual unconscious in individual consciousness. The domain of analytic social psychology is defined and used so as to bring about this understanding.

Chapter Six has made use of Attachment theory to understand the dynamics of the real relationship in psychoanalytic supervision. It is suggested that the concept of the corrective emotional experience, as first suggested by Alexander and French (1946) can be linked to the real relationship in supervision. This sets up the idea that Attachment theory can be linked to the concept of the 'corrective emotional experience' and this is linked, in turn, to the real relationship in supervision. A case vignette is presented to illustrate these thoughts.

Chapter Seven sees the therapeutic relationship as a potentially difficult process to navigate, especially when there is communication being projected through the unsaid or unconscious processes in the room. The therapist is tasked with being able to pick up on the unsaid through the experienced countertransference that is either explicit or implicit. Being able to decipher the communication and how the therapist works with the experienced countertransference is important, as this often impacts on the therapy process. The therapy can either flourish or terminate prematurely. In presenting a case study of such an experience, I explore the concepts of countertransference, enactment and the therapeutic relationship in relation to a particular patient who struggled to engage with her own needs and my struggle of not being heard by the patient.

Chapter Eight seeks to articulate the logic implied in the donations of engenderment material (semen, eggs and embryos), practiced in the field of the new reproductive technologies (NRT), with the system of exchanges of some archaic societies described by Marcel Mauss in his famous article 'The Gift: Forms and Functions of Exchange in Archaic Societies' (1924/1967). The authors also discuss three important interpreters of this essay – Lévi-Strauss, Maurice Godelier and George Bataille – so as to present some interesting thoughts about the consequences that NRT poses to psychoanalysis, and vice versa.

Zelda G. Knight, PhD

In: Psychoanalysis
Editor: Zelda Gillian Knight

ISBN: 978-1-63483-858-0

Chapter 1

PERVERSION TODAY: A LACANIAN PERSPECTIVE

Anne Worthington**, *PhD
Centre for Psychoanalysis, Middlesex University, London, UK

ABSTRACT

While Freud's conceptualisation of perversion was free of disapprobation, as he argued in the Three Essays on the Theory of Sexuality (1905) that human sexuality is founded on a polymorphously perverse disposition, he struggles to make a distinction from a notion of sexual normality. In a climate of increasingly liberal attitudes to certain sexual practices, there is suspicion of situating perversion as a clinical category, from those with an interest in the creative and dissident potential of transgression. Homosexuality is a case in point: no longer criminalized or deemed a perversion. And yet not all sexual practices can be categorized as either progressively transgressive or 'healthily' normal. Can perversion be a category reserved for those who break the law, when the law is so frequently revised and subject to cultural and political revision? My chapter will address some questions about the complexities of the term, perversion, with reference to the history of psychoanalysis, the engagement of psychoanalysis and queer theory and published clinical case histories and will propose that Lacan's nosological framework provides a solution to this problematic concept.

Keywords: perversion, Freud, Lacan, queer, transgression, fetishism, disavowal

INTRODUCTION

Here, then, are factors which provide a point of contact between the perversions and normal life … Perversions are sexual activities which either (a) *extend*, in an anatomical sense, beyond the regions of the body that are designed for sexual union, or (b) *linger*

* Corresponding author: Anne Worthington, PhD. Centre for Psychoanalysis, Middlesex University, The Burroughs, Hendon, London, NW4 4BT. E-mail: A.Worthington@mdx.ac.uk.

> over the intermediate relations to the sexual object which should normally be traversed rapidly on the path towards the final sexual aim.
>
> Freud, 1905, p. 150

> What is perversion? It is not simply an aberration in relation to social criteria, an anomaly contrary to good morals, although this register is not absent, nor is it an atypicality according to natural criteria, namely that it more of less derogates from the reproductive finality of the sexual union. It is something else in its very structure.
>
> Lacan, 1953-4, p. 221

Freud's understanding of perversion in 1905 can be read to imply that it encompasses any deviation from heterosexual genital intercourse, but this definition is undermined by his conceptualisation of human sexuality as unstable and underpinned by a polymorphous perversity as well as by his refusal to pathologise homosexuality[1].

Perversion is a central constituent of Freud's work. If we took him at his word, perversion would need no explanation because, for Freud, the sexual drive is neither unified nor aimed at genital copulation and reproduction (Freud 1905, p. 191). Polymorphous perversity is the root of sex and sexuality. As oft repeated in the *Three Essays,* it is 'normality' that is in need of psychoanalytic investigation.

Nevertheless there is a hesitancy in his approach to perversion as a discreet diagnostic category. His work is littered with references to the 'normal' – whether in aim or object, to the 'majority' of cases, and to words such as 'usually' and 'generally' when he writes about sexuality and sexual difference. Perhaps it is this hesitancy that has contributed to the instability of the term perversion within psychoanalysis, and that results in perversion being a site of contestation for psychoanalysts and their critics.

The concept of perversion has been of particular interest to queer theorists and it has provided a useful locus for engagement with psychoanalysis. In the same way that definitions of the psychoanalytic project are numerous, reflecting the different schools of psychoanalysis, giving particular weight to preferred theoretical constructions, so are those of queer theory. Indeed, it is frequently said that queer theory resists and undermines the very notion of definition, nevertheless, its project could be said to aim at transgressing, transcending and opposing a hetero-normalising hegemony. Queer theory has informed the exploration of perversion as creative and transformative and oppositional to that hegemony. Notwithstanding this approach, there are examples within the literature from those psycho-clinicians who are informed by queer theory, would seem to propose a new normality, new ideals and an imperative to a new conformity. On the other hand, where queer theorists have engaged with Lacanian psychoanlysis, there has been a recognition of its anti-normative potential. Lacan resolves the hesitancy that can be read in Freud, conclusively defining perversion as a clinical category. In this chapter, I will elaborate Lacan's definition which situates perversion as one of three ontological diagnostic structures that describe how the subject resolves the difficulties of being human. How do we understand, make meaning - what is our relation to knowledge? How do we enjoy or, to put it another way, how is the body's libido anchored? (Leader 2011, p. 66-7). For Lacan, a diagnosis of a perverse structure is not dependent on the presence of sexual transgression.

[1] Psychogenesis, 1920; Letter to American Mother, 1935 and elsewhere.

This chapter attempts to investigate the problematics of perversion from Freud to Lacan via queer theory.

FREUD

Freud was alert to the problematics of the category, the diagnosis of perversion, returning to the question 'what is normal in the field of human sexuality?' throughout his work. 'In the sphere of sexual life we are brought up against peculiar and indeed, insoluble difficulties as soon as we try to draw a sharp line to distinguish mere variations within the range of what is physiological from pathological symptoms' (Freud 1905, p. 160).

While Freud was not the first to study the sexual perversions, his originality was that he used the existence of the perversions as a weapon to throw the traditional definition into question. He begins his study of sexuality in 1905 *Three Essays* with the study of the perversions, challenging the definition of human sexuality as being something that does not exist in childhood, develops in puberty and a manifestation of an irresistible attraction between the sexes, with the aim of penetrative sex and reproduction. The whole notion of heterosexual genital intercourse as the norm is disrupted by the idea of the polymorphous perversity of human sexuality, characterized by the absence of any pre-given natural order. All the various ways in which human subjects experience sexual pleasure are but variants of sexual life. Perversion of the *Three Essays* is defined as 'instances in which the sexual function has extended its limit in respect either to the part of the body concerned or to the sexual object chosen' (Freud 1905, p. 52). But even here with this straightforward definition, Freud challenges the received morality of the day by prefacing his definition with the injunction: 'we must learn to speak without indignation of what we call the sexual perversions' (ibid.). In his discussion of fetishism, an extension of both aim and object, Freud characterizes fetishism in general in terms of those cases 'in which the normal sexual object is replaced by another which bears some relation to it but is entirely unsuited to serve the normal sexual aim' (ibid., p. 153). Fetishism includes the overvaluation of the object, and the abandonment of the normal sexual aim (ibid.). But couldn't this be a definition of being in love? When we are in love, normally the object of love is overvalued along with everything associated with her or him. He continues 'The situation only becomes pathological when the longing for the fetish passes beyond the point of being merely a necessary condition attached to the sexual object and takes the place of the normal aim, and further, when the fetish becomes detached from a particular individual and becomes the sole sexual object. These are, indeed, the general conditions under which mere variations of the sexual instinct pass over into pathological aberrations' (ibid., p. 154). And later when 'a perversion has the characteristics of exclusiveness and fixation – then we shall usually be justified in regarding it as a pathological symptom' (ibid., p. 161).

But as Neu (1991) has pointed out this doesn't really work as once it is recognized that the drive/instinct is merely soldered to it object and that there are wide possibilities of variation in the choice of object, thus all choices become problematic. Freud makes this point when speaking of 'inversion' the 'exclusive sexual interest felt by men for women is also a problem and is not a self-evident fact based upon an attraction that is ultimately of a chemical nature.'

So if we apply the criteria of exclusivity and fixation, Neu argues, then an excessively strong commitment to heterosexuality could be seen as perverse (ibid., p. 185). Indeed, being in love with anyone must be situated in this definition of perversion.

According to Freud, psychoanalysis 'shows that it is by no means only at the cost of the so-called *normal* sexual instinct that these symptoms originate – at any rate such is not exclusively or mainly the case; they also give expression (by conversion) to instincts which would be described as perverse in the widest sense of the word if they could be expressed directly in phantasy and action without being diverted from consciousness. Thus symptoms are formed in part at the cost of abnormal sexuality; neuroses are, so to say, the negative of perversions. The sexual instinct … exhibits all the aberrations which we have studied as variations of normal, and as manifestations of abnormal, sexual life' (Freud 1905, p. 165).

This is a famous dictum of Freud's i.e., that the neuroses are 'the negative of perversions' but it is often interpreted the other way round as if Freud said that perversion is the negative of neurosis – treating perversion as the non-repressed manifestation of infantile sexuality and while repression is absent in perversion there is another psychic mechanism at play – disavowal (ibid.). And disavowal for Freud is a normal aspect of the development of sexual difference.

In 1923, Freud argues that children react to the discovery that not everyone has a penis with disavowal. 'They disavow the fact and believe that they do see a penis, all the same' (Freud 1923, pp. 143-4) in order to 'buy some time' to come to terms with castration. He posits that children believe that everyone – girls and women, including their mothers – has a penis. Through a developmental process, a series of transformations will be undergone. As children begin to theorise about the origin of babies, their theory of universal penis possession will be modified – firstly to remove the penis from 'unworthy women,' and then to remove it from their mother (ibid., p. 144). Prior to puberty, Freud argues there is no "femaleness." The distinction the child is able to make is between having a "*male genital* and *being castrated*" (ibid., p. 145; Freud's italics). Freud is signaling that there is a consequence of anatomical difference. In doing so he is also resolving the difficulty at the heart of the *Three Essays* that prevented the achievement of his stated aim to keep psychoanalytic explanations distinct from biological ones. Sexual difference now becomes a psychic operation, rather than a biological or anatomical fact. Later in the child's development, at puberty the "sexual polarity" will no longer be that of active/passive, having a penis/castration, but 'will *coincide* with male and female' (ibid., p. 145, my italics). The notion that this is coincident evokes the coincidental, and the fragility of the process is implied.

Freud traces a chain of experience, fantasy and association that suggests how a foot might come to provide reassurance about castration fears and so become the focus for sex.

In 1927, Freud elaborates the notion that disavowal is the specific mechanism in perversion. He argues that the fetish object is a substitute for the mother's penis that the "little boy" (Freud is not discussing fetishism in women) 'once believed in and … does not want to give up' (Freud 1927, pp. 152-3). But it is not that the boy maintains his belief that his mother has a penis, rather 'he has retained that belief, but he has also given it up (ibid., p. 154). Because the female genital, the 'inferior organs' (ibid., p. 157), signifies the threat of castration, the nascent fetishist boy needs to find a substitute – whether a foot or shoe, piece of velvet or underwear. Furthermore, the substitution of a fetish object representing the female phallus for the castrated female genital functions to 'save the fetishist from becoming a homosexual' (ibid., p. 154).

Freud's argument that the male fetishist is heterosexual is a curious one. The woman can only become a 'tolerable sexual object' (ibid.) for the male fetishist if she has a penis, the sign of masculinity. Arguably then, the male fetishist is homosexual in that his sexual object is masculine, the one that has a penis. The fetish can be interpreted as a manifestation of a homosexual object-choice that 'all human beings have in fact made in their unconscious' (Freud 1905, p. 145). The specificity of the category of perversion – even in the example of fetishism – is problematic for Freud.

In two papers published posthumously, Freud, while not specifically discussing perversion, returns to the problem of the splitting of the ego, which takes place by the mechanism of disavowal. He makes a case for the universality of disavowal. Take for example, mourning. In her account of the year after her husband's death, Joan Didion describes how she knows that her husband has died, but still keeps hold of his slippers – just in case he will need them (Didion 2005). For Freud, whether in terms of "ordinary" childhood development or in the production of a fetish, there is a division between reality and the ego, and between the different agencies – i.e., the ego and the id. In both *The Splitting of the Ego in the Process of Defence* and in *Outline* Freud argues that there is a possibility of disavowal of castration in non-fetishists, as at the heart of the ego there are two psychical attitudes towards external reality in so far as this stands in the way of an instinctual demand. The first of these attitudes takes reality into consideration, while the second disavows it and replaces it by a product of desire. Fetishism is then not an exception, but just a very good example of the rule, that the human subject is structured by a conflict – which in Freudian terms – is a conflict between the demand of the id and the attitude of the ego, between the drive and reality. Thus by 1940 not only has the specificity of fetishism been undermined, but the whole category of perversion.

Queer

Queer theory is a relatively recent, predominantly Anglo-American phenomena. It is too heterogeneous and variously defined to be reduced to a single orthodoxy, nevertheless psychoanalysis and queer theory can be seen as sharing a common area of inquiry. Both disciplines are concerned with the nature of human subjectivity, sexuality and with love. Both disciplines, from their very origins, investigate perversion. Queer theory and indeed queer activism has roots in a dis-satisfaction with "identity politics," and with an assumption of heterogeneity that underpinned demands for equality between LGBT people and heterosexuals. Despite their shared concerns, psychoanalysis and queer theory are distinct disciplines with different aims and methodologies. Queer theory takes up the questions of sex, subjectivity and desire through a persistent engagement within the academy and with the political. While it is said to resist definition, queer theory could be said to aim at transgressing and transcending a hetero-normalising hegemony. Psychoanalysis, on the other hand, is primarily a clinical practice, which takes up the questions by way of the transference and the unique response of each analysand, addressing individual suffering through an analysis of speech as a manifestation of the unconscious. However, the emphasis on the analysis "case-by-case" and the particularity of the position of each individual subject should not detract from the imperative of the analysis of psychoanalysis as a social practice that either complies with or subverts power relations. Queer theory, despite the difficulties of its definition, could be said to have attempted to claim, or indeed, re-claim perversion for its creativity and its dissident potential. Olsen (2012) for example suggests that sado-masochism can subvert categories of (dis)ability and race. West (2012) argues that "kink" offers a containment of cultural anxieties. Rich (1986) argues that lesbian sado-masochistic practices constitute a revolt against the sexual strictures of feminism. For Dollimore (1991 p. 198) 'perversion is a refusal or attempted subversion of those organizing principles of culture which are secured psychosexually, principles which include sexual difference, the law of the father and heterosexuality.'

Queer theory is almost universally underpinned by Foucault. In the *History of Sexuality* (1976) Foucault argued that perversion was an invention of the sexologists, not least for their enjoyment of its regulation. Psychoanalysis, he argues, perpetuates itself and its power through what he calls a 'polymorphous incitement to discourse' (1990, p. 34) thus the notions of prohibition and of repression results in subjects' interest in sexual disclosure. Thus some queer commentators are critical of any kind of engagement with psychoanalysis, defining it as one of the 'murderously pathologising, criminalising and moralising discourse, one of whose comparatively minor effects has been to de-authorise our subjective experiences and to de-legitimise our claims to be able to speak knowledgably about our own lives' (Halperin 1995, p. 420). Any such engagement would represents an abandonment of Foucauldian genealogical enquiry. On the other hand, there are a number of seminal texts in which queer theory has fruitfully deployed psychoanalytic theory in a re-reading that gave emphasis to the instability of identity, the division between the subject and the organism, and the centrality of language are Butler's *Gender Trouble: Feminism and the Subversion of Identity* (1990) and *The Psychic Life of Power: Theories in Subjection* (1997), as well as de Lauretis' *The Practice of Love: Lesbian Sexuality and Perverse Desire* (1994). De Lauretis is frequently credited[2] to have been the first to use the term "queer" in relation to her 1991 work, deploying the term to make possible the delineation and description of certain political and discursive conjunctions, without having to rely on the assumptions of a settled definition or identity.

In the *Practice of Love*, de Lauretis undertakes a Foucauldian reading of some of the key texts of the psychoanalytic debate amongst the analysts on female sexuality in 1920s and 1930s to investigate lesbian sexuality and reclaim the concept of perversion. Emphasising that her contribution is not clinical, she contrasts psychoanalytic theory and clinical material with literary, filmic and critical texts of lesbian self-representation, saying that what she 'likes in Freud … [is] … its ambivalence or systemic instability – less interested in fixing its definitions than registering its transformations (whether that's ego, fantasy or sexuality or whatever)' (ibid., p. 259). Her intention was to go beyond Freud by suggesting a model of desire that was not a response to the Oedipus complex.

She wanted to 'understand lesbian sexuality beyond the commonplace of the masculinity complex and the pre-Oedipal fixation on the mother' (de Lauretis 1999, p. 38); thus, she proposes a model of lesbian desire that she names "perverse." To formulate this, she draws particularly on the Freudian notions of disavowal and retroactivity.

De Lauretis radically departs from Freud, proposing instead that '[w]hat the female subject … must disavow is … the absence … of a female *body-image* [my emphasis]' (de Lauretis 1994 p. 262). She reads the Oedipus complex and the paternal prohibition of incest

[2] Turner, W. (2003), Cooper, S. (2000) and Halperin, D. (2003).

as a prohibition to access the female body, and as a loss of the female body itself. For Freud, however, disavowal is a disavowal of the maternal phallus (Freud 1927) and not a signifier of the masculine cultural and political privilege. In the Freudian schema what is disavowed is castration, the penis signifying a lack that structures subjectivity and desire. De Lauretis proposes, instead, a loss that seems to precede the Freudian castration complex. 'Lesbian desire,' she writes, 'is constituted against a fantasy of castration, a narcissistic wound to the subject's body-image that *redoubles* [my emphasis] the loss of the mother's body by the threatened loss of the female body itself' (de Lauretis 1994, p. 261). Her reading of the mechanism of disavowal acknowledges that castration 'inscribes the irremediable lack – of a *penis* [my emphasis] – and inscribes that lack in the symbolic order of culture, in the terms of sexual difference' (ibid., pp. 261-2); and her privileging of the female *body image* breaks with Freudian psychoanalysis. Paradoxically, her explanation in itself is an example of disavowal, since she knows the nature of the lack and, at the same time, denies it.

De Lauretis is concerned with explaining the particularities of lesbian fetishism through the mechanism of disavowal: 'I would argue … that through the mechanism of disavowal, the female subject of perverse desire displaces the wish for the missing female body and the (non)-perception of its absence onto a series of fetish objects or signs that signify at once the wish and the absence (loss) and re-present the absent (lost, denied) and wished-for female body' (ibid., p. 263). And she continues: 'If the lesbian fetishes are often … objects or signs with connotations of masculinity, it is not because they stand in for the missing penis but because such signs are most strongly pre-coded to convey … the cultural meaning of sexual activity and yearning toward women. Such signs can also most effectively deny the female body (in the subject) and at the same time resignify (her desire for) it through the very signification of its prohibition' (ibid.). Notwithstanding her Foucauldian reading of prohibition, which also broadly characterises the work of queer theorists, these last passages raise the question of why de Lauretis is interested in the penis. In her work, she does acknowledge the phallus but simultaneously denies its operation in the structuring of the subject. In her attempt to detach the penis from the phallus — a move that is of central concern to some feminist and queer scholars, and that anticipates Butler's notion of the lesbian phallus — she re-invests psychoanalysis with biology, through disavowal. This is a question answered by psychoanalysis in 1958, when Lacan says that the penis 'takes on the value of a fetish' (Lacan 1958, p. 160) for heterosexual women. In his re-reading of Freud, Lacan claims that the fetish is not a substitute for the real penis, but that the penis itself becomes a fetish by substituting the woman's absent, and thus symbolic, phallus.

In a later commentary on Freud's *Psychogenesis*, de Lauretis (1999) considers rereading the case history against her model of perverse desire (ibid., p. 38), but concludes that this would be an impossibility since 'a case history belongs to its writer, not to its case' (ibid.). Nevertheless, in her readings of texts authored by lesbians, the inscription of lesbian subjectivity and 'authorial desire' (ibid., p. 39) allowed her to theorise lesbian desire as structured by disavowal. What is disavowed, here, is not sexual difference or love for the mother, but the lesbian's own body — a body that can be recovered in fantasy, and through sexual practices with another woman's body (ibid., p. 50). Of course, the other difficulty de Lauretis would have with her proposed project is that Freud's 'beautiful and clever girl' (1920, p. 147) was neither a fetishist nor perverse. De Lauretis "returns to Freud" in the final section of her essay. Here, she clarifies that the theory of perverse desire in female homosexuality, as elaborated in her *Practice of Love*, is not a psychogenesis of lesbianism but only an account for the 'psychogenesis of lesbianism in some women' (ibid., p. 39). Although she attempts to posit a 'non-Oedipal desire' (ibid., p. 47), she further acknowledges that 'perverse desire may co-exist with some of the effects of the Oedipus complex' (ibid., p. 51), and, indeed, argues that female perverse desire is 'based on post-Oedipal disavowal' (ibid.).

Consequently, she also acknowledges that not all lesbians are perverse, and some have 'gone through the Oedipus complex' (ibid., p. 50). The problematics of her account would be resolved by a reading of psychoanalysis that firmly distinguishes it from biological explanations, and one that does not equate — as she does — Oedipus with reproduction and a normative narrative (ibid., 1999, p. 47). Her account would benefit from drawing on psychoanalytic theorisation of the failure to negotiate the Oedipus complex, and from the distinction that psychoanalysis draws between neurosis, perversion and psychosis.

There is of course another difficulty. The sexual practices investigated by de Lauretis and other queer theorists are those which take place between "consenting adults" and in a political and cultural climate in which the increasing tolerance of what were once deemed transgressive sexual practices, which is not to say that all sexual practices are exempt from disapprobation, even within liberal cultures. Nobus (2006, p. 3) cleverly makes this point with his example of a happily married couple who use a ticklish feather to enliven their sex life. He then poses a question. What would be their thoughts and that of others if they substituted the feather with a whole bird?

Lacan

Lacan resolves this problem and the impasse in Freud's work by defining perversion as a clinical structure, and, in an elaboration of Freud's work – the Oedipus complex, castration and the psychic mechanism of disavowal rather than by a reliance on the diagnosis of symptoms or behaviours.

While some sexual acts are commonly regarded as perverse – albeit such definitions are contested, being contingent on history, culture and politics, from a Lacanian standpoint, it is possible that the non-perverse may engage in such acts and equally possible that the pervert may never engage in such acts. Perversion is not dependent on 'good morals' and social acceptability: 'it is something else in its very structure' (Lacan 1953-4, p. 221).

In common with many psychoanalytic schools, the Lacanian categorical classification system distinguishes between neurosis, psychosis and perversion. Unlike other schools, these categories are regarded as discrete structures, mutually exclusive and constitute all three possible responses to the problem of being human, determined by the neo-subject's response to Oedipus and castration.

The Oedipus complex does three things, as Leader (2011, pp. 64-66) helpfully describes it. The Oedipus complex establishes meaning, as well as the limits to meaning. How do we understand what mother wants, her wanting, her desire? And how do we know what to do with our bodies, our sexual excitements and consequently our attachments and interests? And where do we position ourselves in the world, how do we separate from this mother on whom our very existence depends, and where do we place ourselves in relation to everything/ everyone else?

From a Lacanian perspective it is not possible to "resolve" the Oedipus complex completely – although perhaps the neurotic comes closest to a resolution. In psychosis and perversion, however, there is 'something essentially incomplete in the Oedipus complex' (Lacan 1955-6, p. 201).

How does the person with a perverse structure deal with the problem of being human? What is incomplete for the pervert? Perhaps this question is best answered by first considering how Lacan conceptualised Oedipus in neurosis.

Lacan identifies three "times" of the Oedipus complex. The first is the realization that the mother – like the subject – lacks. She is incomplete, doesn't have it all and thus desires. The child too doesn't have it – otherwise he could satisfy the mother. What is lacking? Something that Lacan designates as the phallus, the phallus that the child is not, and the child's own lack results in anxiety, in response to a hopeless inadequacy at being able to placate the omnipotent, desiring mother.

In the second "time" there is an intervention from the father – who comes between the child and the mother. This is an idea that is more familiar. The father forbids the child's access to the mother, but also denies the mother any access to the phallic object. What is important at this 'time,' is not so much the imposition of the 'no,' the law but that it is registered, recognized. It is important to understand, at this point, that this is not a matter of an ordinary father, a man, a lover within the family. It is that which ensures that the position in which the neo subject aspires to take up i.e., that which provides total satisfaction is in fact, un-liveable and impossible.

The third "time" of Oedipus can be described as the child's acceptance that the father has the phallus, the object that will satisfy the mother and free him from anxiety of the impossibility of satisfying the mother.

But again, we are not talking about a man rather we are talking about a 'function,' a job – and anything might do that job, anything that the child can recognize and that symbolizes for the child that he doesn't have to be that phallus for the mother – something else has it whether that is father, a job, a hobby, a belief. What is important is that there is something that the child recognizes as beyond himself that interests the mother. Thus the child is free to identify with the father, and as Freud argues, the superego is formed out of this Oedipal identification with this father.

It is always tempting, in the service of simplification, to return to an explanation underpinned by environmental failure, the social worker's explanation. Fathers are weak, or absent or mother undermines the father's authority, or mother is too bound up with her infant – and in fact takes the child as her ultimate object of satisfaction. Lacanians do not dismiss these everyday factors, but give emphasis to the subject, the unconscious "choice," that 'decision' that each of us needs to make in relation to the problem of human subjectivity, of how to be human. Furthermore, what is important is the naming and registering of the lack in the mother. It is not coincidental that the chronological time of Oedipus is concurrent with the development of speech and language.

What is incomplete of the Oedipus complex in perversion? Where can this incompleteness be located? Let's look at the response of the neo-subject of perversion to the three tasks of meaning making, dealing with the body – localization of libido and dealing with the law - situating ourselves in relation to the Other.

1. Making Meaning – The Attempt at Finding an Answer to the Question of the Mother's Desire

Freud, following the sexologists, defined fetishism as a perversion and for Lacan too, fetishism is the 'perversion of the perversion.' Today, the deployment of an inanimate object to spice up our sex lives, might be deemed as "kinky," but there would be little disapprobation or indeed, pathologisation of such a creative pursuit of eroticism.

In *Fetishism* (1927), Freud argues that the child who takes up perversion realizes that the mother lacks, that she is castrated but convinces himself that she has a penis all the same. A split in the ego makes it possible for the child to hold both opinions concurrently. For the pervert, he knows the mother lacks, but disavows it all the same. Freud had been using the concept of disavowal, *Verleugnung,* to describe the child's ordinary response to the fact of sexual difference, and even the *Fetishism* paper includes clinical material, in which disavowal is a response in mourning in a case of obsessional neurosis. By 1938, Freud acknowledges that disavowal is a possibility in non-fetishists which seems to undermine the notion of perversion as a diagnostic category altogether.

Lacan, following Freud, claimed that there is a 'fundamental fetish in every perversion as an object perceived in the signifier's cut' (1961, p. 610). Lacan, here, is discussing Ruth Lebovici's case[3] of a transitory perversion and uses this case to make a distinction between a phobic object and a fetish object: the fetish object being a symbolic substitution for the mother's missing phallus.

The anxiety induced by the absence of the phallus of the mother and the subject's own lack of anything that could satisfy her desire, that first time of the Oedipus complex, is disavowed: lack is both present and absent. Without any representation of the mother's desire, its very namelessness, the subject's own no lack of lack will result in a solution: to become the object that stops up, that dams that lack by being that which gives her jouissance. Jouissance can be defined for our purposes as that which has the function of sustaining the illusion (for the neurotic) that pleasure might be obtainable if it were not forbidden (the second time of Oedipus).

Thus the pervert's attempt at making meaning, and finding an answer to the question of the mother's desire is incomplete in that desire is disavowed and is substituted with a different question, the question of the mother's jouissance: how might I give her that pleasure, forbidden to others? The pervert's solution to making sense is to making himself the object cause of jouissance in the (m)other.

In *Seminar X,* Lacan argues that the pervert is committed to offering himself as the object-cause of jouissance. John, for example, took a particular interest in "old women." He did not seek an analysis, but his girlfriend did - who consulted the therapist, it would seem, on his behalf. Nobus (2000, p. 45) puts foreword the view that perverts come to analysis looking for advice as to how they might continue with their sexual practice without getting into trouble and this seemed to be the case with this consultation. John's girlfriend, his proxy, was worried about the risks she was taking in complying with John's request that she used her mobile phone to film her late night taxi rides in which she would expose herself to the driver – whose reaction could be observed in the rear-view mirror. She was worried too about John's

[3] Ruth Lebovici, 1956 Perversion sexuelle transioire au cours d'un traitment psychoanalytique, *Bulletin d'activites de l'Association des Psychoanalystes de Belgique* 25: 1-15.

behaviour. The girlfriend told her therapist, too, about John's sexual life. Seeking introduction through internet introduction sites, John would seek out "old women" who he defined as those who would have no opportunity for sexual satisfaction, taking great interest in descriptions and photographs of their genitalia, which for John – by dint of age alone – signified their lack of jouissance, which he alone would be able to stop up. The women who met with John for sex were "consenting adults" and while such sexual liaisons do not always meet with a wholehearted endorsement from all sections of today's society, nor are they considered unlawful or sinful by all.

Nevertheless, perhaps John's solution to universal human problem of making meaning, to the question of the mother's desire might illustrate something of the perverse solution.

2. Localisation of Libido

Libido is always linked to a loss – at least for the neurotic. The mother is forbidden and unavailable to us and our sexual interests, both practices and objects are now situated anywhere that is not her, or an image of her. For the neurotic this limit, while tragic, also frees us from the necessity of organizing our being around the satisfaction of the mother and creates a place in which other people and interests will come to occupy for us.

In perversion, this task is somewhat incomplete. As I have tried to show above, for some people the problem of libido, what to do about having a body, and having sexual excitations and the question of what to do in relation to the mother's body remains particularly problematic. Separation is incomplete resulting in the tragedy of situating oneself as responsible for the satisfaction, the happiness of the mother. How can the person who is so unhappily attached to the first other effect a sense of separation? The fetish object does just this. In Fink's (1997, pp. 181-6) elaboration of Tostain's (1980) case of a man with a button fetish sets out how a row of identical buttons are used as a creative solution to reclaim his body from the mother, creating a symbolic space for his escape. The child is able to seize on the euphemisms of his parents for genitalia. His mother referred to his penis as '*ton bout*' and his father referred to his mother's genitalia as her '*bouton*' – a simple reversal but one that suggests the maternal phallic lack and sexual difference. In Tostain's analysis (ibid: 258) the button is that which covers the horrifying hole (buttonhole), that annihilating lack in the mother.

And for Fink, the word "button/*ton bout*" replaces and thus saves the child's real penis but in an argument, consistent with the Freudian explanation '*bouton*' names the mother's castration, her lack of the phallus, limiting it as 'only a button' (Fink 1997, p. 184). The naming of her lack delimits it and thus a row of identical buttons, the more buttons the better, gives emphasis to that limit.

3. Situating Himself in Relation to the Other

There is something incomplete about the paternal function for the pervert. Tostain's boy with the button fetish illustrates how there is something that the father has been able to do for his son which was the naming of the mother's lack. But for that child the lack is not interpreted as a desire but as a demand and in terms of *jouissance.*

Something has got in the way of the perverse subject being able to be quite convinced that he is not that which will satisfy the mother. Lacan calls the paternal function the 'Name of the Father' playing on the homophony of 'Nom,' meaning name and 'non' meaning no. The 'no of the father' is a 'no' that lays down the law to both the mother and the child prohibiting incest, and this is what results in a neurotic solution.

In perversion however this hasn't happened completely. Swales (2012, p. 67) explains this lack of conviction as being the result of a lack of 'respect' for the father of either the child or the mother. Verhaeghe (2004, p. 409) writes of a father who 'is reduced to a powerless observer defined as insignificant by the mother,' there has been a 'banalizing' of authority. André (2006, p. 111) writes that the 'father of the pervert disavows the status of the symbolic father' but that this is not due to his behaviour or personality, but rather how he is designated by the mother's discourse. For Lacanians it is this position in relation to the law that supports a diagnosis of perversion.

It is not only the Oedipal law of the father of the prohibition of incest that is not recognized by the perverse subject but all those laws of the replacements of the father. The sexual transgressions are not the diagnostic indicator in themselves, only in so far as they are an effect of the perverse subject's relation to the law.

To describe the pervert as one who has no respect for the law resonates with the popular view of the sexual offender, as one who puts their own sexual enjoyment above the law. The sexual transgression of the pervert, however, can function as a solution to this aspect of the problem of being human. Swales' case history of Ray (2012, p. 183-218) illustrates this point. Ray has been convicted of multiple acts of 'indecent exposure and indecent exposure to minors' (ibid: 185). Ray described his parents relationship as one in which he witnessed his mother 'laughing derisively' (ibid., p. 193) at any attempt of his father for any physical contact. She complained about his inability to make enough money and it was clear to Ray that his mother always got her own way, and that she was 'effectively the head of the household' (ibid.) and was also the one who punished the children for any misdemeanors. Significantly, Ray's father's surname was 'literally associated with something dirty and unwanted' (ibid., p. 218). Ray's acts of exhibitionism are interpreted by Swales as an attempt to bolster the paternal function, as they frequently resulted in the summoning of the police 'a lawgiving Other' (ibid.) and eventually led to his imprisonment, and thus he was 'forced … to respect the authority of a lawgiving Other' (ibid.).

TREATMENT?

I have attempted to address the contestation of the term 'perversion' today with brief clinical illustrations from a Lacanian perspective – a perspective that seems to me to be still valid despite the cultural and technological changes we experience today. Diagnosis does not rely on behaviour, sexual practice or identification. But what about treatment? What does a Lacanian approach have to offer today's clinician? It is frequently claimed in the literature that perverts don't seek analysis. So far that has been the case in my practice. What might be suggested from the case examples I have reported?

John did not seek analysis or any psychological treatment. Perhaps we can surmise that he experienced no suffering, and his activities, at least with regard to his older sexual partners, today do not constitute an 'aberration of an aberration in relation to social criteria, an anomaly contrary to good morals' – well not in London, at least. His girlfriend, his proxy, left him and ended her analysis.

Perhaps for our button fetishist our new technologies and new cultural attitudes to fetishism support his attempts at separation. I didn't search the web for very long I could only come up with numerous of belly button fetish websites – but I suspect a button fetishist site will exist. Or maybe the fetish itself would change along the lines of symbolic equivalence *ton bout → bouton → belly button,* if Tostain's patient had been bi-lingual?

And Ray? He had the law and a Lacanian analyst 'forced on him' (ibid), albeit only for a relatively short time, so I will give the last words to Swales: 'in the course of his psychotherapy, Ray created alternative solutions to propping up his paternal function – namely body piercings and tattoos [*the holes of piercing and front the ink holes related to his father's employment*] ... which functioned as significations of the Other's lack. ... Within his treatment, Ray constructed numerous creative solutions to the problems of the perverse structure. Via the mechanism of disavowal, I often came to function in the transference as a subject-supposed-to-No! knowledgeably putting a stop to Ray's excessive jouissance. ... Ray was beginning to find a way to be something other than *objet a* for the Other" (ibid: 218).

Conclusion

While Freud was clearly opposed to the "moral majority" of his day in his consideration of a psychoanalytic conceptualisation on the perversions, he still expresses his concern with some sexual practices. Describing coprophilia and necrophilia as 'repulsive,' he writes that they 'are so far removed from the normal in their content, we cannot avoid pronouncing them as "pathological' (Freud 1905, p. 161). Queer writers, at least those who tend to celebrate perversion or at least see it as an anachronism that is used to cement particular power relations, seem to evade the difficulties of deeming any sexual practice as problematic. My chapter suggests that Lacan's nosological framework in which a diagnosis is arrived at by the analysis, case-by-case, of the subject's position in relation to the difficulties of being human, provides a way forward for thinking about perversion.

References

André, S. (2006). The structure of perversion: A Lacanian perspective. In: D. Nobus and L. Downing (Eds.), *Perversion: Psychoanalytic perspectives/perspectives on psychoanalysis* (pp. 109-125). London: Karnac.

Butler, J. (1993). *Bodies that matter.* New York, NY: Routledge.

Butler, J. (1997). *The psychic life of power: Theories in subjection.* New York, NY: Routledge.

De Lauretis, T. (1994). *The practice of love: Lesbian sexuality and perverse desire.* Bloomington, IN: Indiana University Press.

De Lauretis, T. (1999). Letter to an unknown woman. In: R. C. Lesser and E. Schoenberg (Eds.), *That obscure subject of desire: Freud's female homosexual revisited* (pp. 37-53). New York, NY: Routledge.

Dollimore, J. (1991). *Sexual dissidence: Augustine to Wilde, Freud to Foucault.* Oxford: Clarendon Press.

Didion, J. (2005). *A year of magical thinking.* New York, NY: Knopf-Doubleday.

Fink, B. (1997). *A clinical introduction to Lacanian psychoanalysis: Theory and technique.* Cambridge, MA: Harvard University Press.

Freud, S. (1905). Three essays on the theory of sexuality. In: J. Strachey (Ed.), *The standard edition of the complete psychological works of Sigmund Freud*, Volume 14 (pp. 123-243). London: Hogarth Press.

Freud, S. (1920). The psychogenesis of a case of homosexuality in a woman. In: J. Strachey (Ed.), *The standard edition of the complete psychological works of Sigmund Freud*, Volumn 18 (pp. 145-172). London: Hogarth Press.

Freud, S. (1923). The infantile genital organisation. In: J. Strachey (Ed.), *The standard edition of the complete psychological works of Sigmund Freud*, Volumn 19 (pp. 141-146). London: Hogarth Press.

Freud, S. (1927). Fetishism. In: J. Strachey (Ed. and Trans.), *The standard edition of the complete psychological works of Sigmund Freud*, Volumn 21 (pp. 149-157). London: Hogarth Press.

Freud, S. (1940 [1938]). An outline of psycho-analysis. In: J. Strachey (Ed.), *The standard edition of the complete psychological works of Sigmund Freud*, Volumn 23 (pp. 141-207). London: Hogarth Press.

Freud, S. (1940 [1938]). Splitting of the ego. In: J. Strachey (Ed.), *The standard edition of the complete psychological works of Sigmund Freud*, Volumn 23 (pp. 271-278). London: Hogarth Press.

Foucault, M. (1976). *The history of sexuality (Vol. 1): An introduction.* (R. Hurley, Trans.). New York, NY: Pantheon.

Halperin, D. (1995). *Saint Foucault: Towards a gay hagiography.* Oxford: Oxford University Press.

Lacan, J. (1953-4). *The seminar of Jacques Lacan, Book I: Freud's papers on technique* (J. A. Miller, Ed.; J. Forrester, Trans.). New York, NY: Norton.

Lacan, J. (1955-6). *The psychoses. The seminar of Jacques Lacan, Book III* (J. A. Miller, Ed.; R. Grigg, Trans.). New York, NY: Routledge.

Lacan, J. (1961). The direction of the treatment and the principles of its power. (A. Sheridan, Trans.). In: *Ecrits.* New York, NY: Norton.

Lacan, J. (1962-63). *Anxiety. The Seminar of Jacques Lacan, Book X.* J.-A. Miller (Ed.). Cambridge: Polity Press, 2014.

Leader, D. (2011). *What is madness?* London: Hamilton.

Olson, I. (2012). Disidentification: Alternative sexuality and gender identities in sadomasochistic praxes. In: A. Worthington (Ed.), *Queer sexualities* (pp. 69-93). Oxford: Inter-Disciplinary Press.

Neu, J. (1991). Freud and perversion. In: J. Neu (Ed.), *The Cambridge companion to Freud* (pp. 175-223). Cambridge, UK: Cambridge University Press.

Nobus, D. (2000). *Jacques Lacan and the Freudian practice of psychoanalysis.* London, UK: Routledge.

Nobus, D. (2006). Locating perversion, dislocating psychoanalysis. In: D. Nobus and L. Downing (Eds.), *Perversion: Psychoanalytic perspectives/perspectives on psychoanalysis* (pp. 3-18). London: Karnac.

Rich, B. R. (1986). Feminism and sexuality in the 1980s. *Feminist Studies*, 12 (3), 525-561.

Swales, S. (2012). *Perversion: A Lacanian psychoanalytic approach to the subject*. New York, NY: Routledge.

Tostain, R. (1980). Fetishization of a phobic object. In: S. Schneiderman (Ed.), *Returning to Freud* (pp. 247-260). New Haven: Yale University Press.

Verhaeghe, P. (2004). *On being normal and other disorders: A manual for clinical psychodiagnostics*. New York; NY: Other Press.

West, D. (2012). 'Acting out': What can we gain by treating hetero-queer fantasy and RT as ritual performance. In: A. Worthington (Ed.), *Queer sexualities* (pp. 149-175). Oxford: Inter-Disciplinary Press.

In: Psychoanalysis
Editor: Zelda Gillian Knight

ISBN: 978-1-63483-858-0

Chapter 2

GUILT AND THE EXPERIENCE OF THE OTHER

Frank Summers**, PhD, ABPP
Northwestern University, Evanston, IL, US

ABSTRACT

Psychoanalysis has traditionally conceived of guilt as the product of superego stricture in response to the desire or intent to violate moral precepts. In this traditional view of guilt, the superego is the main psychic structure involved. While not disputing the importance of this form of guilt, the present paper adds a second form of guilt rooted in the nature of the self. Because self realization and empathy are mutually dependent, the failure to recognize the other as a source of subjectivity, that is, to treat the other as an object, is reflective of a weakened self and, in turn, weakens the self still further. This objectified treatment of the other results in guilt, although there may be no unethical intent. If the self is derailed in the developmental process, the child cannot see the other as a subject and objectifies the other in an effort to use people as manipulable things. Guilt rooted in the objectification of the other is often mistaken for guilt resulting from destructive intent because analysts tend to assume that all guilt is due to the desire or intent to violate moral precepts. The clinical importance of understanding guilt due to objectification of the other is demonstrated in the analysis of two cases.

Keywords: guilt, ethic, de-subjectify, empathy, derailed self

INTRODUCTION

There is perhaps no other psychoanalytic concept that has had a more extreme oscillation in the history of psychoanalytic ideas than guilt. In the early days, it occupied the very center of the psychoanalytic firmament as it was regarded as the very cause of repression, the source

* Corresponding author: Frank Summers. Address: 333 East Ontario Suite 4509B, Chicago, IL 60611. E-mail: franksumphd@gmail.com.

of neurosis. And, in fact, for many of classical persuasion guilt remains the center of neurosis and therefore unconscious guilt is the primary dynamic in analysis. Nonetheless, one sees remarkably little about guilt in today's analytic literature. Shame, which early on was virtually ignored as an analytic dynamic, is seen today by many analysts as central to the narcissism of many patients (e.g., Morrison 1997, Miller 1993, Wurmser 1977).

As a matter of fact, Fairbairn (1943) regarded guilt as "pseudoguilt," a defense against shame. Fairbairn's argument was that guilt makes us feel strong, but bad, whereas shame makes us feel weak. He and his colleague, Harry Guntrip (1961) contended that Western people prefer to think of themselves as "strong and bad" rather than weak, and therefore, the feeling of guilt is preferred to shame, the pain of feeling inadequate against which guilt provided a ready defense.

In addition to this argument, the recognition of the role of narcissism in defenses and symptoms has resulted in an emphasis on shame. Kohut's (1971) pivotal shift away from classical psychoanalysis was motivated by his belief that many of his patients were defending not against guilt, but against a fragile sense of self. He pithily summed up this theoretical transformation by saying we have moved from Oedipus to Hamlet (Kohut 1984).

Nonetheless, there is not analyst who has been practicing very long who has not had a patient whose life is burdened with unbearable guilt. One of my patients says that every move she makes that lacks perfection evokes a feeling of guilt and concomitant self attack. Now such perfectionism can be regarded, as Fairbairn would have undoubtedly seen it, as a defense against shame, the feeling of exposing an inadequacy. But, one cannot be so quick to dismiss guilt because the patient's experience is a feeling that she has done injury to others with a resulting feeling of guilt rather than shame.

So, here we come to the fundamental distinction between guilt and shame. Guilt is a feeling of doing injury to the other, while shame is the *exposure* of inadequacy. It is inadequacy as *seen by the other* that characterizes shame. By contrast, in guilt, my concern is *for the other*: I am guilty if I do injury to the other.

In shame, failure to comply with one's grandiose standard is an injury to the self, typically experienced as vulnerability to self esteem (e.g., Kohut 1971). By contrast, when the grandiose ethical standard is not met, it is the other who is failed, not the self, and the result is guilt, not shame. The key difference then is the way in which the other enters the picture. Guilt is not fundamentally narcissistic; it is about transgression of an ethical obligation to the other. Granted that in recent years, in the era we might call the Age of Narcissism, more are concerned with exposing their own vulnerability than doing harm to others, this preoccupation can hardly be said to have eliminated guilt as a dynamic force.

While both shame and guilt include the other, in shame the other is there only as a source of my injury, the experience is of my insufficiency, which is why we see the close association between narcissism and shame. From an analytic perspective, we wish to know what the inherent relationship is between self and other. And here I believe we confront the irony that in contemporary psychoanalysis we recognize, as never before, the inextricable connection between self and other, and yet we have greatly reduced the role of guilt which shows as no other concept the very self-other interrelationship on which so much of today's psychoanalysis is built.

THE CONTEMPORARY ETHIC OF PSYCHOANALYSIS

The role of guilt can be explicated only within the contemporary analytic framework, so the foundation of the relationship between self and other must be articulated, however schematically. The child becomes a self only in the gaze of the other, the caretaker who sees the child's subjectivity (e.g., Beebe and Lachmann 2002). No one becomes a human on an island apart from the human world. What Benjamin (2005) adds is that eventually the child must see the other as a subject in order for the gaze of the other to bring forth the subjectivity of the growing child. This critical fact means that the self is not simply reliant on others; for the self to become who she is others must be seen as subjects of experience. It is this recognition and appreciation of the other as a subject in his own right that makes the other's gaze a source of one's own subjectivity. It is in this way that the evolution and growth of the self is inextricably linked to experiencing the other as a subject. It is here that we find the inherent tie between ethics and self development. The pursuit of one's own ends at the expense of the other constitutes an objectification of the other, the treatment of the other as an object in the world to be utilized for my gain.

Only if the other is a subject can that gaze provide recognition of one's own experience and therefore the means by which I may become a subject in my own right.

This evolution of analytic thought leads us to a pivotal point in the development of contemporary psychoanalysis: the realization that the self is dependent on the experience of the other as a subject and therefore the ethic of empathy is imprecated in self realization and, perforce, in the very goals of analysis. This is what I mean by "the emerging psychoanalytic ethic" (Summers 2013).

There is in the very fabric of contemporary psychoanalysis an ethic of treating the other as an experiencing subject. Whatever the outcome of a given analysis, the analytic process may be said to have failed if the analysand is unable to treat others as subjects. The unethical from an analytic perspective is any behavior that *fails to recognize the experience of the other as an existing subject.* This ethic is an inviolable analytic principle implicit in the recognition of the pathology of splitting, ostracization, demonization, and scapegoating, but has become explicit in the contemporary world in which subjectivity is recognized as our fundamental human attribute and being seen as such is inherent in becoming who we are.

It follows then that the unethical is inherently pathological because to fail to grasp the other as a subject is to damage the ability to become oneself. There is no self realization outside of the world of human subjects. To treat others as objectified in any way is to demean one' own ability to be a full subject. The outcome will be a perversion of self realization, a derailment of the self from its evolution in the subjective world toward an its becoming an objectified entity, much like any material object.

One sees such obvious destructive treatment of others in egregious violations of human rights, such as physical and emotional violence and torture, but one may well ask what objectification of the other has to do with more typical and less dramatic ethical transgression, such as cheating on tests. The link is not difficult to perceive once we reflect on what makes such acts unethical. It is wrong to cheat on a test, for example, because it gives one an unfair advantage over another whose full subjectivity as a test taker with the same experience as the cheater is not recognized.

In order to cheat, one has to deny the experience of others taking the test, and that is precisely what one finds in asking for the experience of cheating. The cheater does not think about what it is like for the others taking the test. The quickest way to communicate the unethical nature of any act is to ask the cheater what it would be like to be the object of cheating. It is in the nature of the unethical to deny the experience of she who is transgressed upon. In fact, it is this very denial that makes it possible to act unethically.

The point here is that to commit an unethical act is to de-subjectify an other or group of others. An act is regarded as unethical precisely because it in some way uses others as a means and therefore compromises the subjectivity of other people. The author of an unethical act obliterates the experience of the other precisely because to be aware of the other's experience is to be aware of doing damage to the other and therefore to feel guilt.

This is a very different basis for moral behavior than the superego; it is an ethic of inclination, rather than an ethic of imposition. There is substantial evidence that moral behavior motivated by imposition is fragile, whereas those who understand the principles of ethics tend to be stable in their ethical behavior (Kohlberg 1981). What psychoanalysis now adds to this finding is that it is that same group who is most likely to realize their self potential.

The Guilt-Ridden Patient

The patient suffering from oppressive guilt is not *necessarily* someone who either has or wished to violate a moral precept. It is true, of course, that guilt-ridden patients believe they are not treating others as they should be. Such patients may even attack themselves in a manner consistent with a harsh superego, but some patients of this type, despite the onerous guilt that burdens their lives, do not feel the guilt of malevolent intent. The surprising feature in the dynamics of such patients is that they do not feel they have done injury despite their unrelenting guilt.

Consider my patient, Rebecca, who feels she is never doing enough for others, that she is neglectful of other people and therefore responsible for much of their distress. She can turn in a work project for which she receives strong compliments, but if she senses any slight dissatisfaction in any part of her report, she will feel she has let down her boss, feels guilty, and obsesses about what she should have done better. Like many of today's guilt-ridden patients, Rebecca is a conflict avoidant accommodating person who fears doing anything that may cause the other discomfort. Any "no" is felt as doing injury, resulting in guilt as though she has done damage, perhaps irreparably. For example, Rebecca tends to take on more than her share of work responsibility because she feels guilty saying "no," but one day she was so overwhelmed she could not complete a project for a co-worker that she had taken on as a favor to the other woman. While her colleague winced in dissatisfaction, she set off to see if she could find another to help her, and my patient became preoccupied with the immediate reaction of distress. She became wracked with guilt and doubt. Perhaps she could really do it? If she stayed late and pushed other projects to the side, perhaps if she changed priorities, she might be able to complete the co-worker's assignment after all.

These thoughts initiated an obsessional thought process regarding whether Rebecca could find a way to complete the work for her colleague. I of course illuminated the fact that the issue was not "finding a way," but that she felt guilty saying "no." When I inquired into what damage she felt she had committed, she expressed chagrin that her colleague might get into trouble, would not be able to finish the project on time. She averred that it is quite realistic to believe that her colleague would be in trouble for not getting her work done on time. My patient could not separate herself from the co-worker's presumed distress. She felt guilty and of course responsible for any difficulties experienced by the other worker. If in fact the work had been turned in late, she would have felt guilty and responsible for that malfeasance.

Her concern for her colleague's plight stands in stark contrast to the unethical person who denies the injury suffered by the other, and my patient did no harm, but believed that her colleague was undergoing great distress due to her own lack of cooperation. In conventional terms, the issue is my patient's exaggerated belief in her own destructiveness, the fantasy that her aggression is damaging, and therefore she feels guilty for the aggressive act of saying "no." While belief in the damage of her "no" is certainly excessive, we would do a disservice to this patient and others of the same type if we reduce the guilt to a presumed exaggerated fear of aggressivity.

Although this interpretation has been the most common way psychoanalysis has explained overburdensome guilt when no malfeasance has taken place, there was no evidence for it in Rebecca's present life or history. In fact, Rebecca's family history did not fit a fear of aggression. She was not excessively prohibited from aggressive expression as a child and in fact she had been a very angry adolescent. She could see that the fear of her ability to do damage was wildly exaggerated, but she continued to feel guilty. The idea that she feared her aggression did damage to others was a purely speculative hypothesis that did not fit her experience and had no impact on her guilt.

Here we have come upon what may appear to be a subtle but psychoanalytically meaningful distinction between two sources of guilt: violating a moral precept, such as cheating or lying, and failing to help out another human being in distress.

In the latter case, there is no clear ethical standard transgressed, as there is when one lies, cheats or steals. While Levinas (1969) claims that there is such an ethical imperative for the recognition of our fellow human beings, such a moral stance operates at a different level from the usual precepts. The guilt due to the objectification of the other is rooted in a violation of our very humanity. In that sense, Levinas' principle is not in disagreement with the view advanced here that there is an ethical imperative in human relating, but here we distinguish that from violating a societal stricture because the two have different dynamic sources. No societal standard dictates a morality of extending oneself or even sacrificing oneself to relieve the plight of another. For that reason, psychoanalysis must recognize a difference between two sources of guilt. Of course it is regarded as praiseworthy to make sacrifices to come to the aid of others, but that praise is meted out because the individual has gone beyond the normal moral precepts. It is not at all clear that we as a society expect a selfless placing of the other before our own self interest. In fact, we tend to call those who act that way as "martyrs," or "uber" moral souls. That is because we do not set our moral principles at a selfless level. Seeing the other in distress, we may we tend to feel we should do something, but there is wide latitude in what responses we regard as fulfilling our moral duty. Granted that not helping may be considered morally callous in most cases, it is often acceptable to do something simple, such as give out a phone number that might be useful or hand an indigent person a coin. We do not call the person who helps in this minimal way "unethical," even if we know that have done little.

Now consider the person who feels guilty for not having done more to help the indigent or the person in distressful circumstances. My patient Rebecca would be wracked with guilt whenever she saw another person in abject circumstances, saw another depressed, or hear of another's misfortune, such as an illness or injury. The guilt here is not a result of violating a societal moral precept, as it is for those who feel guilty for lying or cheating.

Rebecca's standard for her moral behavior well exceeded that of most mortals, and when she violated her own strictures, which she had no choice but to do, she attacked herself with ruthless condemnation. One might justifiably say her moral standards reflected a form of ethical grandiosity, but despite the fact that Rebecca's moral standards were grandiose, failing to comply with them made her feel guilty, rather than ashamed.

Most importantly, Rebecca's moral standards do not simply differ in magnitude from conventional societal standards. First, they applied only to her.

Unlike those who feel guilty for cheating, the guilt over insufficient response to another's pain is not a general precept applicable to all equally. Rebecca, like other patients who suffer from this harsh form of guilt apply it only to themselves. Rebecca never considered the possibility of applying this standard of morality to herself. Only she was the object of vituperative attacks for a failure to be selfless in the interest of the other.

Second, this form of guilt has a different underlying dynamic than the conflict that tends to give rise to guilt for violating a societal standard. The obsessive, circular self-attacks one sees in patients like Rebecca consist of a negative synergy in which the ethical imperative to relieve the other's distress is never met because it cannot be, resulting in guilt and the punishment of endless self flagellation. This guilt is not fueled by aggressivity and is not fueled by intent to do harm. Rebecca was caught in a vicious cycle of attacking herself for not ameliorating the pain and suffering of others, and then castigating herself for her irrational expectations of herself, she then felt guilty for her irrationality. This cycle repeated with the frequency with which she witnessed misery or even milder forms of distress.

Note that there was no hint of shame in her failure to meet what she regarded as her ethical obligation. She did not even feel "moral shame;" she felt no shame at all. She did not feel ashamed, but guilty for how she treated the other, or more correctly, how she failed to treat the other. Rebecca's history fit in broad outline the developmental dynamics of many patients who are trapped in vicious cycles of guilt. Her grandiose moral standard originated in her mother's need for her to relieve the older woman's pain and emotional suffering when Rebecca was a child. She could recall her mother seeking her out, telling her about her life problems, especially with Rebecca's father, and seeking succorance she could not get from her husband. Rebecca's father was a distant man and the mother had undisguised contempt for him, devaluing and belittling his lack of interpersonal skill at every opportunity. Her mother sought relief from Rebecca, even when her daughter was a young child. Rebecca could remember her mother seeking comfort from her, even crying in distress.

Rebecca of course felt the need and desire to soothe her mother's pain and had never resolved her inability to do so. Throughout her adult years she bore the guilt of not having relieved her mother's pain and depression, which she believed it was her duty to do. In the usual form of guilt rooted in dark wishes, such as feelings of excessive aggressitivity and intent to do harm, the guilt is due to the feeling of "badness" for one's desires or fantasies, if not deeds. But, in the guilt suffered for the failure to relieve the other's distress, the guilt is typically a product of a childhood need to "cure" a parent, or perform some other miraculous ethical feat.

In the years of discussing this issue in analysis, Rebecca became aware of anger at her mother, but she did not feel guilty due to the anger to which she in fact felt entitled. Rebecca's guilt was due to her feeling that she let her mother down by seeking from her, rather than attending to her pain and suffering.

The underlying, but unconscious assumption of her life was that she should have been able to repair her mother's pain but failed in the task. She felt responsible for her mother's unabashed life of distress and depression because she had not improved her mother's lot in life, and she felt the same toward anyone with whom she had any degree of emotional contact or any sense of connection. Having failed to relieve her mother's pain, Rebecca felt she should at least make the world a better place by improving the life of almost everyone to whom she came into contact (This is undoubtedly the origin of Searle's (1979) observation that patients are failed psychotherapists). When she did not succeed in this goal, she felt she was once again failing in her moral duty. Such a failure is easily misinterpreted as her fantasy of doing injury, but in fact she had no such fantasy. She had a grandiose belief in a moral duty she was unable to fulfill.

It is of course true that under her inability to repair her mother's distress was a great deal of anger at her mother for needing and attempting to exploit her. However, to attribute her guilt to this anger is a theoretical imputation rather than a clinical finding. Rather than guilt over her anger, Rebecca felt she was entitled to be angry with her mother for reversing roles and exploiting her as a maternal function.

Rebecca's guilt then was embedded in the way she experienced other people. She did not feel guilty primarily due to any desire, wish, or state or even act of her own. She engaged others as human beings with a variety of different experiences, but when that experience included the other's suffering, she felt responsible for the other's pain, resulting in an overwhelming sense of guilt. Once she noted a negative experience in the other, no matter how great or small, it became magnified in her mind, and she was unable to contain her guilt for failing to relieve it.

While guilt is often the result of intent, in cases like Rebecca, no intent is necessary for the induction of paralyzing guilt. The connection between guilt and intent is so embedded in the analytic mind (e.g., Freud 1923) that it is indeed difficult for analysts to see guilt where there is no intent to transgress or do harm, but that is because we have a limited view of guilt. And this may account for the paucity of discussion of guilt in the current analytic literature. Guilt is still so identified with the intent to do harm or violate accepted norms that where there is no such intent, we miss the guilt even if it stands before us, as we say, "hidden in plain sight." What we see in many of today's patients is guilt that is hidden because it is not wrapped in malevolent intent, but in a different kind of morality.

Of course guilt is the force behind making wishes unconscious, but we must also come to grips with other forms of guilt that are motivated and produced by a different set of dynamics, as we saw in Rebecca.

Cases like Rebecca are not uncommon. Many people avoid conflict and fail to assert their own interests and desires not because they bear the guilt of unconscious desires, but because they are mercilessly attacking themselves for failing to be sufficiently humane to others, even if that means abject self sacrifice. The source of guilt lies for them in the nature of the experience of the other, irrespective of motive.

The Therapeutic Process

As one might expect, Rebecca was exquisitely sensitive to the slightest indication of distress or discomfort shown on my face or behavior. She was concerned that not only her emotional problems, but also the job itself, might be taxing for me, and she felt that she needed to titrate the emotional drain on me.

When I noted that she was excessively concerned about my well being and was trying to find a way to relieve me of my emotional pain as she had so often done with her mother, she readily agreed. She felt that she was consuming an excessive amount of my time with her guilt and self flagellation, and that her repetitiousness was wearing on me. She feared that by not improving fast enough she was depleting my emotional resources, and her best options were to quit therapy to make my life easier, or work harder to make her symptoms abate. With another patient the thought of leaving therapy to "help out" the therapist would be defensive, but with Rebecca, it was the primary dynamic. She wanted to get better for me, as she feared her obsessiveness and guilt were creating too much difficulty for me, thus adding to her already overbearing guilt. As with her mother, she believed that she should be able to make my life better, but by obsessing on the same issues, she was draining me rather than bolstering my lot in life, and therefore, failing in her moral obligation. In this way, Rebecca's personal morality emerged in the analysis, and its needs were not being met. It should be noted that although grandiosity was in play, she felt none of the shame-filled vulnerability characteristic of the narcissistic injury suffered by the punctured grandiosity of the narcissistic personality disorder.

Of course, as is typically the case, there was some truth in Rebecca's perception of my experience of her. I often felt her repetitious self flagellation, guilt, and unquenchable moral preoccupations with the same issues to be tedious and difficult to listen to, but no more so than I feel with many patients. This was the truth in her experience of me, but as was characteristic of her, Rebecca magnified this piece of truth almost beyond recognition. In her mind, she was draining me, depleting me of resources, and she attempted to restrain her repetitious self attacks to diminish the debilitating impact she believed they had on me. When I noted that she seemed to feel protective of me, Rebecca acknowledged that she felt she had to "take care of" me by not expressing too much negative emotion for fear she would do me harm. She went on to say that she felt keeping herself under emotional control was the best route to preserving our relationship and me.

The primary transference dynamic was the parallel between her relationship with her mother and me. She saw that she regarded me as fragile in a way that she had experienced not only her mother, but also all others with whom she had significant emotional contact. She felt that it was her responsibility to ensure the well being of others in any way she could. If she could not, she felt like a failure in a moral sense, and so with me, she often felt that a strong sense of guilt for not improving my state of mind.

My response was both to acknowledge the strain I felt in being subjected to her continued and seemingly endless self attacks and guilt while clarifying that my feelings were not even close to the depth she feared and, above all, they did not have the injurious impact she believed them to have. Over time the distinction between the degree of my frustration with the repetitiousness of her self attacks and the catastrophic reaction from which she believed me to suffer helped Rebecca sort out the difference between her beliefs about her impact on others and the impact she, in fact, did have on other people. So, there were two components to Rebecca's transference guilt: her exaggerated belief in the distress she caused me and the belief in my need for her to care for me to relieve the suffering.

Rebecca was certain with me as she was with others that if she was at all difficult or negative that I was injured, perhaps irreparably, and therefore she felt guilty and had a responsibility to sooth my psychic state. In every relationship, if the other experienced even slight distress, Rebecca felt guilty and assumed the responsibility to relieve the suffering of the other, even when she had no means of so doing. The difference, of course, between her relationship with me and others is that I questioned her assumptions that I was deeply hurt and needed her help. In fact, I told her that I did not experience the degree of hurt that she imputed to me, thus setting into question her assumption of having done injury. It was after I made clear that I did not feel injured that Rebecca was willing to question her previously bedrock assumption that she was continually doing me harm. We talked about her experience as a perceptual process between us rather than a concrete reality on which she had an obligation to act. The process of inquiry in itself was an advance because the very discussion of Rebecca's need to care for me and relieve my presumed emotional distress in itself shifted Rebecca from the mode of repair to a discourse about the need to repair. By engaging in discussion, Rebecca was already out of the concrete level in which she had made her assumptions of others' experience.

While I conveyed with utmost sincerity that I was not deeply injured or strongly disaffected by Rebecca's repetitious her thoughts of doing injury without any recognizable change, I also made it clear that I was not free from a sense of tedium that I felt was inevitable in hearing these persistent musings. When I expressed the strain for me in acknowledging my difficulty in listening to her repeated self accusations, she not only saw, but also experienced me as a whole person who was not diminished by the need to endure her repetitious ruminations. I did not require caring from her despite a certain emotional strain in the relationship. Rebecca made contact with my mind for the first time, but most important, she made contact with the mind of someone who had been affected by her without a diminished sense of self. The realization that I was functioning before her without any special care from her was the primary impetus in questioning her previously rock hard assumption of doing injury. All the interpretations over many years had not convinced her that I did not have such a need for her to fix me, but seeing is believing, and she required seeing my mind function, even contacting me as a functioning person for her to see that she was not required to repair all the world's damage. The essence of the therapeutic action for Rebecca lay in her being able to see that she in fact did put a strain on me, but it did not have the catastrophic impact she had assumed it would have. This combination was a new experience for her and brought her from the concrete to the level of discourse in her effect on others.

Now this realization of course did not come without a cost. In realizing that she did not have the catastrophic impact she imagined, Rebecca was forced to confront the reality that I did not need her as she had imagined.

It took something from her sense of self to accept the reality that I did not need her to soothe my pain. She was at a loss for how to understand my continuing in the relationship if I was not wounded and did not require her to soothe the wound. To be unable to relieve my emotional distress felt like a blow to her sense of self. One trait she took pride in was her ability to do for others. With her realization that I did not need her to fix a wound, Rebecca lost her excessive moral expectation.

In this way, much of her guilt was relieved, but along with it her sense of self was being reluctantly brought down to earth. Ultimately, Rebecca believed that she gained more in losing her inflated expectations of herself than she lost in the pride of her grandiose morality.

It is of course true that many guilt ridden people feel guilty over treating others with disrespect or for having the intent to mistreat others. But, even in these cases we cannot be satisfied with an explanation that ends with aggression or envy. Consider the typical case of envy and competition in which the guilt is due to the desire is to see the other fail. The hope to see the other falter violates one's precepts of how one's fellow man should be treated and that results in guilt for the transgression of ethical principle. But, as analysts we may ask a further question: Why do we have such a principle? As we saw earlier the very existence of the self is dependent on seeing the other as a subject in her own right. We cannot be a subject if the other is not seen as a subject, so if the analytic goal is the realization of self potential then the recognition and appreciation of the other as a subject is the ethic built into the very nature of what it is to be human. To become realized as a full subject requires the appreciation of the other, and when the self is derailed by a developmental arrest, a substitute emotional investment is sought in an easily measureable achievement, such as income, investment portfolio, sales figures, or business growth. When emotional investment is placed is such quantifiable forms of self appreciation, others' success is threatening. It is then that envy and competition become a source of aggression and hostility to others.

It is rare that aggressivity is a bottom line dynamic; more typically, aggression is a product of a failure in the ability of the self to achieve its destiny. The point for our purpose is that the guilt is not a direct product of aggression, but a product of the inability of the self to treat others as full human beings which in turn is a function of the failure of the self to realize its potential. When the self falters, others' demise may be sought as a desperate maneuver to achieve temporary relief, but guilt is the steep price paid. Guilt, even when it appears to be due to envy and malevolent intent, can be analyzed back to its root in the de-subjectification of the other. Any splitting of the other's full subjectivity is to some degree an objectification of the humanity of the other, the self, or both, and violates the nature of what it is to be a human subject. This guilt dynamic and the therapeutic process for its amelioration are illustrated in my patient Dan, who was highly competitive, always seeking to move ahead in the business world and fearful of being outdone by others. Whenever a friend or colleague embarked on a project or made an effort to achieve, Dan expressed support, but in his unguarded therapy moments admitted to wishing that the friend or colleague would fall on his face, and Dan felt an extreme sense of guilt for this secret wish. In subtle ways Dan sabotaged his own efforts at success, which we analyzed as his guilt-induced self punishment for his envy and malevolent intent toward others. However, here too, Dan's guilt was far more complex than can be accounted for by reference to the destructiveness of aggressivity. Dan had a desire to see his friends and colleagues fail, but, contrary to conventional wisdom, he did not feel guilty because of any hostility toward them. To impute such hostility to Dan, like the effort to attribute anger to Rebecca, would be born of theoretical presuppositions and not the clinical reality of his experience. Dan hoped that if he were able to see the person fail, he would boost his view of himself in comparison and feel inflated, but that feeling immediately came into conflict with his guilt. Dan's guilt was not a result of anything he did to the other, it was a product of his feeling of exploiting the other to enhance his self esteem.

So for Dan, as for Rebecca, the oppressive guilt from which they suffer is not attributable to unacceptable intent, but to the way the other is experienced. Dan's guilt was rooted in the diminution of the other and the resultant objectified use. Insofar as I seek the other's failure, I delegitimize her as a human. I am not regarding the other as a human with whose subjectivity I seek to connect, but as an objectified entity the failure of which I hope to put to my advantage. It is this experience of the other as a means, a means to my own perceived concrete advantage that leads to the guilt. So, to leave guilt at the intent is to depart the analysis at a point that fails to get to the root of Dan's guilt. As analyst, we need to recognize that Dan feels guilty for removing others from the human world, and in the process he dehumanized himself. It is not that I object to saying that Dan feels guilty over his desire to see his colleagues fail; it is that when we inquire into the reasons for the intent, we find that the envy and mean spirited desire to see the others fail is a product of a disturbed sense of self. When we see the derailed nature of the self, we find at times extraordinary guilt, but that has more to do with the experience of the other than with the intent per se. We saw this principle in the analysis of Rebecca. Her intentions were presumably positive, not small minded as were Dan's, but in both cases, the guilt was a product of a weak self that sought a certain experience with the other to feel strengthened. Rebecca needed to be needed, and Dan was envious and small minded, but in both cases, the guilt was due to the way the other was objectified for the purpose of the self, not the intent to do harm.

This dynamic difference is critically important for two reasons. First, it means that the therapeutic action lies in a new experience in which the analyst will be experienced as a subject in her own right. It is in the struggle to see the analyst as a subject of experience that patients like Dan can gain their own full subjectivity, thus obviating the need to see others falter. We saw this in detail with Rebecca and the same holds with Dan. Solidifying the sense of self relieves severe guilt, and that begins with a new experience with the analyst.

Second, this is perhaps one place that psychoanalysis may make a contribution to understanding the nature of what it is to be a human being with implications for the wider world. We can learn from our analysis of guilt that when we treat others as a means, we feel guilty. Psychoanalysis has assumed for too long that guilt requires unacceptable wishes. The source of guilt in many human situations is the violation of the fundamental meaning of what it means to be a human being. By recognizing the role of empathy in the very fiber of the human condition, we understand guilt as an index of having thought of the other in violation of the very nature of our humanity. So, ironically, to feel guilty is to affirm our humanity. When Dan feels guilty about his desire to use the other to relieve his anxiety over his potential failures or Rebecca feels guilty that she is not doing all she can to relieve others' suffering, for others, both are standing forth in their humanity by affirming the principle of how they know others should be treated, that is, as subjects in their own right. And, by affirming their own need to make contact with others' subjectivity, they make possible their own humanity.

CONCLUSION

A major breakthrough in contemporary analysis is Benjamin's insight that recognition of the other as a subject in her own right and self development are mutual processes. This essay has extended the implications of this pivotal insight. When we de-subjectify another human being, we treat that person as an entity, much like any natural object, as though "it" has no ability to experience the world. Our only options then are to feel guilty at violating the other's humanity or to defend against awareness of having dehumanized the other in order to defend against guilt feelings. As we have seen, ethical transgressions can be violations of ethical norms, as in the traditional superego conception of guilt, or the de-subjectification of the other that can occur without either an unethical act or even the intention of doing harm in the fantasy world. It is the latter form that breaks new ground for understanding the power and influence of guilt. We have gone beyond the traditional analytic assumption that if no unethical act has occurred, guilt is due to the fantasy of doing injury or violation of an ethical precept. In contrast to this traditional view, we have seen in the cases of Rebecca and Dan that the de-subjectification of the other carries with it a burden of guilt that can be as debilitating as any moral transgression. As we have seen, it is the inability of the self to realize its potential that issues in the de-subjectification of the other.

Guilt is the visible legacy of the spiral of a derailed developmental process, much of which is unconscious. But, as we have seen, if we follow the guilt trail back through the thread of de-subjectification to its origins without halting our inquiry prematurely due to theoretical presuppositions, we find an ineffective self that cannot subjectify the other. The self is then given to desperate measures to repair the defects in its ability to function. The exploitation of the other for this purpose issues in guilt.

This form of guilt then is the dis-ease of the self, the symptom of a self gone awry. By assuming theoretical preconceptions we have missed a fundamental purpose of guilt. It is a signal, indeed, but not necessarily a signal of a threatening feeling. It is a signal of the degree to which we have strayed from our fundamental humanity. For our guilt is there to show us that we are suffering from a distressed and weakened self. Guilt is a signpost, and if we can read it, we will be brought back to who we most fundamentally are. Guilt is an all too common human experience not because we all feel sinful, but because guilt is a correction to our inevitable human foibles and derailments.

It follows that guilt is not simply a painful or pathological experience, but a valuable index of our very humanity. It is not Dan and Rebecca we need worry about when we ponder the future of humanity, for in their guilt they affirm their belief in the humane treatment of others. On the contrary, potential evil lies in those who are willing to objectify others without guilt and therefore vilify, scapegoat, and even attempt to destroy others. We all tend to objectify others to some degree, but those who feel no guilt about it and therefore no conflict while treating others as material entities or worse who show us the lowest level to which humanity can descend. Such people are either without guilt or defend against it, but either way they lack the guilt that tends to oppose the objectification of others. And it is that unambivalent objectification that leads down the slippery slope to maltreatment and, if unchecked, can result in the worst form of evil of which human beings are capable. Such a disconnection from our very humanness is the peril of contemporary humanity, and a danger to which contemporary psychoanalysis might well address itself.

References

Beebe, B. and Lachmann, F. (2002), *Infant research and adult treatment: Co-constructing interactions*. London: Routledge.

Benjamin, J. (2005), *Like subjects, Love objects*. New Haven, CT: Yale University Press.
Fairbairn, W. R. D. (1943/1952). The repression and the return of bad objects (with special reference to the 'war neuroses'). In: *Psychoanalytic studies of the personality* (pp. 59-81). London: Tavistock.
Freud, S. (1923/1966). The ego and the id. *Standard edition of the complete psychological works of Sigmund Freud*, Volume 19 (pp. 12-59). London: Hogarth Press.
Guntrip, H. (1961). *Personality structure and human interaction*. New York, NY: International Universities Press.
Kohlberg, L. (1981). *Essays on moral development*, Volume 1. The philosophy of moral development. San Francisco, CL: Harper and Row.
Kohut, H. (1971). *The analysis of the self*. New York, NY: International Universities Press.
Kohut, H. (1984). *How does analysis cure?* Chicago: University of Chicago Press.
Levinas, E. (1969). *Totality and infinity: Essays in exteriority*. Philadelphia, PA: Duquesne University Press.
Miller, S. (1993). *The shame experience*. London: Routledge.
Morrison, A. (1997). *Shame: The underside of narcissism*. Hillsdale, NJ: The Analytic Press.
Searles, H. (1979). The patient as therapist to his analyst. In: H. Searles, *Countertransference and related subjects: Selected papers of Harold Searles* (pp. 380-459). New York, NY: International Universities Press.
Summers, F. (2013). *The psychoanalytic vision: The experiencing subject, transcendence, and the therapeutic process*. New York, NY: Routledge.
Wursmer, L. (1977). *The mask of shame*. New York, NY: Aronson.

In: Psychoanalysis
Editor: Zelda Gillian Knight

ISBN: 978-1-63483-858-0

Chapter 3

PSYCHOANALYTIC SENSIBILITY IN A BEHAVIOURAL WORLD: SUPERVISING INTERN COUNSELLING PSYCHOLOGISTS IN AOTEAROA, NEW ZEALAND

***Mark R. Thorpe**, PhD**
Department of Psychology, Auckland University, New Zealand

ABSTRACT

Psychoanalysis passed its heyday in the seventies and has been usurped by short term cognitive behavioural therapies. Counter to this trend, in the past two decades there has been a small, but significant, growth of psychoanalytic psychotherapy in Aotearoa, New Zealand. This chapter describes my experience of using a psychoanalytic sensibility when teaching and supervising intern counselling psychologists in a mental health and university system which is subtly dominated by a cognitive behavioural worldview. The differences between the cognitive behavioural and psychoanalytic therapeutic styles are briefly outlined. This is followed by a few examples used to illustrate the systemic foreclosure of potential space, meaningful symbol formation, and the development and understanding of the therapeutic relationship and the transference-countertransference matrix. The implications of using behavioural techniques and homework assignments are viewed from a psychoanalytic perspective. Supervision vignettes are then presented to illustrate how I attempt to open the space and introduce a psychoanalytic sensibility in supervision. A foray into my supervisory and systemic countertransference is presented followed by some thoughts on supervising different styles of breaks and endings in therapy.

Keywords: supervision, psychoanalytic sensibility, counselling psychology, cognitive behavioural therapy

* Corresponding author: Mark R. Thorpe, PhD. Department of Psychology, AUT University, Private Bag 92006, Auckland 1141, New Zealand. E-mail: mark.thorpe@aut.ac.nz.

Introduction

In this chapter I describe my experience of trying to maintain a psychoanalytic sensibility while teaching and supervising intern counselling psychologists in a mental health and university system dominated by the biomedical and behavioural world views. I start with a short introduction to psychology in Aotearoa New Zealand and the recent emergence of Counselling Psychology. This is followed by a vignette, describing an aspect of my experience as an external examiner, to illustrate how the system inhibits the development of certain aspects of the therapeutic relationship and the development of potential space and meaningful symbol formation.

At this point, I introduce the research on the differences between cognitive therapy and psychodynamic therapy. The next example, set during the process of selecting counselling psychologists, illustrates the effects of employing behavioural techniques on the therapeutic process. Continuing the discussion on behavioural homework assignments, I discuss my experience of supervising cognitive behaviourally oriented final year students. I then explore the psychoanalytic style of the identification of recurring themes and patterns through the use of computer software analogies.

Finally, I provide a few signposts to my academic and supervisory countertransference and reflect upon my motivations for writing this chapter. My hope is that you read the chapter playfully, curiously, critically, and deeply, i.e., with a psychoanalytic sensibility.

Psychology and Psychotherapy in New Zealand

Shortly after World War II the Boulder conference, with its "…uncritical acceptance of the medical model, the organic explanation of mental disorders, with psychiatric hegemony, medical concepts, and language" (Albee 2000, p. 247) ushered in the scientist-practitioner model, the "…new discipline of cognitive science and neuroscience" (Corballis 1990, p. 2). Psychology in Aotearoa New Zealand, at times flippantly referred to as the 'last bastion of behaviourism' (Oakes 1999), has followed this trend.

A survey by Kazantzis and Dean (1998) showed that registered practicing psychologists in New Zealand use cognitive approaches more often, and psychodynamic approaches less frequently, when compared to their British and American colleagues. Recent research indicates that New Zealand psychologists experience a high degree of confidence in using CBT techniques in the clinical arena (Kennedy-Merrick, Haarhoff, Stenhouse, Merrick and Kazantzis 2008). Reflecting on a related theme, Thorpe and Farrell (In Press) point out that research evidence on the importance of the therapeutic relationship (Norcross and Wampold 2011) has had less of an impact on practice in Aotearoa New Zealand than in other parts of the world. Culturally this is congruent with Hofstede's (1983) review of the work practices of 53 countries which placed New Zealand firmly on the individualist rather than the collectivist end of the continuum.

Anecdotally, in Aotearoa New Zealand counsellors adopt a humanistic approach, psychotherapists are psychodynamic, and clinical psychologists follow a behavioural or cognitive behavioural path. The country has evidenced a small but substantive growth of psychoanalytic influence in the past 20 years.

This has partly been fuelled by the immigration of senior psychoanalytic psychologists and psychotherapists from South Africa, South America, United Kingdom, Europe and America. The New Zealand Institute of Psychoanalytic Psychotherapy (NZIPP), part of the Psychoanalytic Psychotherapy Association of Australasia), has run five psychoanalytic psychotherapy trainings of four years duration. The International Association of Relational Psychotherapy and Psychoanalysis (IARPP) has grown significantly and hosts an annual conference as does the Centre for Lacanian Analysis (CLA). The Australian and New Zealand Society of Jungian Analysts (ANZSJA), AUT University Department of Psychotherapy and the Institute of Psychosynthesis New Zealand provide psychoanalytically oriented trainings. There are a few clusters of private practitioners who are known for their psychoanalytic orientation.

Counselling psychology, a new registration in New Zealand (Farrell 2013, Thorpe 2013), sees itself as occupying a philosophically pluralistic space (McAteer 2010) which values an integrative and holistic approach, a focus on context, therapeutic reflexivity, and the therapeutic relationship (Kliem and Feather 2013). Although counselling psychology is a few degrees to political left of clinical psychology, I will argue, through the use of vignettes, that these values are sometimes undermined by the long shadows cast by Pavlov, Skinner and Eysenck.

INTO THE HEART OF DARKNESS

One aspect of an academic's role is to act as an external examiner and moderator for other universities. The following is my experience, dreamed into writing (Ogden 1997, 2005), of moderating the final oral exams of ten clinical psychology intern students.

The students were all female (not uncommon in the present climate) young, intelligent, hardworking, compassionate, intuitive and potentially psychologically sophisticated. Many of them had completed a six month practicum rotation at the Department of Corrections, the New Zealand term for the prison services. Associating to the word 'corrections' provides an indication of the primary task of that specific arm of the Department of Justice. I was curious to see if the prison culture of 'correcting bad behaviour' may have influenced the therapeutic style of the psychology department and its clinical students.

Years ago I had been on the same department's external advisory board and knew my way around the beautifully spacious campus. On this visit the uncanny made an appearance. An image arose in my mind that I was entering a jail. I tried to shake off the disturbing feelings of entrapment, blame and punishment. The more I denied and tried to push these pernicious projections away, the stronger the prison walls grew around me.

Gradually, imperceptibly, the fundamental aspects of my worldview were stripped from me. The process began at the initial contact; agreeing to the external examiner's covert duties, perusing the course outline, reading the case reports, and watching the case study videos. Upon entering the psychology department in the university I heard the click of the well-oiled steel door close behind me. My last feeble thought was that it was going to be impossible to think, feel or reflect in this heart of darkness. Then the lights went out.

By the end of the two days of examining my mind was numb. Missing thoughts without a thinker, broken links and empty containers (apologies to Dr Bion). I defensively oscillated between my standard style of dissociation (planning the next holiday in Bali), sadistic fantasies of arrogant and superior revenge, and most importantly, identification with the imprisoner.

Enter another student (perhaps a prisoner) to be examined for a position in the prison services (read registration as a psychologist). This woman was a recent immigrant, naïve about the New Zealand culture, but firmly grounded, relational, and resonating empathy and curiosity. I was woken by a weakly flickering beam of psychoanalytic light from the darkness. Hope? I cautiously crawled into the light to meet this strange new creature. She skilfully presented the case study of an elderly man, cleared by the cardiologist, who presented with atypical heart palpitations and anhedonia. Six months ago he had lost the eternal love of his life when his wife had unexpectedly died of a heart attack. The student hinted at ideas of unprocessed loss and grief and the examiners' positively reinforced her with approving nods. Dispatching with the short history of the past, the business end of the formulation focussed on the physiological symptoms. I heard a silent scream: "What is she doing? Surely not this student?" The patient was skilfully and compassionately educated about 'symptom focusing,' 'symptom attribution' (Broadbent and Petrie 2007) and the 'competing cues theory' (Pennebaker 2000). His heart palpitations were caused by his continuous focus on them (somatic focussing), resulting in noticing previously unfelt twinges, and creating an increasing self-reinforcing cycle of anxiety and negative anticipation. The effective management plan consisted of mutually agreed upon (to improve the therapeutic relationship) distractions in order to focus his attention away from his heart and break the vicious cycle. A brief informative lecture on medical information on the signs of a heart attack was efficiently added to counter his somatic attributions based on his faulty thinking patterns. For good measure some effective empirically supported techniques, grounded in Beck's (Beck, Rush, Shaw and Emery 1979) trifold theory of depression - negative view of self, world and future – were added to reduce his depression. Spiritual, cultural and ethnic valences were respectfully raised.

My heart was breaking, for the patient and the student. Deus ex machina: "This is what is most alive and real in the presentation (Ogden 1997). The heart of the matter. Mark, stop being a coward and help the student bring the patient back to life." Relying on my authority as the senior examiner, I gently asked a few questions about the man's loss of his wife. A look of sad relief fleetingly crossed the student's face, only to be followed a few milliseconds later, by a look of panic and fear. To her credit, she paused for a second, steadied herself and waited for the next question. I went on to ask if she thought there may be a connection between the man's loss and his atypical heart palpitations. My feelings came flooding back, my mind reconnected, I was back in the world of people. A breakthrough was imminent. The student said: "Do you mean he had a *broken heart*?" "Eureka – she got it. The selected fact." Out of left field came a terrible sound – snorts of derisive laughter from the superintendent and her second-in-command. The stench of our humiliation, stupidity and wrong doing became suffocating. The hard concrete jail floor opened up and swallowed the student and the external examiner, delivering them into the depths of incarceration. With a sickening thud the lead door closed on humanity, compassion, love, gratitude and curiosity.

The incident was over in the blink of an eye. Order was restored. We were back in the oral examination, behaving ourselves. Nothing had happened. Years later, I shamefully confess, to my psychoanalytic reader, that the student and the department passed with flying colours.

Retrospectively, I considered the embarrassing possibility that I had willingly handed in my psychoanalytic sensibility in exchange for acceptance, belonging, admiration, importance, and seniority, along with a promise that I would not be sentenced as a difficult, trouble making outsider who thought and behaved in unacceptable ways. A cowardly abandonment of the subversive mission of psychoanalysis - to oppose the destructive imperatives of our economic, political and social systems (Grey 1993).

This is an opportune time to consider the differences between the cognitive behavioural and psychoanalytic styles of practice. In a review of recent psychotherapy process literature Blagus and Hilsenroth (2000, 2002) identified those specific techniques and interventions which distinguished cognitive behavioural from psychodynamic therapy. The distinctive activities which characterised cognitive behavioural therapy are; use of homework and outside-of-session activities, the therapist's active direction of session activity, teaching skills to assist patients to cope with their symptoms, emphasis on the patient's future experiences, the provision of information to the patient about their treatment and symptoms, and an intrapersonal/cognitive focus. On the other hand, the distinctive features of psychodynamic psychotherapy (Shedler 2006, 2010) are; a focus on affect and the expression of emotion, exploration of attempts to avoid distressing thoughts and feelings (defences), identification of recurring themes and patterns, discussion of past experiences (developmental focus), emphasis on interpersonal relationships, focus on the therapy relationship (specifically the transference and countertransference dimension), and the exploration of fantasy life. Using this template how could the vignette be understood? The student therapist ticked all the boxes in the cognitive behavioural manual. She firmly directed the content of the therapy sessions (not allowing the patient to talk too much about the death of his wife, etc.), provided a cognitive focus (identification and directing the patient's thoughts) which was future oriented (clear goals identified) by educating the patient on the treatment of his disorder and symptoms (explaining symptom focusing and attribution, education on signs of heart attacks), and taught him skills (distraction away from somatic focussing) to be practiced as homework assignments aimed at reducing the presenting symptom (atypical heart palpitations). From a psychoanalytic perspective she focussed less on the patient's feelings (abandonment, loss, grief and anger) and symptomatic defences against them (expressive and defensive use of heart palpitations), identifying recurring themes or patterns from past experiences (wife's recent death linked to his previous losses and separations), fantasy life (associations, dreams), and interpersonal relationships (loss of his wife). Considering Gelso's (2014) tripartite model of the therapeutic relationship, the student facilitated a convivial 'real relationship and a clear 'working alliance,' with the patient, but paid no heed to the transference or countertransference dimension (patient's desperate longing for his therapist/wife who abandoned him?). Thinking of the oral exam itself, we can see the lack of containment provided by the examiners, the system, and my spectacularly unsuccessful attempt to turn the tide. There are many possible ways of analysing the overdetermined 'broken heart' vignette. I wish to focus on the attack on potential space and symbol formation.

Potential Space and Symbol Formation

Winnicott (1953) coined the term 'potential space' to describe an intermediate area of experiencing which lies between fantasy and reality, and includes the therapeutic encounter, area of play, creativity and symbolisation as well as the location of the cultural experience Winnicott (1967). Potential space has been seen as a developmental facilitator which assists the child's movement towards emotional independence (Litt 1986). Elaborating on Winnicott's ideas, Ogden (1985) has put forward the concept of a dialectical process as a paradigm for understanding the form and mode of the psychological activity used to generate potential space and meaningful symbol formation. Ogden proposes that potential space may be understood "…as a state of mind based upon a series of dialectical relationships between fantasy and reality, me and not-me, symbol and symbolized" (1985, p. 9).

Based on Hegel (1807) a dialectic is seen as a process in which two opposing concepts each create, inform, preserve, and negate each other. Ogden argues that meaning accrues from difference. In a homogenous field, with no point of difference, there is not even a recognition of the existence of the homogeneous field itself because there are no other terms than itself to attribute to it. The dialectic becomes possible when there is an optimal level of contrast between the opposite poles. The dialectical process has to be created and maintained by a third component of the system, an interpreting subject. This gives rise to a dynamic interplay of three differentiated entities, a triangularity as opposed to a homogeneous oneness. Ogden postulates that it is within the triangularity of interpreting subject and the two other poles of the system (symbol/symbolised, me/not-me, fusion/separateness, etc.) that potential space originates. When the patient's degree of freedom is limited, it is the therapist who takes on the role of the interpreting subject or metasystem (Rey 1986).

Ogden lucidly describes how the presence of potential space gives rise to the emergence of the psychological subject, endowed with the quality of thinking their own thoughts and feelings their own feelings. A rich psychological life emerges with the freedom to think and imagine in a world made up of the layering of symbolic meanings.

Ogden (1985) then goes on to develop a model of the psychopathology of potential space. A collapse of the dialectic in the direction of either of the two poles, or the unavailability of a third to recognize the dialectic, inhibits the production of potential space. Four possibilities options are; reality subsumed by fantasy, reality as a defence against fantasy, dissociation of fantasy and reality, and when the mother/therapist is unable to provide the interpreting function.

I would argue that the second form of psychopathology of potential space, reality as a defence against fantasy, best explains the broken heart vignette. There was an unavailability of a third, interpreting subject, to recognise the dialectic between the symbol (atypical heart palpitations) and the symbolised (grief of the loss of his wife through a heart attack). The strong shift towards reality (techniques to direct the patient's thoughts) defended against exploring the fantasy (the meaning of the heart palpitations). To use Ogden's phrase, reality was employed to 'drain the blood out of the fantasy.' There was no layering of meaning between the somatic symptoms and psychological history. The therapist and client became imprisoned in the realm of the thing in itself and no personal significance was generated.

The broken heart story contains a few twists. I would hazard a hypothesis that the student could have easily become the third in the system, generated potential space and assisted the patient to create meaningful symbolization, if she had been left alone. It was the snorts of derisive laughter from the two examiners that viciously attacked the links and effectively blocked any creative and imaginative process on the part of the student in the examination. Pushing this line of reasoning even further, I would wager that neither of the examiners would treat their own bereaved uncles in the same manner. My experience of them is that they are both creative and insightful people, outside of the oral examination room. So who is left to blame? The system? Enter the concept of 'system domain defences.' Based upon the earlier work of Jacques (1955) and Menzies (1960), Bain (1998) proposed that system domain defences are stronger than, and tend to undermine, the individual players. In academic based psychotherapy these defences are at their height during formal periods such as oral examinations. In order words, although the student and the two examiners may have been able and willing to work in a more creatively symbolic manner, the system domain defences of cognitive behaviourism, managed care, fiscally focussed economy and globalisation were too powerful on the day. This destructive process is increasingly happening throughout the therapy world. To see psychoanalysis' lack of immunity, read Kernberg's (1996) paper on thirty methods to destroy the creativity of psychoanalytic candidates.

TECHNIQUES, TECHNIQUES, TECHNIQUES

The basic assumption of cognitive behavioural therapy is that replacement of maladaptive thinking with realistic and effective thoughts changes the symptomatic behaviour. As simple as ABC: The Activating event is interpreted through the person's Beliefs resulting in the Consequences, including behaviour, feelings and further thoughts (Ellis and Dryden 1987). Change the thought and you change the psychological problem. However, this emphasis on the primacy of cognition in mediating psychological disorder has been increasingly questioned. Longmore and Worrel (2007) in a review of recent studies write that there is: "...little empirical support for the role of cognitive change as causal in the symptomatic improvements achieved in CBT" (p. 173). The most commonly prescribed technique, to support the maladaptive thinking hypothesis, is Socratic questioning which explores the patient's cognitive processes, challenges and changes the irrational beliefs. This is supported by additional techniques such as behavioural activation, and self-monitoring of automatic thoughts and behaviours (particularly negative ones). Therapists are taught to select specific techniques based on the patient's problems and specific goals. The type of techniques may include environmental, biological, behavioural, supportive, experiential or interpersonal. Interestingly, Waller et al. show that that CBT therapists: "...commonly "drift" away from using proven therapeutic techniques" (2012, p. 171). Their research indicates that with eating disorders, the implementation of CBT techniques was far lower than expected, "...particularly for clinicians who are anxious, older or more experienced..." (2012, p. 171).

In the following section I use a group based vignette as a spring board to discuss how the use of behavioural techniques are conceptualised from a psychoanalytic perspective. This is followed by a description of my own supervision style in relation to understanding the implementation of techniques by supervisees.

The Ubiquitous Whiteboard

The scene: after four years of university study, the best psychology students are being selected for eight places in master's degree in counselling psychology. The gate is narrow and persecutory anxieties, and their defences, are at their height. Part of the selection process is a one hour leaderless group in which students discuss the topic of what makes a good counselling psychologist. Four selectors watch the video link from a nearby room. On this occasion we decided that after 40 minutes the students' interactions had become somewhat repetitive and no additional information was being gleaned. Had selectors and candidates withdrawn from the anxiety of the primary task? As the group process co-ordinator, I knocked, entered the room, and told the students that the panel would like to see more interaction and discussion on what makes a good counselling psychologist. Paranoid anxiety bubbled up into the room. A few forays into authentic interpersonal communication was followed closely by another wave of anxiety. One courageous, enthusiastic and proactive student leapt up and stood at the whiteboard with a pen in hand. Displaying excellent leadership and synthesizing skills she started facilitating a brainstorm session of the essential characteristics of a counselling psychologist. Two of the panel members, both card carrying CBT members, burst into peals of embarrassed laughter. Out of earshot, and unaware of the disturbance a few rooms away, the students continued.

The whiteboard was quickly filled with insightfully ordered bullet points. Job well done. (I will spare you my associations to "bullet" points, given my compulsory national service stint in the South African Defence Force many years earlier).

One of my free floating thoughts during the event came in the form of a question. Why did the cognitive behavioural, and not the psychoanalytic or systems based selectors, laugh openly? What was going on? Speaking for myself, I could see the disruption in group process coming and was able to maintain analytic neutrality (translation: stifled any overt response). Perhaps the laughing selectors were reacting to an inherent contradiction in the cognitive behavioural system. I tried to read the unconscious interpretation (Casement 1995, Langs 1995) eloquently delivered by the students: "We tactfully demonstrated to you how this course is really structured, rather than the sales pitch in the course outline. We copied the way you teach and do therapy and showed you what professional counselling psychologists should do. Authentic personal communication is all very well, up to a point, but the real work comes in the form of clear, rational, observable and measurable techniques, such as making logical lists on whiteboards. CBT without a whiteboard is like classical psychoanalysis without a couch." Another question which piqued my curiosity was why the group 'chose' the student with a strong Pacific ethnicity to take charge of the whiteboard technique. Traditionally Pacific and Maori cultures give pride of place to the relationship and dialogue. A frequently quoted Maori proverb is "He aha te mea nui o te ao? He tangata. He tangata. He tangata," Translated it means "What is the most important thing in the world? It is people, it is people, it is people." So why select such an unsuitable candidate for the role? Perhaps colonization and other forms of Stockholm syndrome, demand evidence of a strong bond and identification with the aggressor.

A psychoanalytic reading of techniques may go as follows: A technique may be introduced to defend the therapist, client and system against conflictual feelings and thoughts leaking into the therapy. This effectively blocks and reverses any psychoanalytic penchant to explore difficult feelings. Therapy is nipped in the bud at the very point at which it starts to bloom. A well-chosen technique draws the client and therapist's attention away from their developing relationship to more practical and technical issues. When potential space is foreclosed, and there is no place for reverie, alpha function (Bion 1991), 'lying fallow' (Khan 1997) or 'wasting time' (Ogden 2005), it is virtually impossible to identify important recurring themes. Paraphrasing Langs (1995) 'one frame break begets another.'

Individual Supervision of Cognitive Behavioural Techniques

As a supervisor my first duty is to do no harm, to monitor the risk of the patient to self and others, and to support the therapist. Once risk and therapy interfering behaviours have been effectively addressed it is time to focus on supervising the therapist's cognitive behavioural work. I try to understand their therapeutic world view, style, overt and covert rules of conduct. I immerse myself in the work and support the student to do better cognitive behavioural therapy. Throughout the supervision (we have 45, 60 minute supervision sessions in their internship year) I attempt to use cognitive behavioural language as frequently as possible. This process follows the psychoanalytic style of making a 'trial identification' (Casement 2002) and using the patient's own metaphors, images and language. The breath of permissible language has expanded considerably since the assimilation of Buddhist mindfulness practices into cognitive behavioural practice, making my work somewhat easier. However, on those days when I get out of bed on the wrong side, I still find speaking one language, while thinking in another, trying and frustrating.

Employing a psychoanalytic sensibility to supervision, my first level of intervention is to listen with an evenly hovering analytic ear with no memory, desire or understanding. As the supervision progresses, and the supervisee and I become better acquainted, trusting and confident, I try to facilitate a deeper level of exploration of the behavioural techniques introduced by the therapist. This includes reflecting upon the symbolic significance of the chosen technique and what it may mean to the patient and therapist. For example, we may use the patient's 'thought records' – a form of homework used to identify, debate and alter the patient's negative cognitions. I encourage the therapist to play with, and reflect upon, the possible symbolic meaning of the patient's carefully noted thoughts. The content of the technique thus becomes grist for the psychoanalytic mill and one of the clandestine royal roads to the unconscious of the patient, and possibly the cognitive behavioural therapist.

I find that one of the most difficult, and rewarding, supervisory tasks is to assist the therapist to reflect upon the precipitating factor. In order words, what was happening in the therapy that prompted the therapist to introduce a technique? In the back of my mind I am wondering which unconscious process was arising in the patient, the supervisee and the therapeutic relationship, that needed avoiding. My experience is that supervisees initially say that they felt they were 'not doing anything' but 'merely listening' to the client and in the session. This results in a cognitive dissonance between 'doing' and 'being.' The therapy manual, reinforced by other trainers and supervisees, demands good face validity, something that can be measured and audited. However, if sufficient supervisory rapport is available, students often then drop into a deeper level of reflection, considering what was it about the process that made them anxious enough to shut the client up and disrupt the developing transference-countertransference, by finding a useful technique.

The best timing for this type of supervisory intervention is when the patient consistently refuses, or forgets, to do their homework assignments.

A message from the patient's unconscious requesting entrance into the therapy? Non-compliance with homework raises a red flag for the supervisee. Clearly they are not doing what is expected. Therapy without efficiently completed homework assignments is simply directionless navel gazing, or, horror of horrors, psychoanalysis. An example: The supervisee tells me that his patient has failed to do the prescribed homework, repeatedly. My countertransference knocks loudly.

After years of in vivo exposure, as a supervisor, to sentences containing the phrase: "failed to do his homework" my PTSD has been reinforced rather than extinguished. I regressively lose 52 years. I am tiny, the school is menacing, and I shamefully can't remember whether I did my homework or not. "Focus – back to your current homework – write about the supervision vignette."

In a mildly irritated tone, the supervisee says that the client has on a few occasions actually asked him for some more homework and then 'forgotten' to do it. A plethora of excuses were offered, none of which cut any ice with the therapist. What should he do? It is not uncommon at this point, for me to have received little specific information on the technique in question. "I did the five part model," "we did some mindfulness" or even "I gave him homework" are seen as sufficient explanatory statements. Nuanced specificity is somehow not required. This is similar to a psychoanalytically oriented supervisee blandly saying "I interpreted the transference" or "we dealt with the resistance." These type of statements merely provide a form of face validity indicating that the therapist has ticked the boxes of the model. So I ask for details about the techniques and why they were chosen. Being a non-behaviourist, I can play the naïve card and ask stupid questions.

Knowing that this is a psychologically sophisticated supervisee, and sensing his openness to further exploration, I ask what he 'feels' about the patient's repeated requests and refusals. The supervisee replies: "I think he just can't organise his life." Notwithstanding the unwritten rule that professional CBT therapists are not allowed feelings in the consultation room, I persist in trying to get blood out of the stone. "I agree, but what do you 'feel' about his refusal to do your homework?" The supervisee produces a few more theoretical answers and then guiltily admits that he may feel disappointed, frustrated, perhaps a bit hurt, unwanted, powerless, inadequate, rejected and… angry. Naturally these feelings are not presented in summary form as they are in the last sentence, but rather in a sporadic fashion throughout the session (vis-à-vis free-association). It is my supervisory task to collect them, think about them, and replay them to the supervisee at an opportune time.

A shadowy image of an object-relationship starts forming in the corner of my mind. I ask the supervisee to remind us, so that we can hear it in this context, about the patient's relationship with his father, and recent difficulties with landlords. Father, with his own history of rejection, was prone to be unavailable emotionally to the patient and frequently left the home for long periods of time. In the supervisee's mind, the patient never really lost his father, but neither did he really have him. Perhaps an ambivalent attachment? I ask: "What do you think the patient felt?" "Uh... perhaps hurt, unwanted, powerless, frustrated and angry." A smile of recognition crosses the supervisees face.

What about the incident with the landlord – the precipitating event for the referral to therapy? Initially the landlord was a pleasant man who enthusiastically invited the patient to stay in the communal house. An amicable relationship was forged. One day, out of the blue, for no rhyme or reason (according to the patient) the landlord kicked him out of the house. "And what did the patient feel about that?" - Cut and paste the above mentioned sets of feelings.

Half-way there, with a cursory understanding of subject pole of the object-relationship. "What do you think the landlord (and then the father) felt about the situation?" Warmed up to the task the student says: "Relief, freedom, triumph, pity and some guilt." I continue: "What role does it feel like you are being drawn into?" "uh… being the father?"

I respond: “How would it feel if you, as therapist/father/landlord, gave up on and rejected this difficult patient?”

After playing with the dynamics for some time, the supervisee and I think we have a clearer idea of this “merry dance” (supervisee’s phrase) of push-pull which activates the transference-countertransference of “help me but I won’t let you,” “I want to be close but I am terrified of rejection,” and “I promise, seduce and then reject you, as I expect you to do to me.” The next question, loosely formulated by the supervisee, is: should the therapist address this pattern directly with the patient, or should he use the information indirectly to inform the choice and style of techniques to be implemented? In my experience CBT supervisees are fascinated, curious and fearful about learning how to use the information directly with the patient (see Schaeffer 2007 for a discussion on this double-edged sword).

Paradoxically, students periodically produce a memory of when their own therapist, frequently psychoanalytically oriented, has explicitly brought the transference into the session. However, this style, which is good for the goose, is out of bounds for the CBT therapist and system. This irony is verified by research (Norcross and Grunebaum 2005, Norcross and Guy 2005) indicating that 44% - 66% of behavioural practitioners seek personal therapy, but primarily from non-behaviour colleagues such as psychoanalytic, psychodynamic, eclectic, and existential-humanistic therapists.

Pattern Recognition

One of Shedler’s (2006, 2010) proposed distinctive features of the psychoanalytic technique is the identification of recurring themes and patterns. The therapeutic and supervisory sensibility which I aspire towards is a specific style of pattern recognition elucidated by authors such as (Matte Blanko 1975). The task of the therapist or supervisor is to recognise the patterns in the other distinctive areas of psychoanalytic practice including feelings and defences against them, past experiences, interpersonal relations including the therapeutic relationship, and fantasy life.

In an attempt to moderate my critical academic superego and introject the psychoanalytic emphasis on free-association and symbol formation, I will employ a computer software analogy (personal communication K. van Oldenborgh) to elucidate some aspects of pattern recognition as employed in cognitive behavioural and psychoanalytic thought. At times I have found computer language a useful way of engaging students and supervisees who live in the digital era and are three standard deviations younger than me. The images complement Freud’s original hydraulic model and its iceberg icon.

Therapeutic pattern recognition software works as follows: Web crawlers systematically and comprehensively browse the vast stores of information available to the therapist. This is sorted and categorized. Desirable information is passed through the firewall where it is processed and used to inform the therapist on how to conduct the therapy. Malware and spyware which may interfere with, or corrode, the operating system, is detected, blocked and quarantined by the virus protection. The therapist can choose to destroy the quarantined viruses, or allow their information into the system.

The CBT Application Programme seeks out, categorises, processes and uses large amounts of technical, logical, numerical, information from the left hemisphere.

This app has a highly effective and hyper vigilant antivirus function. Information classed as dangerous or irrelevant includes: a) information from the therapist such as; personal and deeper thoughts, fantasies, dreams, symbolic logic, parapraxes, memory of what the therapist said in the sessions, therapist's personal history, etc. b) information from the client; feelings are restricted by complex algorithms (greater freedom than what the therapist is allowed), as are the client's spontaneous discussions. Information from the real relationship and the working alliance (Gelso 2014) is permitted, but transference information is generally blocked. Alarms sound when dreams, symbolism, fantasies and information from specific areas of the right hemisphere (see Schore 2003, 2011) are detected.

Most students purchase the premium version of the pattern recognition software. This add-on powerfully scours the information web for critical information on the conflicting demands of the university, placement organisation, supervisors and examiners. Patterns are extracted, analysed, and hyper-linked with other students. While this process hones the student's reflective and analytic skills, it also uses up much of the working memory and the system slows down considerably. Academic supervisors cannot afford this option.

There is a fierce ongoing battle between hackers and virus protection programmers. As hackers becomes more devious at finding different 'backdoors,' the virus protection software identifies and blocks more effectively. The protection sensitivity is turned up and a vicious cycle ensues. Since Freud, supervisors with psychoanalytic tendencies, have been trained in the dark arts of subversion and hacking. My task is to leave an attractive Trojan horse at the gate, in the hope that it gets taken into the city under the cover of darkness. The supervisee can then make full use of their own feelings, fantasies and listen uninterruptedly to the patient's story. However, in the light of day, the system defences recover quickly and expel the disruptive unconscious material – something I have tried to illustrate in the vignettes presented above.

One of the problems with the starter versions of the psychoanalytic app is that, although the links are all in place, the bandwidth is compromised. Superficial links are easily made between current and past relationships, a process termed 'parallel process' by other depth therapists. However, the links to the hidden feelings and their defences need to be made and worked through first. In Malan's (1979) terms, the triangle of conflict (defence, anxiety and hidden feeling) needs to be interpreted and worked through, before links are made to the triangle of person (recent relationships, parents or past and the transference). I would argue that this is a sophisticated form of foreclosure on conflicting affects and it forms the lion's share of my supervision with some psychoanalytically oriented supervisees.

SUPERVISORY COUNTERTRANSFERENCE

While writing this chapter, I have been hoping, that you, the sophisticated psychoanalytic reader, has not come to any incisive trial interpretations about my hidden psychic structure. Naturally I have attempted, in defiance of my psychoanalytic sensibility, to stay one step ahead of you. Unfortunately, my formulations of what object-relationship I have been enacting with CBT remain feeble and half-baked. I bolster my confidence with a reminder from Paula Heimann (1950) that therapists can never see their own countertransference because it is, by its very nature, unconscious.

What follows are some 'partially' free associations to my supervisory countertransference of living in a behavioural world. Clearly I cannot begin to help my supervisees understand the schisms and double binds in which they find themselves without some attempt to understand and process my own entrapment in the 'therapy wars' (Saltzman and Norcross 1990).

Plagiarism, Ignorance and Arrogance

I find it extremely irritating and disconcerting when my well-crafted projections refuse to sit still. Frequently, without a 'by your leave,' they up sticks and move away when I most need them! They are parts of me, and although I don't want them back at that time, I certainly miss them and feel depleted when they are not close. In the past two decades CBT has become an inconsistent and unreliable container of my projections. Like a shape-shifter, it continually reinvents its form and identity. The most popular of the so called third wave CBT therapies used in Aotearoa New Zealand include Dialectical Behaviour Therapy (Linehan 1993), Acceptance and Commitment Therapy (Hayes and Smith 2005), Mindfulness-based cognitive therapy (Segal, Williams and Teasdale 2013), and Mindfulness-integrated CBT (Cayoun 2011).

The following experiences spring to mind. In the past five years, a good colleague, whom I appointed when I was head of department, has delivered conference presentations on existentialism and CBT, play therapy and CBT, mindfulness and CBT, environmentalism and CBT, spirituality and CBT, compassion and CBT, indigenous Maori culture and CBT. Recently I attended a one day workshop entitled 'Transference and Countertransference in Cognitive Behavioural Therapy' hosted by the Aotearoa New Zealand Association for Cognitive Behavioural Therapy (NZACBT). I cry "foul." The referee looks the other way.

One of my reactions to old wine in new bottles goes something like; "How dare these ignorant, Johnny-come-lately upstarts, plagiarize and rob my - I mean psychoanalysis' - religious essence and family values? Have they never read Freud or Klein, let alone Ogden, Shedler, Mc Williams, Bateman, Schore or Stern? Is there no end to this vicious colonization under the politically correct guise of helping people more efficiently? The university plagiarism officer is going to hear from me, or was she replaced by another marketing manager? I give up. Withdraw to a safe place of splendid isolation, arrogance and omnipotent holding of the truth. Wait a minute, is that not one of the reasons why psychoanalysis fell from grace?" Parallel to my moral high ground stance, comes a wave of relief. Excitement and admiration for the 'new concept.' I am no longer an Amalekite banished to wander through the wilderness. Here is a bridge, albeit rather rickety, that could span the opposites. Some relevant common ground? A promised route out of the paranoid-schizoid position? I find that I am less defensive when a supervisee introduces one of these newly discovered concepts than when I read them in a journal article. Perhaps, the relational field with the supervisee, helps mitigate my opposition. There are two real people in the room, not two ideas in a book. Admiration and gratitude are attacked by their nemesis. Envy (Klein 1975) shows its destructive face. "Who is this new baby that has wounded my narcissistic specialness by stealing my mother, father and transitional toys?" In response a weak voice says: "in this 'impossible profession' (Freud 1937, Malcolm 1980) it is important to defer gratification in the service of the therapy and client. When your client comes to a brilliant insight, the 'selected fact,' you don't blurt out "but that is my idea. Don't you remember when I lovingly gifted that interpretation to you six months ago? Almost word for word!" Winnicott whispers about how he looked back in horror at how much growth he had prevented by needing to be clever. Perhaps if I can sublimate the need for admiration and specialness, I could gain a greater satisfaction by watching the patient or supervisee discover their truths for themselves, in their own way and at their own pace. This is reminiscent of the bitter sweet process of supporting my children on their journey to separation-individuation.

Snuggled somewhere between these dynamics lurks Sophocles' child - Oedipus. Laius was a practical, fix it, 'doing' rather than 'being,' Health and Safety Advisor who distanced himself from his working class family. During the salad days of undergraduate training I explained to him the difference between depth therapy and behaviourism. In a kind fatherly way, he asked why I would choose to work in a more complex, difficult and time consuming manner. Perhaps this chapter is an attempt to answer the question? Jocasta, trained in the fine arts, read voraciously, loved talking about the meaning of life and relationships, and came from a well-known academic family. Perhaps continually finding myself trying to understand and negotiate between different therapeutic world echoes my oedipal drama. How do I fight in the arena without gauging out my eyes?

One aspect of the Mark-CBT relationship is possibly a displacement of my struggle to adapt as a newly arrived immigrant (21 years) to New Zealand (see Thomas 2014, Thorpe and Thorpe 2008 for a discussion how immigrant psychologists adapt to New Zealand). Here I will simply invite Kafka to speak:

> ...your ignorance of the local situation is so appalling that it makes my head go round to listen to you and compare your ideas and opinions with the real state of things. It's a kind of ignorance that can't be enlightened at one attempt, and perhaps never can be, but there's a lot you could learn if you would only believe me a little and keep your own ignorance constantly in mind. ...wherever you may be, never forget that you're the most ignorant person in the village, and be cautions (Kafka 2008, p. 494).

Gradually I move to a position of curiosity and delight. I enjoy the fascination of observing someone discovering the 'old' idea anew, from a different perspective. Reflecting on my own experience, I never cease to be surprised how I get a flash insight while reading my favourite undergraduate psychodynamic teaching book (Malan 1979) only to notice my own thick underlining of the exact sentence. 35 years ago! The insight vanished and I rediscovered it, numerous times. As Freud and Breuer (1893), and more recently Ogden (2009), argue, psychoanalysis has to be continually rediscovered. Is this any different to when a dyed-in-the-wool behaviourist discovers a new concept which sounds like interpretation, the unconscious or transference? This process of vicarious rediscovery, from a different worldview, helps me revaluate my understanding of the concept. "And the end of all our journeying, will be to arrive where we started, and know the place for the first time" Eliot (1944, p. 86).

Termination

There are different styles of ending sessions and terminating therapy. A cognitive behavioural therapist may start winding down an individual session 15 minutes before time.

The therapist stops the patient talking freely and summarises the session, in bullet format on the whiteboard. The therapist reminds the patient about the next week's homework and clarifies the rationale for its implementation in a positively reinforcing manner. Then the therapist hands the Scott Miller Session Rating Scale (to measure the working alliance with the aim of improving the therapeutic relationship) and the Outcome Rating Scale to the patient. The therapist scores, analyses and discusses the results with the patient openly and efficiently.

The content and process of the next session is then planned by the therapist who explains it to the patient by logically linking it to the remaining symptoms. The therapist ends the session on time and writes up the updated therapeutic plan for the next session, linked to the overall treatment goals, in the clinical notes. A modified version of this process is applied to the ending of the therapy itself in addition to long breaks in the treatment. The process of supervision, with a few caveats, mirrors the style of therapy. Themes of loss or separation as they manifest in the therapy are not intentionally tracked by the therapist. Overt signs that the patient is reacting 'negatively' to the ending or separation are seen as a hindrance to the treatment, understood behaviourally and dealt with through the application of appropriate techniques.

I once observed a clear example of this during a Dialectical Behavioural Therapy (DBT) demonstration supervision group at the annual personality disorders conference.

One of the therapists, sporting a glowing and health look, started the session by describing his wonderful three week skiing holiday. He went on to say that he was somewhat shocked when his patient started screaming at him in the next session. The therapist skilfully applied a variety of behavioural techniques to stop this 'therapy interfering' screaming behaviour, whereupon the patient simply screamed longer and louder.

There was no attempt, by the therapist or the supervisory group, to try and understand the patient's screaming as a reaction to the three weeks gap in the therapy and the therapist's wonderful holiday without the patient. Conference delegates were allowed to observe and learn from the supervision group but forbidden from making any comments. Once again my screech of despair remained muffled.

Psychoanalytically oriented therapists have a different style of working with separations and endings in therapy. Themes of separation are therapeutically privileged and seen as an additional opportunity to work through fundamental issues of separation-individuation. The therapist becomes increasingly sensitive to the patient's communications on loss around breaks and terminations of the therapy. Ideally this is done by keeping in mind the history of separations, and linking it to themes presented in the patient's free associations, feelings, behaviours, fantasy material including dreams (transference), and the therapist's countertransference. Without ongoing interaction and feedback between the therapist and patient, filtered through a psychoanalytic sensibility, themes of endings are avoided and cannot be dealt with effectively in the therapy. Clearly supervising students working in a cognitive behavioural world is a complex process if these nuances are seen as important.

Here, in the termination phase of this chapter I find myself at a loss of how to end before the editor stops me at the word limit. In the case of a book chapter, unlike journals such as Psychoanalytic Dialogues which facilitate debate, there is no right of reply with the exception of a post-publication email discussion. Without the ongoing interaction between the reader and writer, I am alone with my projections, internal working models (Bowlby), object-relations, or basic schemas (Beck). Instead of providing you with a bullet point summary, I will rather reflect upon my feelings about the chapter and a few unsaid points.

I have thoroughly enjoyed writing this chapter for you. To be more precise, I have curiously watched the chapter write itself. Similar to the process of most therapy and supervision the writing has been led by the unconscious. The chapter has disregarded my initial instructions to divide the writing equally into the Shedler's seven categories of psychoanalytic psychotherapy as discussed above. There has been a strong gravitational pull towards the description of group vignettes from my individual supervisory work.

I partly understand this as having to understand the pernicious influence of the system before working on the individual level. Counselling psychology theory argues that without a thorough understanding of the broader context, supervision and therapy would be hamstrung. The system defences would continually trip the supervisory couple up, mostly outside of their awareness. I feel I have gained a deeper understanding of the effect of the biomedical and behavioural system on my relationship with supervisees and their patients. I hope that the chapter has, in some small way, facilitated your thoughts in the area of supervision and therapy in the 2010s.

In retrospect I find the process of using a psychoanalytic sensibility to supervise counselling psychology intern students difficult, stressful, challenging, fascinating, enjoyable, enlivening, intriguing, and rewarding. To illustrate my thesis I seem to have chosen the most dramatic and, for me, memorable examples. However, I would like to add that individual supervision sessions frequently reach a greater depth than I have illustrated, particularly in the second part of the year and in the last three months after the final oral examinations. My sense is that over the past few years, this form of supervisory process has become easier for me and for my supervisees. Perhaps the system is changing and there is greater reflective space? I certainly feel a sense of relief, and trepidation, that after 21 years of being in Aotearoa New Zealand, I have finally managed to start writing about my experience of working and supervising here.

References

Albee, G. W. (2000). The Boulder model's fatal flaw. *American Psychologist*, 55(2), 247-248.

Bain, A. (1998). Social defenses against organisational learning. *Human Relations*, 51(3), 413-429.

Beck, A. T., Rush, A. J., Shaw, B. F. and Emery, G. (1979). *Cognitive therapy of depression*. New York, NY: Guilford Press.

Bion, W. R. (1991). *A memoir of the future*. London: Karnac Books.

Blagus, M. D. and Hilsenroth, M. J. (2000). Distinctive activities of short-term psychodynamic-interpersonal psychotherapy: A review of the comparative psychotherapy process literature. *Clinical Psychology*, 8(167-188). doi:10.1093/clipsy.7.2.167.

Blagus, M. D. and Hilsenroth, M. J. (2002). Distinctive activities of cognitive–behavioral therapy: A review of the comparative psychotherapy process literature. *Clinical Psychology Review*, 22(5), 671-706. doi:10.1016/S0272-7358(01)00117-9.

Breuer, J. and Freud, S. (1893). Studies on hysteria. In: J. Strachey (Ed.), *The standard edition of the complete works of Sigmund Freud*, Volume 2 (pp. 1-252). London: Hogarth Press.

Broadbent, E. and Petrie, K. J. (2007). Symptom perception. In: S. Ayers, A. Baum, C. McManus, S. Newman, K. Wallston, J. Weinman and R. West (Eds.), *Cambridge handbook of psychology, health and medicine* (pp. 219-222). Cambridge, UK: Cambridge University Press.

Casement, P. (1995). *On learning from the patient*. London: Routledge.

Casement, P. (2002). *Learning from our mistakes: Beyond dogma in psychoanalysis and psychotherapy*. New York, NY: Guilford Press.

Cayoun, B. A. (2011). *MiCBT - Principles and practice*. West Sussex, United Kingdom: Wiley-Blackwell.

Corballis, M. C. (1990). The two profiles of psychology. *New Zealand Journal of Psychology*, 18, 2-8.

Eliot, T. S. (1944). Little Gidding V. In: *Four Quartets* (pp. 67-90). Retrieved from http://www.davidgorman.com/4Quartets/4-gidding.htm.

Ellis, A. and Dryden, W. (1987). *The practice of rational-emotive therapy (RET)*. New York, NY: Springer Publishing Co.

Farrell, B. (2013). Counselling psychology in Aotearoa/New Zealand – What is it, where has it come from, and where might it go? *New Zealand Journal of Psychology*, 42(3), 11-17.

Freud, S. (1937). Analysis terminable and interminable. *International Journal of Psycho-Analysis*, 18, 372-405.

Gelso, C. (2014). A tripartite model of the therapeutic relationship: Theory, research, and practice. *Psychotherapy Research*, 24(2), 117-131. doi:10.1080/10503307.2013.845920.

Grey, C. C. (1993). The subversive mission of psychoanalysis. *International Forum of Psychoanalysis*, 2, 13-17.

Hayes, S. C. and Smith, S. (2005). *Get out of your mind and into your life*. Oakland, CA: New Harbinger Publications.

Hegel, G. W. F. (1807). *Phenomenology of spirit* (A. V. Miller, Trans.). London: Oxford University Press (Reprinted from 1977).

Heimann, P. (1950). On counter-transference. *International Journal of Psycho-Analysis*, 31, 81-87.

Hofstede, G. (1983). The cultural relativity of organizational practices and theories. *Journal of International Business Studies*, 14(2), 75-89. doi:10.2307/222593.

Jacques, E. (1955). Social systems as a defense against persecutory and depressive anxiety. In: P. H. M. Klein and R. E. Money-Kyrle (Ed.), *New directions in psychoanalysis* (pp. 478-498). London: Karnac Books.

Kafka, F. (2008). *The castle*. London: Vintage.

Kazantzis, N. and Deane, F. (1998). Theoretical orientations of New Zealand psychologists: An international comparison. *Journal of Psychotherapy Integration*, 8(2), 97-113. doi:10.1023/A:1023236406807.

Kennedy-Merrick, S. L., Haarhoff, S. J., Stenhouse, L. M., Merrick, P. L. and Kazantzis, N. (2008). Training cognitive bahavioural therapy practitioners in New Zealand: From university to clinical practice. *New Zealand Journal of Psychology*, 37(2), 8-17.

Kernberg, O. F. (1996). Thirty methods to destroy the creativity of psychoanalytic candidates. *The International Journal of Psychoanalysis*, 77(5), 1031-1040.

Khan, M. M. (1997). On lying fallow: as aspect of leisure. *International Journal of Psychoanalytic Psychotherapy*, 6, 397-402.

Klein, M. (1975). *Envy and gratitude and other works, 1946-1963*. London: Hogarth Press.

Kliem, A. and Feather, J. S. (2013). Collaborative partnership and reflective practice: An intern counselling psychologist and client share their therapeutic journey. *New Zealand Journal of Psychology*, 42(3), 59-65.

Langs, R. (1995). The therapeutic relationship and deviations in technique. *International Journal of Psychoanalytic Psychotherapy*, 4, 106-141.

Linehan, M. M. (1993). *Cognitive-behavioural treatment of borderline personality disorder*. New York, NY: Guilford Press.

Litt, C. J. (1986). Theories of transitional object attachment: An overview. *International Journal of Behavioral Development*, 9(3), 383-399. doi:10.1177/016502548600900308.

Longmore, R. J. and Worrell, M. (2007). Do we need to challenge thoughts in cognitive behavior therapy? *Clinical Psychology Review*, 27(2), 173-187. doi:10.1016/j.cpr.2006.08.001.

Malan, D. H. (1979). *Individual psychotherapy and the science of psychodynamics*. London, UK: Oxford University Press.

Malcolm, J. (1980). *Psychoanalysis: The impossible profession*. New York, NY: Random House.

Matte Blanko, I. (1975). *The unconsicous as infinite sets*. London: Duckworth.

McAteer, D. (2010). Philosphilosophical pluralism: Navigating the seas of diversity in psychotherapeutic and counselling psychology practice. In: M. Milton (Ed.), *Therapy and beyond: Counselling psychology contributions to therapeutic and social issues* (pp. 1-19). West Sussex, UK: Wiley-Blackwell.

Menzies, I. (1960). A case-study in the functioning of social systems as a defence against anxiety: A report on a study of the nursing service of a general hospital. *Human Relations*, 13(2), 5-121. doi:10.1177/001872676001300201.

Norcross, J. C. and Grunebaum, H. (2005). The selection and characteristics of therapists' psychotherapists: A research synthesis. In: J. D. Geller, J. C. Norcross and D. E. Orlinsky (Eds.), *The psychotherapist's own psychotherapy: Patient and clinician perspectives* (pp. 201-213). New York, NY: Oxford University Press.

Norcross, J. C. and Guy, J. D. (2005). The prevalence and parameters of personal therapy in the United States. In: J. D. Geller, J. C. Norcross and D. E. Orlinsky (Eds.), *The psychotherapist's own psychotherapy: Patient and clinician perspectives* (pp. 165-176). New York, NY: Oxford University Press.

Norcross, J. C. and Wampold, B. E. (2011). *Evidence-based therapy relationships: Research conclusions and clinical practices*. 48(1), 98-102. doi:10.1037/a0022161.

Oakes, L. (1999). Psychotherapy in Aotearoa. *Psychotherapy in Australia*, 2(2), 60-65.

Ogden, T. H. (1985). On potential space. *The International Journal of Psychoanalysis*, 66, 129-141.

Ogden, T. H. (1997). Reverie and metaphor: Some thoughts on how I work as a psychoanalyst. *The International Journal of Psychoanalysis*, 78, 719-732.

Ogden, T. H. (2005). On psychoanalytic supervision. *The International Journal of Psychoanalysis*, 86(5), 1265-1280. doi:10.1516/BEE8-C9E7-J7Q7-24BF.

Ogden, T. H. (2009). Rediscovering psychoanalysis. *Psychoanalytic Perspectives*, 6, 22-31.

Pennebaker, J. W. (2000). Psychological factors influencing the reporting of physical symptoms. In: A. A. Stone, J. S. Turkkan, C. A. Bachrach, J. B. Jobe, H. S. Kurtzman and V. S. Cain (Eds.), *The Science of self-report: Implications for research and practice* (pp. 299-316). London: Lawrence Erlbaum Associates.

Rey, H. (1986). The schizoid mode of being and the space-time continuum (beyond metaphor). *Journal of the Melanie Klein Society*, 4, 12-52.

Saltzman, N. and Norcross, J. C. (Eds.). (1990). *Therapy wars: Contention and convergence in differing clinical approaches. Jossey-Bass social and behavioral science series.* San Francisco, CA: Jossey-Bass.

Schaeffer, J. A. (2007). *Transference and countertransference in non-analytic therapy: Double-edged swords*. Plymouth: University Press of America.

Schore, A. N. (2003). *Affect regulation and the repair of the self.* New York, NY: W. W. Norton.

Schore, A. N. (2011). The right brain implicit self lies at the core of psychoanalysis. *Psychoanalytic Dialogues*, 21(1), 75-100. doi:10.1080/10481885.2011.545329.

Segal, Z. V., Williams, J. M. G. and Teasdale, J. D. (2013). *Mindfulness-based cognitive therapy for depression*. New York, NY: Guilford Press.

Shedler, J. (2006). That was then, this is now: An introduction to contemporary psychodynamic therapy. *Unpublished paper: University of Colorado School of Medicine*. Retrieved from http://www.jonathanshedler.com/PDFs/Shedler%20%282006%29%20 That%20was%20then,%20this%20is%20now%20R9.pdf.

Shedler, J. (2010). The efficacy of psychodynamic psychotherapy. *American Psychologist*, 65 (2), 98-109.

Thomas, A. (2014). *South African immigrant psychologists' experiences of the therapeutic relationship with their New Zealand Pakeha clients.* AUT University, Unpublished dissertation.

Thorpe, M. R. (2013). The process of conducting qualitative research as an adjunct to the development of therapeutic abilities in counselling psychology. *New Zealand Journal of Psychology*, 42(3), 35-43.

Thorpe, M. R. and Farrell, B. (In Press). The client-professional relationship. In: W. Waitoki, J. Feather and N. Robertson (Eds.), *Professional practice of psychology in Aotearoa New Zealand*: Manuscript submitted for publication.

Thorpe, M. R. and Thorpe, K. M. A. L. (2008). Immigrant psychotherapists and New Zealand clients. *The Journal of the New Zealand Association of Psychotherapists: Forum*, 14, 30-45.

Waller, G., Stringer, H. and Meyer, C. (2012). What cognitive behavioral techniques do therapists report using when delivering cognitive behavioral therapy for the eating disorders? *Journal of Consulting and Clinical Psychology*, 80(1), 171-175. doi:10.1037/a0026559.

Winnicott, D. W. (1953). Transitional objects and transitional phenomena. *International Journal of Psychoanalysis*, 34, 89-97.

Winnicott, D. W. (1967). The location of cultural experience. *International Journal of Psychoanalysis*, 48(3), 368-372.

In: Psychoanalysis
Editor: Zelda Gillian Knight
ISBN: 978-1-63483-858-0

Chapter 4

TRAUMA OR LOSS: INTERVIEWS WITH HOLOCAUST SURVIVORS

C. Fred Alford*, PhD
Professor of Government and Distinguished Scholar-Teacher,
University of Maryland, Maryland, US

ABSTRACT

What is the precise relationship between loss and trauma? Recently it has been argued that they should be more sharply distinguished. Drawing upon extended interviews with survivors of the Holocaust, this essay argues that traumatic loss has the quality of an intrusion, and in this regard is similar to psychic trauma associated with less dramatic and total losses. Unlike those who recover from trauma with the help of therapy, most Holocaust survivors recovered through the process of doubling, a practice originally suggested by one of the founders of trauma theory, Sándor Ferenczi. The practice is not without its costs, particularly among older survivors.

Keywords: trauma, loss, Holocaust survivor, post traumatic stress disorder, doubling, Ferenczi

INTRODUCTION

Is loss a component of chronic long term trauma? If so, how best to understand and deal with it? Some, such as Horowitz (2009) argue that loss is not central to trauma. To be sure, extreme loss generates many of the familiar symptoms of trauma, such as the flashback, and more generally the inability to believe what one knows to be true (Horowitz 2009, p. 29). In what is generally considered traumatic loss, it is impossible to say "this happened then." For "then" never stops being now; the past is never past. But, Horowitz continues, loss is not trauma (p. 34). For even traumatic loss is always related to normal loss, even losses with

* E-mail: calford@umd.edu.

which we never come to terms. Put simply, there is a continuum, however fragile, between normal and traumatic loss.

This is not the case with traumatic suffering. Traumatic suffering breaks the link between the suffering of loss and normal suffering via the compulsive repetition of the moment of victimization. Not the return of the past (as in loss), but the persistence of the thing itself, "a broken-off piece of suffering," marks traumatic suffering (Horowitz 2009, p. 38). Trauma in this regard is special, for there is nothing to be learned from it, no connection to normal experience.

Whether it is useful to separate trauma and loss in this way is the topic of this essay. Rather than simply speculate about their relationship, I consider a particular group of traumatized men and women who, perhaps more than any other, seem to have suffered both trauma and loss. Or rather, trauma and loss seem to be inseparable in their experiences: survivors of the Holocaust. Important about these survivors for our purposes is that they are looking back on their experiences from a distance of a quarter century and more, often as many as forty years later. The persistence of loss as a feature of their trauma is striking. Of course, theirs was a particularly terrible and intense trauma, but there is increasing interest these days in what has come to be called C-PTSD, chronic or complex post traumatic stress disorder, often associated with captivity or entrapment (Roth, Newman, Pelcovitz, van der Kolk and Mandel 1997). The Holocaust is incomparable, but not incommensurable.

METHODS

The witnesses quoted are among the first witnesses to have their testimony videotaped. The Fortunoff Archive for Holocaust Testimony at Yale University was co-founded by a psychiatrist and child survivor, Dori Laub (www.library.yale.edu/testimonies/about/founders/laub.html). This accounts for one of the striking aspects of the testimonies. They are long and relatively unstructured. In this regard they are quite different from the interviews undertaken for Steven Spielberg's Shoah Foundation (sfi.usc.edu). Under the Fortunoff model the interviewers ask relatively few questions, allowing long responses, and long uncomfortable pauses, often punctuated with tears, and sometimes moans. Some interviews run over four hours. Most run about two hours. The interviews began in the 1970's, and for many survivors it was the first time they had talked about the Holocaust, even to their families. Even, or especially, within the Jewish community, discussion of the topic was not encouraged until years later. Instead, survivors were encouraged to get on with the task of building a new life, not dwelling on the past. Many survivors were themselves often shocked by the emotional intensity with which their memories and feelings, damned up for so many years, seemed to come tumbling out. Of course, we will have to question this familiar but not necessarily accurate hydraulic metaphor. I have viewed over two hundred-fifty hours of testimony, often several times over (Alford 2009, 2013).

One of the most influential, and best, books on Holocaust testimonies in recent decades is Lawrence Langer's *Holocaust Testimonies: The Ruins of Memory* (1991). It was particularly valuable as a corrective to Victor Frankl's *Man's Search for Meaning* (1984), originally published in 1946, which argued that even the assault of the Holocaust could be withstood, if one was fortunate enough to survive, with the right attitude. On the contrary, Langer argued that in many respects survivors were ruined by experiences they could not recover from. Consider the titles of his chapters: "anguished memory," "humiliated memory," "tainted memory," and "unheroic memory." Langer comes closer to the truth than Frankl, but in my experience Langer fails to convey the vigor and vitality with which many survivors lived even their haunted lives.

Trauma Is Loss

What does the trauma suffered by Holocaust survivors look like decades after their survival? Does it look like loss? Like fear? Like a combination of both? Judith Herman's *Trauma and Recovery* (1997) is still one of the single most influential books on the topic, particularly among clinicians like herself. Yet, her clinical focus is far from narrow. For Herman, trauma is not just an assault on body and mind. It is an existential crisis.

> Traumatic events destroy the victim's fundamental assumptions about the safety of the world, the positive value of the self, and the meaningful order of creation. The traumatic event challenges an ordinary person to become a theologian, a philosopher, and a jurist. [The victim] stands mute before the emptiness of evil, feeling the insufficiency of any known system of explanation (Herman 1997, pp. 51, 178).

Or as Muncie K. (T-503), a Holocaust survivor interviewed in 1984 put it, "I see the bodies, the trucks, all my life, that I am normal, that I have children, that I can live. I don't know how. It is just amazing that I can have a normal life after all I went through."[1]

This, though, is not the experience that Muncie K. cannot put into the past. What astonishes Muncie is how unbelievable it all was, and by unbelievable Muncie means the moral and human unbelievability. "Absolutely unbelievable that they did this to us. Why? This is the question I always ask." She repeats a version of this statement at least a half dozen times during her interview for the Fortunoff Video Archive, an interview that lasted about two hours. By the end of the interview she is practically screaming her question-as- statement.

Herman's claim that trauma is an existential crisis, a claim exemplified by Muncie K., raises the question of what trauma really is. In looking at Holocaust survivors who suffered chronic and extreme trauma, I will not be answering the question in general. There are traumas, not trauma. I will be attempting a preliminary answer for a special population. It has implications for other survivors of trauma, particularly severe chronic trauma, but the larger and more general relevance of these conclusions is not clear, though I will speculate in the conclusion. (See Appendix on the changing status of Post Traumatic Stress Disorder in the fifth edition of the *Diagnostic and Statistical Manual of Mental Disorders* of the American Psychiatric Association, known as *DSM-5*.)

For Herman, trauma therapy is not just about the recovery of memory. This certainly fits the Fortunoff witnesses, none of whom seem to have forgotten their experiences, even if they are sometimes incredulous.

[1] The interviews in the Fortunoff Archive are not anonymous. However, the Archive prefers this method of citation. Summaries of the interviews are available on the Yale Orbis catalog, open to the public, and accessible by typing HVT before the accession number (T-xxx).

The final problem the trauma victim faces is learning how to mourn the world she has found herself in. "The descent into mourning is at once the most necessary and the most dreaded task of this [late] stage of recovery." (Herman 1997, p. 188) Patients fear that that once they start grieving they will never stop.

As one Holocaust survivor put it, "even if it takes one year to mourn each loss, and even if I live to be 107 [and mourn all the members of my family], what do I do about the rest of the six million?" (Danieli 1988, p. 292) Curiously, Herman frequently illustrates a point about chronic childhood abuse, usually sexual, with quotations from Holocaust survivors. "`Never again' is the survivor's universal cry." Herman (1997, p. 206) is referring to a survivor of childhood sexual abuse, but one can see how the two atrocities are interwoven in her thinking about trauma. One might argue that she is painting trauma with too broad a brush. Perhaps, but she is not drawing all trauma under this horizon, only the chronic and extreme. Chronic or complex post-traumatic stress disorder (C-PTSD) is not yet recognized in the *DSM-5* (American Psychiatric Association 2013), as a distinct subtype, but there is no reason to think that its sequela are identical to those suffered by an adult who was brutally assaulted, or another adult who watched helplessly as her partner died in a car accident. A singular event, no matter how terrible, may have different psychic consequences than years of continuous and severe trauma.

Horowitz (2009) argues, as we have seen, that it is misleading to assimilate trauma and loss. Even loss that we never make good on, loss that we can never truly accept in our heart of hearts, is part of or related to normal development, according to both Freudian (1917) and Kleinian (1940) perspectives. Trauma, on the other hand, is in many respects the opposite of loss. Trauma is not the absence that never can be made whole. Trauma is the intrusion that insures that the future will always be like the past. "Trauma is the absolute assurance that the past, present, and future cannot be mediated. It is the certainty of no [new] experience" (Horowitz 2009, p. 35).

Like so many contemporary theorists of trauma (Caruth 1996, van der Kolk and van der Hart 1995), Horowitz argues that trauma cannot be spoken, and it cannot be treated as though it were a normal emotional disturbance. Horowitz's is the phenomenological version of the claim by Caruth, van der Kolk, and others, that traumatic knowledge is not knowledge in the ordinary sense of the word. Trauma is not knowledge, because it is not experienced as thought, but rather as thing. "Trauma cannot be thought. It can only be halted" (Horowitz 2009, p. 40).

It is hard to know what these last lines mean. Trauma cannot be thought. It can only happen. But trauma can be thought *about*. Horowitz thinks about trauma and writes down what he thinks. Many of the Fortunoff witnesses think about the trauma they have experienced, and reflect upon it in their testimonies. Since Horowitz fails to define trauma (in terms of magnitude, chronicity, or any of the usual parameters) we are left with the question of whether it is useful to separate trauma and loss without knowing what constitutes trauma. Still, it remains an interesting question.

Consider a couple of testimonies about loss.

Eva L. (T-71) lost her first family to the Holocaust and has gone on to have a second one. Her current husband and children are her life. Yet Eva dreads large family gatherings. "So hungry for family." She means, I think, "I am so hungry for family," but the sentiment is so primordial that it is expressed as hunger in the absence of an "I." (Eva L. T-71) No matter how much love she feels for her second family, it cannot erase the loss of her first. Nothing can. They are incommensurable, and a part of Eva will always remain inconsolable, the part that cannot say "I."

Abe L. (T-1394) saw his parents shipped off to Auschwitz from the Vilna ghetto. Just 16, he joined his brothers in the woods who were active with the Bielski Partisans. Too young to take part in major actions, he reports his brothers bombing trains, taking whole villages, and generally fulfilling the role of the heroic Jewish resistance fighters. A junior partisan, Abe is not the sort of person one would expect to be vulnerable to PTSD, primarily because his wartime experience was associated with more action and less passivity and helplessness than most survivors. Yet, helplessness is all he can talk about. Not his several years with the partisans until the war's end, but his previous life in the ghetto. "Every night I think of my brother's 2 kids, shot in cold blood by the local police." He thinks of the impious burial of his grandmother in the garden of his house. He thinks of what must have become of his parents at Auschwitz. He can't stop crying.

> I thought that when the years go by, the Holocaust would go further away. It will never go away until the end of time. I dream about it. I can't get something like that out of my system. We were all, all the Jews in all the shtetls around us like brother and sister. All gone now, especially the children. You can't get that out of your mind. The hole in your heart gets bigger. The Holocaust is getting closer not farther. I think I'll finish up here. The people and children, they don't go away. I have to stop. I'd like to cut it off. It's too much.

Existential Loss?

Should one argue that Eva's and Abe's losses are so traumatic because what they *really* lost is faith in a world in which loss makes sense. Eva L. (T-71), it should be noted, asks almost the same question as Muncie K. It is a common question. "If I could come here and have a family and live a normal life, more or less, then how could it have happened? How could I survive? Who would believe if I can't believe it myself?"

Are losses like Eva's and Abe's not losses in the ordinary sense? For they do not seem to fit Horowitz's claim that "loss is the incomprehensible relationship to something that is easy enough to grasp, but we cannot bring ourselves to believe." For not only can Eva and Muncie, especially, not believe what happened, but one cannot say that their experiences were easy enough to grasp. They were imprisoned in another world, in which the rules of ordinary loss do not apply. As Leon put it,

> People hadn't become ciphers yet. They were still, up to that moment, human beings. With a name, with a personality. And when they were gone, their image was retained. But the mass disappearing into the gas chambers—they're just a mass of people going—like into a slaughterhouse. There was a difference. A qualitative and quantitative difference (Greenspan 1998, p. 159).

These were not ordinary losses. Not only were they difficult to believe, but they were not "easy enough to grasp."

Would it help to call these losses "existential"? What would make them "existential" is what Muncie, Eva and Abe have learned about the world, the knowledge to which Herman refers. Eva, Muncie and Abe “stand mute before the emptiness of evil, feeling the insufficiency of any known system of explanation.” Only Muncie, at least, does not remain mute. She screams for an answer, and one is reminded of Albert Camus' (1955, p. 45) definition of the absurd. The absurd arises from the experience of the gulf between humanity’s demand for meaning and nature’s unreasoning silence. Only in this case absurdity takes on a new and strictly human meaning. Humans demand a meaning comprehensible to the pre- (and post-) Auschwitz self. The world of death that was Auschwitz replies with a meaning no longer comprehensible in the discourse of ordinary human life and death, in which death is measured by individuals, not piles of nameless corpses.

The absurd cannot be grieved. It has the quality of what Maurice Blanchot (1995, p. ix) called "knowledge as disaster," in which one learns too much. Traumatic loss *is* intrusion. In that sense it fits the traditional definition of trauma (van der Kolk and Saporta 1991). As Julia S. put it, "You’re not supposed to see this; it doesn’t go with life. It doesn’t go with life.” (T-934) To undergo an experience so alien to life is not merely a loss; it is the intrusion of anti-life, sometimes in the guise of unbelievable life. To recover from this knowledge, which is not absurd, just incomprehensible, the victim must mourn. Because it is incompatible with life, some victims like Abe must mourn forever. All of which suggests that trauma itself is sometimes experienced as the reality that occludes meaningful narrative, meaningful life. This does not mean that trauma is somehow beyond narrative. On the contrary, trauma is the last narrative, after which there can be no other, for there is no more meaning left in the world. Or at least that is how it is experienced by the victim. To render these real, concrete losses “existential” is not wrong, and yet it seems unnecessarily abstract. Traumatic losses are overwhelming not because they fit a particular definition of trauma as the inability to not repeat the past, but because the past has become unbearable. The past is so depleted and filled with pain that it destroys every present moment: that is trauma as loss. The category of “existential loss” is created by real, actual losses. What else could it mean? One does not become traumatized by loss in the abstract, only by loss of the concrete person or way of life. Unless, of course, one has experienced mass, nameless death. Then the loss is not of a person, but a belief that there are things humans do not do to each other, things that cannot happen on this earth. Not just persons, but places, and all that goes with them, are subject to loss: a home, an extended community, a way of life, a history--all may be subject to devastating loss. And all may be lost together. Annette Wieviorka quotes Richard Marienstras in an effort to understand what life was like for those who survived the Holocaust.

> Let a Frenchman try to imagine—but could he imagine this fully?—France erased from the map, and finding himself with a handful of French speakers among people totally ignorant of the collectivity to which he belonged and whose language, manners, landscape, history, cuisine, institutions, religion, and economy now defined the concrete modalities according to which he could belong to the human race. What then would be his sense of life, what possibility would he have to participate in the *project* of the community that welcomes him, except in the most superficial way? (Wieviorka 1997, p. 26, quoting Marienstras).

The Theory of Assumptive Loss

Muncie, Eva, and Abe have been betrayed by humanity. By their expectations of what humanity is capable of even at its worst is traumatic loss (DePrince and Freyd 2002). We create a stable world that we subsequently discover to be real. All that is required is what D. W. Winnicott (1953) called the “good enough mother,” or what John Bowlby (1973, p. 203) called “internal working models.”

All that is required is in fact a lot: that mothers and other primary caretakers cooperate with the infant and young child’s naïve expectation that the world will be there to meet his or her needs. The infant and young child does not think “I expect mother to be there and feed me.” But when the infant is hungry, cries out, and is fed in a predictable manner, he or she develops a basic trust in the world, especially if he or she is physically held in a comfortable and comforting fashion (Winnicott 1992).

Adults do not need to be held and fed in this way, but the need for a secure holding environment, as Winnicott called it, never goes away. It just changes its form, such as the need for a stable job, a meaningful culture, family, food, and shelter.

An implication of this assumption is that the world that is shattered by trauma, a world that appears to be an outer world of order, stability, predictability, goodness, and value, is actually an inner world, a self-made world. Or rather it is both, for this good enough world that the child discovers, and the adult goes on to live in, is actually the creation of the self in cooperation with a world that acts enough like one’s internal expectation that there is no need to question one’s basic assumptions about the world. Seen from this perspective, trauma is the shattering of an unwritten social contract between self and world: that the world will, with all its dangers, be good enough and safe enough to support my original experience of having discovered a good enough world to live in (Kauffman 2002).

Trauma takes place where my expectation meets the world’s reality. If I am supremely fortunate throughout my life, I will never know this or learn this.

The suture will remain unnoticed, for it will be unnecessary to notice it. Conversely, if I am unfortunate, the world will become filled with antimen, dedicated to the destruction of me and my kind.

Then I will be traumatized, not only in the realm of fear, but in the realm of loss of my assumptive world. Since this world that is destroyed is also inside me, I will fall apart. One reason Muncie and Eva keep saying they can’t believe what happened to them is because to do so they would have to say that everything they ever believed about the world was wrong: wrong then and wrong now. Knowledge as disaster, as Blanchot calls it. Better to doubt oneself, at least a little bit.

Jean Améry, who was interned in Auschwitz, decided never to return to his native Austria after the war (Alford 2013, pp. 157-192)[2]. The experience led him to think long and hard about exile. To be without a home, Améry concluded, is to lack a fundamental security. Security stems from not having to constantly respond to chance occurrences, because we have confidence in our understanding of the culture in which we live, while trusting our ability to interpret the language, gestures, and expressions of the citizens among whom we live. “One feels secure, however, when no chance occurrence is to be expected, nothing completely

[2] The “antiman” is Jean Améry’s (1980, p. 40) term. Améry was a resistance fighter in Belgium who was tortured before being interned at Auschwitz, Buchenwald, and Bergen-Belsen.

strange to be feared."(Améry 1980, p. 47) Even if this is an idealization from a man writing in exile, his point is provocative. "There is no `new home.' Home is the land of one's childhood and youth" (p. 48).

To be sure, over time the exile can learn the subtleties of the language and culture of his or her new home. However, this will always be a mental acquisition, an intellectual act. He or she will always have to think about it; it will never be entirely natural. Améry is a fine example of the mental self-holding of the exile, who can never feel simply held again, but who must always live on the surface of his skin in the new culture. The exile can never just be, or so Améry argues, and his life seems to attest. Améry (1980, 44) puts it succinctly, "I was no longer an I and did not live within a We." Were he to belabor the point, he might have said, "Because I no longer lived within a We, I could no longer afford to be fully and spontaneously an I."

Home is Where We Start From (1990), the title of a collection of Winnicott's essays, reflects the same idea. One can build new homes, in new lands, and eventually come to feel that one belongs there. One can even have what Améry (1980, 41) calls a "transportable home," by which he means a religion or ideology. But one can never replace one's first home, and the security it provided (Améry 1980, p. 46).

One can never replace one's first home, and when it and everything associated with it is taken away, one can never regain the security associated with it. It might seem that Améry is talking about fear, for that is how we have learned to think about chronic trauma: a perpetual, often low level, occasionally dramatic eruption of fear that never goes away. But perhaps that is not the best way to think about the loss. In characterizing his loss as loss of home, Améry seems to be writing about the loss of a world he could rely on in order to just be. Such a world is the basis of security, and one might as well categorize insecurity not as a dimension of fear, but of homesickness (*Heimweh*). That is, the loss of the freedom to just be. Kauffman (2002, p. 210) calls it "a caesura in becoming." Following Winnicott, it might be more accurate to call it a gap in spontaneous being, a gap that must be constantly minded and mended, so that one can never just freely exist in the world. This, at least, seems closer to Winnicott's theory and to the experience that Améry is writing about. But the words do not matter as much as the idea.

DOUBLING

There are no constants among survivor testimonies, no universal themes. The two that come closest, are "no one can understand who wasn't there," and "even today I live a double existence." Kraft (2002, p. 2) argues that doubling is the near universal theme.

> Almost all witnesses state that they live a double existence. There is a Balkanization of memory, where Holocaust memories and normal memories are assigned to two, sometimes hostile territories. Consider a few phrases that witnesses use: "a double existence," "another world," "a schizophrenic division," "two worlds," "two different planets," "double lives."

What requires understanding is not so much the frequency with which witnesses refer to "doubling," for that is an observational given, but whether they are all referring to the same process, and what that process or processes might be. For some the process is almost like that of watching another testify. "I made a videotape for my daughter. She said `mommy, you must be so sad.' But when I see it, it's like it happened to another person. At moments you get mushy, but at moments you think you're telling someone else's story" (Sonia P. T-1681).

Reuben experiences doubling in a less literal fashion. A concentration camp survivor, he speaks of himself as "like a *gilgul*," a ghost, a soul that comes back without a body to wander the world uneasily, lost. "Reuben's death" is how Henry Greenspan (1998, p. 66) refers to Reuben's life. Yet, of all Greenspan's "recounters" (his preferred term, though he uses "witness" and "survivor" as well), Reuben lived out his days surrounded by the most abundant life: wife, six children, and a big dog with puppies wandering in and out of the room in which Greenspan interviews Reuben for hours. Additionally, Reuben is constantly being called to the phone. Often, it seems, to settle a community dispute, a role for which he appears well suited but which is entirely informal. What to make of a ghost who seems so alive, or at least so surrounded by life? Greenspan says simply "The ongoing death that Reuben describes, therefore, should not blind us to the substance of his ongoing life" (p. 67).

For Reuben, doubling is a double-helix, the strands of life and death wrapped around each other in a complex pattern that in the end favors life over death, without ever forgetting, or allowing the witness to forget, that every moment of life is twinned with a moment of death.

And vice-versa. By focusing solely on the living deaths of those who died at Auschwitz, we "miss the vitality of their ongoing lives, memories and legacies that have nothing to do with the destruction but which allow survivors to recount at all" (Greenspan 1998, p. 169). This is important to understand--what is broken and what remains, and how these two parts of survivors' lives live on close, but not always intimate, terms. Some perspectives, those focusing exclusively on survivors' trauma, make it is easy to miss in the vigor with which many survivors have taken up their lives, even at the price of having to abandon parts of themselves that contain these memories. As Charlotte Delbo (2001, pp. 2-3) puts it,

> Auschwitz is there, unalterable, precise, but enveloped in the skin of memory, an impermeable skin that isolates it from my present self. Unlike the snake's skin, the skin of memory does not renew itself. Alas, I often fear lest it grow thin, crack, and the camp get hold of me again. I live within a twofold being. The Auschwitz double doesn't bother me, doesn't interfere with my life. As though it weren't I at all. Without this split I would not have been able to revive.

Having experienced the unthinkable, many survivors can never quite believe their own story. They know it happened, but they can't quite believe it happened to them, even though they know it did. If this sounds contradictory, it is. It is the basis for doubling.

Eva L. elaborates.

> The older I get, the more questions I ask. Why am I the only one of the whole family to survive? Who would believe if I can't believe it myself? When I was young it was easier, I was busier. I can't believe it happened to me. People ask me to tell the story, and I refuse. I can't believe a human could go through this. Every day was a year. How can they believe a human can survive under this if I can't believe it? (T-71)

Auschwitz for one who has lived inside it is evidently incomparable. Not merely the pre-Auschwitz self, but the post-Auschwitz self can hardly believe it. In a sense, this was the Germans' greatest and most perverse victory. They created a regime of death so horrendous that not merely those who were not there, but those who were, can hardly believe it. The persistence of doubling is explained not only by the survivor's inability to translate between two separate realities, two worlds. The persistence of doubling is also an expression of perpetual mourning, a loss that cannot be worked through, a loss that is as real, vivid and painful as it was fifty years ago in some cases.

Robert Jay Lifton (1986, p. 420) used the term "doubling" to refer both to the way in which the Nazi doctors, as he called them, as well concentration camp inmates, survived. This seems misleading. The Nazi doctors doubled in order to cope with a world of death they lived within and made their own. It was a temporary coping mechanism. For survivors, doubling may have begun in the camps, but it became a lifelong way of coping. For survivors, doubling serves life. What I take from Lifton is his distinction between doubling, on the one hand, splitting and dissociation on the other. Using the metaphor of a tree, Lifton writes that "doubling takes place still higher on a tree whose roots, trunk and larger branches have previously experienced no impairment." (p. 423) What Lifton means to suggest is that doubling is functionally "holistic," allowing the double to function as whole. While Lifton's seems an inadequate explanation, and more certainly needs to be said on the subject, it is an accurate empirical description of the behavior of a large number of survivors over many decades. Late in his career, one of the founders of trauma theory, Sándor Ferenczi stated that "forgetting" is sometimes the best path. "Now is the time for encouragement to the tasks of life and future happiness, instead of pondering and digging in the past." Ferenczi understands that the result is to "sequester" or "encapsulate" traumatic experience. But this is now the goal (Ferenczi 1988, p. 181, Ferenczi 1994, pp. 260-261). This isn't doubling, but doubling and Ferenczi's late conclusion have more in common than divides them.

The problem with this strategy is that it tends to work best with younger victims of extreme chronic trauma. As they age, as more and more of the "tasks of life" lie behind them, the memories of the Holocaust return. Recall Abe L's comment that "the Holocaust is getting closer not farther." Abe was 65 when he made that statement, and did not appear to be in robust health. Studies of older survivors support the observation that the trauma that receded for decades frequently reappears in later years (Eitinger, Krystal 1995, Barak and Szor 2000).

A strategy that is functional for decades should not be dismissed. Especially when it is ethically sound. With the term "ethically sound" I mean that it allows survivors to be honest about the reality of their experience. They do not deny, downplay, or dismiss the horror. They hardly ever identify with the aggressor. This allows the survivors to be genuine witnesses, martyrs (μάρτυς) in the original meaning of the term. We need not learn about the Nazi horror only by seeing the deformations it has imposed upon its victims, but also from the insights passed on by its witnesses. One might argue that the integration of traumatic memory into ordinary memory would better serve the survivor. It hardly matters. Perhaps it would help the survivor, but the goal was beyond the reach of most survivors. Certainly doubling is no cure. However, it allowed many survivors to live "normal" lives for decades, while remaining true to the reality of their experiences, and to history. That is not a bad trade off.

Conclusion

How generalizable these conclusions are is an important and difficult question. The Holocaust is unique. But the experience of loss as intrusive trauma is not. It seems to fit the survivors of childhood sexual abuse, as Herman (1997) and others have argued. And its fits the survivors of other large scale disasters, in which not only lives, but entire ways of life, have been lost. It would seem to fit the survivors of the Buffalo Creek disaster, in which a poorly constructed dam gave way. The resulting flood destroyed not only lives, but a community and way of life.

> By collective trauma, on the other hand, I mean a blow to the basic tissues of social life that damages the bonds attaching people together and impairs the prevailing sense of communality. "We" no longer exist as a connected pair or as linked cells in a larger communal body (Erikson 1976, pp. 153-154).

Interesting and challenging is whether the disasters collected in Erikson's later book, *A New Species of Trouble* (1994), would also be illuminated by the Holocaust. For while the trauma of the Holocaust will always be a unique horror, what is learned from it survivors about chronic trauma may be relevant to the chronic traumatization of special populations studied by Erikson. These include people living in persistent poverty, or institutionalized in asylums and prisons, or living on American Indian reservations. Migrant labourers and their children, and the socially marginal generally, such as the aged, the isolated, and unwelcome strangers in new lands, aliens and immigrants, are also included. Among these groups, says Erikson, one can hardly avoid seeing the familiar symptoms of trauma: numbness of spirit, a susceptibility to anxiety, rage, and depression, a sense of helplessness, loss of various motor skills, a heightened anxiety about threats from their social and physical environment, preoccupation with death, retreat into dependency, and a diminution of ego function (Erikson 1976, pp. 255-256).

In almost every case, Erikson is studying chronic trauma that destroys not just individuals, but their families, along with entire ways of life. In this respect the trauma involves a loss that cannot properly be mourned, for there is no community remaining within which to mourn it. In this respect, at least, there is something to be learned from the way in which trauma and loss became one in the Holocaust. Interesting too is that trauma and loss, while always bound, are not always inseparably bound. The degree depends, in good measure, on whether the loss involves entire families and communities, and whether the remnant that remains is capable of collectively mourning that loss.

Appendix on the Definition of Trauma

Trauma is not restricted to Post Traumatic Stress Disorder (PTSD). I assume this point throughout this essay. Nevertheless, for most people working in the psychological professions, as well as other scholars, PTSD has come to define trauma. Therefore, it is worth paying attention to its changing definition in the *Diagnostic and Statistical Manual of Mental Disorders* (DSM) of the American Psychiatric Association.

The diagnosis is in flux. The edition used by Horowitz, (DSM IV text revision 2000), classifies PTSD as an anxiety disorder, characterized by an individual's experience of intense fear, helpless, or horror in response to an etiologic event. In 2013, DSM-5 was published. PTSD now has its own category, "trauma and stress related disorders." (309.81) In addition, "language stipulating an individual's response to the event—intense fear, helplessness or horror, according to DSM-IV—has been deleted because that criterion proved to have no utility in predicting the onset of PTSD" (www.dsm5.org/Documents/ PTSD%20Fact%20Sheet.pdf).

In fact, these categorical changes make virtually no difference in how the disorder is diagnosed. PTSD still requires that "the person experienced, witnessed, or was confronted with an event or events that involved actual or threatened death or serious injury, or a threat to the physical integrity of self or others." Symptoms of PTSD include the following:

- Intrusive and recurrent recollections of the event, including dreams, and flashbacks.
- Avoidance and numbing, in which people, places, activities, and even consciousness are avoided, the latter through drink, drugs, sleep. Feelings of detachment and estrangement from others, as though no one else could possibly understand. Restricted range of affect: all the emotions are turned down, including love, affection, pleasure, as though every powerful emotion were a danger.
- Sense of a foreshortened future. "What's the point in planning anyway? I don't expect to be around that long."
- Hyper-arousal: Difficulty falling or staying asleep. Irritability or outbursts of anger. Hyper-vigilance. Exaggerated startle response. These symptoms must last for at least a month for the diagnosis of PTSD to be met.

DePrince and Freyd (2002, p. 72) claimed that the definition of PTSD has likely influenced research inasmuch as fear tends to be the reaction most frequently examined and considered in theories about PTSD onset, maintenance, and recovery. The focus on fear can be seen in the current classification of posttraumatic stress disorder as an anxiety disorder and the requirement that the traumatic stressor invoke fear or helplessness in the individual (DSM-IV). This is no longer technically accurate. PTSD is now no longer classified as an anxiety disorder, and fear and helplessness are no longer part of the stressor. Nevertheless, it will take some time for research to catch up with the new definition. Furthermore, this reconceptualization may not make much difference in practice, as the symptoms remain almost identical. PTSD became its own category partly because of the presence of PTSD "at the center of public as well as professional discussion," as the previously quoted fact sheet states. Perhaps the most valuable change is the recognition that PTSD is really not just one disorder, but several. One of the new subtypes is dissociative, and some who have commented on the new category believes this opens the door to better understanding of chronic or complex PTSD (C-PTSD), associated with long term captivity. Judith Herman (1992, 1997) has long advocated for the inclusion of C-PTSD.

Perhaps the clearest conclusion at this point is that while the definition of trauma in the DSM remains in flux, this makes little difference in how we apply the term "trauma" to victims of the Holocaust and other instances of severe and chronic trauma.

REFERENCES

Alford, C. F. (2009). After the Holocaust. New York, NY: Cambridge University Press.

Alford, C. F. (2013). Trauma and forgiveness: Consequences and communities. New York, NY: Cambridge University Press.

American Psychiatric Association. (2000). Diagnostic and statistical manual of mental disorders, (4th ed.). Washington, DC: American Psychiatric Publishing.

American Psychiatric Association. (2013). Diagnostic and statistical manual of mental disorders, (5th ed.). Washington, DC: American Psychiatric Publishing.

Améry, J. (1980). At the mind's limits: Contemplations by a survivor on Auschwitz and its realities. (S. Rosenfeld and S. P. Rosenfeld, Trans.). Bloomington, IN: Indiana University Press.

Barak, Y. and Szor, H. (2000). Lifelong posttraumatic stress disorder: Evidence from aging Holocaust survivors. *Dialogues in Clinical Neuroscience*, 2, 57-62.

Blanchot, M. (1995). The writing of the disaster. (A Smock, Trans.) Lincoln: University of Nebraska Press.

Bowlby, J. (1973). Attachment and loss: Separation: anxiety and anger, Volume 2. New York, NY: Basic Books.

Camus, A. (1955). The myth of Sisyphus and other essays (J. O'Brien, Trans.). New York, NY: Vintage Books.

Caruth, C. (1996). Unclaimed experience: Trauma, narrative, and history. Baltimore, MD: Johns Hopkins University Press.

Danieli, Y. (1988). Treating survivors and children of survivors of the Nazi Holocaust. In F. Ochberg (Ed.), Post-Traumatic therapy (pp. 278-294). New York, NY: Brunner/Mazel.

Delbo, C. (2001). Days and memory. (R. Lamont, Trans.). Evanston, IL: Marlboro Press/Northwestern University Press.

DePrince, A. P. and Freyd, J. J. (2002). The harm of trauma: Pathological fear, shattered assumptions, or betrayal? In J. Kauffman (Ed.), Loss of the assumptive world: A theory of traumatic loss (pp. 71-81). New York, NY: Brunner-Routledge.

Eitinger, L. nd. The aging Holocaust survivor. Retrieved from: www.holocaustechoes.com/93Etinger2.pdf

Erikson, K. (1976). Everything in its path: Destruction of community in the Buffalo Creek flood. New York, NY: Simon and Schuster.

Erikson, K. (1994). A new species of trouble: The human experience of modern disasters. New York, NY: W.W. Norton.

Ferenczi, S. (1988). The clinical diary of Sándor Ferenczi. Cambridge, MA: Harvard University Press. [original 1932]

Ferenczi, S. (1994). Final contributions to the problems and methods of psychoanalysis. London: Karnac Books. [original 1955]

Frankl, V. (1984). Man's search for meaning. New York, NY: Simon and Schuster.

Freud, S. (1917). Mourning and melancholia. In J. Strachey (Ed.), The complete psychological works of Sigmund Freud, Volume 14 (pp. 243-260). London: Hogarth Press.

Greenspan, H. (1998). On listening to Holocaust survivors: Recounting and life history. Westport, CT: Praeger.

Herman, J. (1992). Complex PTSD: A syndrome in survivors of prolonged and repeated trauma. *Journal of Traumatic Stress,* 5 (3), 377–391.

Herman, J. (1997). Trauma and recovery. New York, NY: Basic Books.

Horowitz, G. (2009) A late adventure of the feelings: Loss, trauma, and the limits of psychoanalysis. In K. B. Golden and B. Bergo (Eds.), The trauma controversy (pp. 23-44). Albany, NY: SUNY Press.

Kauffman, J. (2002) Safety and the assumptive world: A theory of traumatic loss. In J. Kauffman (Ed.), Loss of the assumptive world: A theory of traumatic loss (pp. 205-213). New York, NY: Brunner-Routledge.

Klein, M. (1940). Mourning and its relationship to manic-depressive states. In Love, guilt and reparation and other works, 1921-1945 (pp. 344-369). New York, NY: The Free Press, 1975.

Kraft, R. (2002). Memory perceived: Recalling the Holocaust. Westport, CT: Praeger.

Krystal, H. (1995). Trauma and aging: A thirty year follow up. In C. Caruth (Ed.), Trauma: Explorations in memory (pp. 76-99). Baltimore, MD: Johns Hopkins University Press.

Langer, L. (1991). Holocaust testimonies: The ruins of memory. New Haven, CT: Yale.

Lifton, R. J. (1986). The Nazi doctors: Medical killing and the psychology of genocide. New York, NY: Basic Books.

Roth, S., Newman, E., Pelcovitz, D., Van Der Kolk, B., and Mandel, F. S. (1997). Complex PTSD in victims exposed to sexual and physical abuse: Results from the DSM-IV field trial for posttraumatic stress disorder. *Journal of Traumatic Stress*, 10, 539–555.

van der Kolk, B. and Saporta, J. (1991). The biological response to psychic trauma: Mechanisms and treatment of intrusion and numbing. *Anxiety Research*, 4, 199-212.

van der Kolk, Bessel and van der Hart, Onno. 1995. The intrusive past: The flexibility of memory and the engraving of trauma. In C. Caruth (Ed.), Trauma: Explorations in memory (pp. 158-182). Baltimore, MD: Johns Hopkins University Press.

Wieviorka, A. (2006). The era of the witness. (J. Stark, Trans.). Ithaca, NY: Cornell University Press.

Winnicott, D. W. (1953). Transitional objects and transitional phenomena. *International Journal of Psychoanalysis*, 34, 89-97.

Winnicott, D. W. (1992). The child, the family, and the outside world. New York, NY: Perseus Books.

In: Psychoanalysis
Editor: Zelda Gillian Knight

ISBN: 978-1-63483-858-0

Chapter 5

Some Thoughts about the Individual and the Social Unconscious

Siegfried Zepf*[*]*, MD
Former Director of the Institute for Psychoanalysis,
Psychotherapy and Psychosomatic Medicine,
University of Saarland, Saarbrücken, Germany

Abstract

This chapter addresses the problems that arise if social unconscious is defined as a generalization of parts of the individual dynamic unconscious. It is argued that the contents of the social unconscious are not mental but social in nature, and moreover that the social unconscious stands in opposition not to a generalized individual consciousness but rather to social consciousness. It is shown that the social unconscious appears in social consciousness in a manner akin to how the individual unconscious appears in individual consciousness. The domain of analytic social psychology is defined in the present context.

Keywords: individual unconscious, social unconscious, analytic social psychology

Introduction

Starting with Freud's assumption that an individual's unconscious develops on the basis of a prehistoric drama recorded in man's archaic heritage - that of the killing of the primal father who had a monopoly of women by the horde of brothers (Freud 1939a, p. 99) - in which, according to Busch (2001), the existence of social unconscious in individuals is asserted, all definitions of the social unconscious locate this phenomenon in individuals, and is understood as relating to mental contents.

[*] Corresponding author: Siegfried Zepf, MD. Narzissenstr. 5, 66119 Saarbrücken, Germany. E-mail: s.zepf@rz.uni-sb.de.

Fromm (1962), for example, defines the "social unconscious" as "those areas of repression which are common to most members of society" (p. 88), while Devereux (1956) in an identical fashion declares the "*ethnic unconscious*" to be "that portion of the total unconscious segment of an individual's psyche that he shares with most members of his given cultural community" (p. 6, see also Adams 2002, Herron 1995). Erdheim (1962) too, who makes a class-specific differentiation, supports this conception: "The social unconscious is that part of the unconscious of an individual which he has in common with the members of his social class" (p. 220, translated).

The conception of the social unconscious as a generalization of the individual unconscious seems self-evident. The individual dynamic unconscious contains instinctual wishes of an individual, the fulfillment of which in his or her socialization would have led to conflicts that could not have been tolerated on the conscious level. For this reason, consciousness was withdrawn from them by means of defensive operations. Since individuals are socialized in the same society, it appears legitimate to assume that conflicts that induce them to undertake defensive operations are common to them all.

On the surface, there seems to be no reason why consciousness should not be limited to individuals and the social unconscious to those instinctual wishes that fall victim to defense processes in most individuals in a society. Closer consideration, however, reveals certain problems associated with this attribution. My discussion of these problems will lead to the insight that there is a social consciousness that is distinct from its individual counterpart, and that the social unconscious stands in opposition not to a generalized individual consciousness, but to social consciousness, and, moreover, that it relates not to mental but to social contents. After considering the extent to which the social unconscious, understood in this way, deserves that name, I shall show that it in fact appears in mystified form in social consciousness in the same way as individual unconscious manifests in individual consciousness.

In the final section, I shall define the domain of analytic social psychology in the present context. In view of the controversy that surrounds all psychoanalytic concepts, I shall commence by setting out my understanding of the Freudian concept of the unconscious, to which I shall confine myself to the following. In so doing, I shall, for the time being, disregard the possible role of an archaic heritage of humanity in the formation of the individual unconscious, and shall save my discussion of that issue for the beginning of the following section.

THE INDIVIDUAL UNCONSCIOUS

If we disregard not only Freud's assumption of an archaic heritage, but also his untenable hypothesis of a life instinct and a death instinct[1], he is seen to consider the individual, dynamic unconscious as made up of instinctual sexual wishes that are warded off. Freud (1915d) initially distinguished two kinds of such instinctual wishes. The first had never been conscious, and was subject to a "primal repression … which consists in the psychical (ideational) representative of the instinct being denied entrance into the conscious" (p. 148),

[1] Freud (1920g) himself regarded his doctrine of Eros and Thanatos as an "often far-fetched speculation" (p. 24), as "hypotheses" concerning which he did not know "how far I believe in them" (p. 59). For a more detailed critique of this Freudian concept, see for example Becker (1973), Braun (1979), Fenichel (1945, pp. 59-61), and Zepf (2006, pp. 35-39).

while the second had been conscious and was repressed because in their fulfillment "the motive force of 'unpleasure' [would] have acquired more strength than the pleasure obtained from satisfaction" (p. 147).

However, the distinction between primal repression and repression proper has proven problematic (see Zepf 2012). Keeping in mind that the subject of psychoanalytic investigation is the patient's inner life conceptualized as "representational world" (e.g., Sandler 1993, p. 337; Sandler and Rosenblatt 1962, p. 128), it is impossible to localize the primal repressed. At first sight, it seems as if one could localize it in the unconscious or the id respectively. Yet, if one goes along with the idea that the representational world is the genuine subject of psychoanalysis, concepts such as "conscious," "unconscious," "id" and the like prove to be abstractions subdividing the representational world analytically into different aspects with the aim of reconstructing conceptually the historically established interplay of psychic representations. Being satisfied with such a localization would mean that one were to localize the repressed in an abstraction, thus dissolving it in it.

Brenner's (1957) argument rules this problem out. Brenner points out that ten years after introducing the concept of primal repression, Freud (1926d) no longer understood it as referring to a state experienced passively but as one initiated by "quantitative factors such as an excessive force of excitation" (p. 94), and that after 1926 Freud substituted the term "primal" in repression by "earliest" (p. 140) and "first and original" (1933a, p. 94). Brenner (1957) concludes that Freud's final view of primal repression was that its cause and mechanism did not essentially differ from those of "*repression proper*" (Freud 1915d, p. 148; italics in the original) in later life.

If one accepts Brenner's (1957) assessment and abandons the view of primal repression as a process qualitatively different from repression proper, it follows that primal repression also is only a step in a defensive operation. As a 'rule,' Freud (1915d) writes, repression "creates a *substitutive formation*" (p. 153), so that, in another step, the instinctual wishes that have become unconscious reappear in consciousness in the distorted form of substitutive formations.

Substitutive formations of the repressed differ from the repressed itself in content, but have something in common with it. Throughout his work, Freud uses the term "substitute" in a similar sense to how he uses the term "symbol" - as codified by Jones (1916) - in *The Interpretation of Dreams* (e.g., Freud 1905e, p. 77, p. 97; 1910a, pp. 27-35; 1916-17a, p. 110, p. 156; 1926d, p. 90; 1940a, p. 190), treating both as issues which always have a "common element, the *tertium comparationis*" (1916-1917a, p. 152), with the symbolized unconscious. The assumption that Freud regards the content of repressed ideas as being represented in a distorted manner in substitutive ideas (e.g., 1915d, p. 154) is validated by the example Freud (1915e) gives in this context. He cites an obsessional neurotic patient who "suffered from having to take a long time over putting on his stocking" and - "after overcoming his resistance" - "found as the explanation that his foot *symbolized* a penis, that putting on the stocking stood for a masturbatory act …" (p. 200, my italics).

These substitutive formations of repressed contents - which Freud (1896b) also calls "structures in the nature of a compromise between the repressed ideas and the repressed ones" (p. 170) - are not generated by repression. Freud (1915d) explicitly stresses "that it is not repression itself which produces substitutive formations … but that these latter are indications of a *return of the repressed* and owe their existence to quite other processes (p. 154). Freud points out that "there are a great many different mechanisms of forming substitutes" (ibid.), and emphasizes that "repression … is more sharply differentiated from the other mechanisms than they are from one another" (1937c, p. 236). He illustrates the difference between repression and these mechanisms, which include, for example, displacement and reaction formations, by the analogy of a book in the days when books were not yet issued in editions but written out individually. Undesirable passages, Freud writes, were crossed through by the official censorship; however,

> if the authorities were not satisfied with this, but wanted also to conceal any indication that the text had been mutilated, [another way] would be for them proceed to distort the text. Single words would be left out or replaced by others, and new sentences interpolated. Best of all, the whole passage would be erased and a new one which said exactly the opposite put in its place. The next transcriber could then produce a text that aroused no suspicion but which was falsified (p. 236).

In this example, "repression has the same relation to the other methods of defence as omission has to distortion of the text," and the distortions of the text, the "different forms of falsification" (ibid.), correspond to substitutive formations whose "distinguishing characteristic … is the far-reaching distortion to which the returning material has been subjected as compared with the original" (1939a, p. 127).

For the purposes of the following discussion, the point I wish to emphasize is that Freud sees an individual's dynamic unconscious as consisting of instinctual wishes which are warded off, but which find their way back into individual consciousness in distorted form by various mechanisms[2].

The Social Unconscious

I indicated at the beginning of this paper that the usual definitions of the social unconscious give rise to difficulties. For instance, whereas Freud's (1939a) thesis of an "archaic heritage of human beings" which "comprises not only dispositions but also subject-matter - memory traces of the experiences of earlier generations" (p. 99) - can explain the existence of a trans-social consciousness, it cannot account for that of a social consciousness, in the sense of one that is generated socially and is therefore specific to a given society.

Furthermore, as Busch (2001) also stresses, Freud's thesis is highly speculative3. Freud (1921c) considered the thesis presented in *Moses and Monotheism* and *Totem and Taboo* as a "just so story" (p. 122), standing "not at the end, but rather at the beginning of an understanding of this phylogenetic factor" (1985a, p. 20). He had given the first version of the study of Moses the subtitle "A historical novel" (Yerushalmi 1989, p. 375), and in a letter to Max Eitingon dated 27 November 1934, he has the following to say about his *Moses*, which he did not at first want to publish: "Experts would find it too easy to discredit me as an

---

[2] Ogden (1997) refers as follows to the appearance of the unconscious in consciousness in the form of substitutive formations: "The unconscious is not "subconscious'; it is an aspect of the indivisible totality of consciousness" (p. 9).

[3] The same goes for Jung's (1928) concept of a "collective unconscious," which he defines as "the all-controlling deposit of ancestral experience from untold millions of years, the echo of prehistoric world events to which each century adds an infinitesimally small amount of variation and differentiation" (p. 162). I shall not discuss this concept further here.

outsider" (quoted in Jones 1957, p. 194). It was in particular the historical part that incurred his dissatisfaction. In a letter to Arnold Zweig dated 11 November 1934, he writes that

> This historical novel won't stand up to my own criticism. I need more certainty and I should not like to endanger the final formula of the whole book, which I regard as valuable, by founding it on a base of clay ... (Freud 1968a, p. 97).

In this context it should also be borne in mind that, in the discussion of a lecture given on 8 November 1911 entitled "On the supposed timelessness of the unconscious," Freud warns against overhasty conclusions as to "memory contents that are phylogenetically acquired":

> As long as it is possible for us to explain these things by an analysis of psychic phenomena, we are not justified in coming to the conclusion that a store of memories had been carried along phylogenetically (Nunberg and Federn 1974, p. 307).

However, an argument against the assumption that Freud doubted the scientific validity of his thesis is that, in the last year of his life, in answer to Jones's (1957, p. 313) request that he "alter ... a sentence ... in the Moses book in which he expressed the Lamarckian view in universal terms ... since no responsible biologist regarded it as tenable any longer," Freud states "that they were all wrong and the passage must stay."

Furthermore, he writes in the same year:

> My position, no doubt, is made more difficult by the present attitude of biological sciences, which refuses to hear of the inheritance of acquired characters by succeeding generations. I must, however, in all modesty confess that nevertheless I cannot do without this factor in biological evolution (Freud 1939a, p. 100).

Whatever view is taken of Freud's position, the hypothesis of a change in DNA structure through psychic contents, shaped by the psychic experiences of humanity, and their transmission from one generation to the next, was already disputed in Freud's day (e.g., Mitchell 1982, Schur 1972) and has since been abandoned (e.g., Freeman 1967, Moore and Fine 1990, p. 147). Whereas we must relinquish the assumption that the social aspect of the unconscious enters into the individual unconscious in the form of an "archaic heritage," the common problem with the definitions of the social unconscious used by Fromm, Devereux, and Erdheim is that these authors are thereby asserting the existence, alongside the part that is socially determined, of another part of the unconscious that is not socially determined but is, so to speak, private. For instance, in defining the social unconscious as a "*part* of the unconscious of an individual," Erdheim (1982, p. 220; my italics) implies that there is also another, nonsocial, part, while Fromm (1962) explicitly distinguishes the social unconscious from the "*individual unconscious*" by claiming that the latter relates to non-generalizable contents "which an individual represses for reasons of individual circumstances peculiar to his personal life situation" (p. 88, see also Adams 2002, Herron 1995). Devereux (1956) defines the "*idiosyncratic unconscious*" in similar terms: "*The idiosyncratic unconscious* is composed of elements that the unique and specific stresses the individual has experienced have obliged him to repress" (p. 7). Yet this distinction, as Busch (2001) and Herron (1995) point out, lacks an objective foundation. At any rate, the assumption of an interactive, and hence always socially influenced, formation of unconscious personality structures from the beginning is now accepted as one of the key insights of psychoanalysis. The social demands relating to the molding of the instincts are enforced in the family, which must to that extent be seen as a "psychological agency of society" (Fromm 2000, p. 163). This implies that, from the point of view of Fromm, Devereux, and Erdheim, not just a part, but the whole of the unconscious would have to be regarded as socially determined, i.e., as a social unconscious.

Although psychoanalysis focuses on the individual as a subject whose essential aspect is his or her uniqueness, if a common social etiology is responsible for the unconscious of different individuals, the unconscious must itself possess common elements, and therefore be generalizable in terms of these elements too. These generalizations are the subject of analytic social psychology. Its attention centers not on that which is unique in each case, but on the general contained in the unique. The focus of interest is not on a specific individual fate, but on how and under what conditions unconscious contents can come into being at all in individuals. Since a "new-born child is no more than a preliminary sketch of a person" (Elias 1939, p. 22) - the possibility of a person, so to speak - the specificity of his or her development lies not in himself but eccentrically in the social conditions in which he grows up and lives. Thus, neuroses are not mere individual vicissitudes, but a socially conditioned, general phenomenon that is manifested in individuals in specific form in each case[4]. From the point of view of analytic social psychology, account is taken of the etiologically essential, and this essential general element is carried forward into individuals by way of the "psychological agency of society." Although this process assumes different forms, the society concerned is always the same.

If the psychoanalytic perspective is combined with that of analytic social psychology, the concrete particularities of Fromm's "individual unconscious" or Devereux's "idiosyncratic unconscious" prove to be specific phenomenal forms of the general that is essential to their genesis. In other words, society is reproduced at psychological level in individuals not in specific conflicts, but in supra-individual conflict *structures* whose content varies from one individual to another. The substrate of Fromm's "social unconscious" or Devereux's "ethnic unconscious" comprises not parts of individually unique conflicts, but their typical *structures* which are specific for a society.

Besides this topic, there is another problem. The social unconscious is seen as a generalization of the individuals' unconscious conflicts in terms of their common structures, so that social consciousness turns out to be nothing more than a generalization of the individual's consciousness. But social consciousness possesses attributes that are not present in individual consciousness. Individual consciousness is the product of an individual, reproduces his or her practice ideationally, is formed anew by each individual, and disappears with his or her death. Social consciousness, on the other hand, as Leontyev (1959) writes, is the "ideal, mental form of the crystallisation of mankind's social experience and social practice" (p. 226), and this consciousness does not perish with the death of an individual. Instead, it is handed down from one generation to the next by a process in which it is not created afresh, but modified.

Examination of the relationship between social and individual consciousness shows also that individual consciousness is formed on the basis of social consciousness (e.g., Delgado

---

[4] As Ferenczi (1908, p. 290) puts it, neurosis is a "sickness of society."

1969, p. 27, p. 38), and that social consciousness appears in individual consciousness in a particular form which, being individualized, is therefore always narrower. This gives rise to a further difference - namely, that social consciousness is appreciably more extensive than its individual counterpart, so that it takes on a reality of its own that must be distinguished from individual consciousness.

Social consciousness is the result of the social activity of acquiring knowledge. Although the foundation of social knowledge is admittedly the knowledge-acquiring activity of individuals, no individual gains knowledge like a Robinson Crusoe marooned on an uninhabited island while still a child. Before individuals can produce knowledge, they must first appropriate to themselves the concepts of their scientific discipline in which earlier knowledge is stored and which have entered into social consciousness. Again, the insights contained in social consciousness are no more the product of different individuals working solipsistically in isolation from each other than are the recording and processing of information and the production of new ideas based on that information.

Because individuals - in the very appropriation and, in particular, the production of knowledge - enter into social "knowledge-acquiring relationships" (Wittich et al. 1978, p. 102; translated) in which they to some extent cooperate with each other and at least engage in exchanges by way of publications, both existing and new knowledge is always socially determined. Individuals can develop their knowledge-acquiring capacity only on this basis and only by collaborating with others.

As a precondition for their knowledge-acquiring activity, individuals appropriate the knowledge of their field of interest that is stored in social consciousness and process, and deepen it in mutual cooperation; the results of their knowledge-acquiring activity can then in turn enter into social consciousness. That is why, in the production of knowledge, "the gnoseological subject proper is not the individual but society," and the "individual subject represents the manner of existence of the social subject" (Lektorskii 1965 [translated from the German edition: 1968, p. 130f.]). The knowledge admitted into social consciousness reproduces in generalized, ideational form situations that belong to the shared world of individuals.

This has consequences for the understanding of the social unconscious. If the social unconscious is lacking the social consciousness, and this consciousness relates not to mental contents of individuals but in general form to situations in their world, then the social unconscious too cannot be made up of particular mental contents of individuals. Instead, the concept of the "social unconscious" must relate to situations which exist and have effects in the world, and which have also become known at least to some individuals - otherwise no one could know about them - the knowledge of which, however, has not been able to enter into social consciousness.

Some psychoanalysts who have also taken an interest in sociological issues may perhaps be reminded in this context of the "invisible hand[5]" invoked by Adam Smith (1776, p. 477) as a metaphor of the social forces that operate independently of individuals' conscious interests.

[5] The passage that includes this concept reads as follows: "He generally, indeed, neither intends to promote the public interest, nor knows how much he is promoting it. By preferring the support of domestic to that of foreign industry, he intends only his own security; and by directing that industry in such a manner as its produce may be of the greatest value, he intends only his own gain, and he is in this, as in many other cases, led by an invisible hand to promote an end which was no part of his intention" (Smith 1776, p. 477, my italics).

Few, however, will recall that Marx and Engels stripped this "invisible hand" of its metaphorical cloak and revealed it as the action of material social conditions - as a force that asserts itself even though it is unconscious in terms of social consciousness. This thesis is supported by quotations such as the following:

> *Development of the productive forces* of social labour is the historical task and justification of capital. This is just the way in which it *unconsciously* creates the material requirements of a higher mode of production (Marx 1894, p. 259; my italics).

> The *determination of the market-value of products* ... is a social act, albeit a socially *unconscious* and unintentional one. It is based necessarily upon the exchange-value of the product .... (ibid., p. 661; my italics).

> But when we see that the three classes of modern society, the feudal aristocracy, the bourgeoisie, and the proletariat, each have a morality of their own, we can only draw the one conclusion: that men, consciously or *unconsciously*, derive their ethical ideas in the last resort from the practical relations on which their class position is based - *from the economic relations* in which they carry on production and exchange (Engels 1878, p. 87; my italics).

> When, therefore, it is a question of investigating the driving forces which - consciously or *unconsciously*, and indeed very often *unconsciously* - lie behind the motives of men in their historical actions and which constitute the real ultimate driving forces of history, then it is not a question so much of the motives of single individuals, ... as of those motives which set in motion great masses, whole peoples, and again whole classes of the people in each people (1886, p. 50, my italics).

> That the *material life conditions* of the persons inside whose heads this thought process goes on, in the last resort determines the course of this process, remains of necessity *unknown* [in German: *unbewusst* - literally, "unconscious"] to these persons, for otherwise there would be an end to all ideology (ibid., p. 56; my italics).

I shall endeavor in the following to establish whether, and if so to what extent, this definition remains consistent with the psychoanalytic definition of the dynamic unconscious.

Social Consciousness and the Social Unconscious

Before proceeding further, I should like to make a preliminary comment. It may seem antiquated and out of tune with the times if, in discussing the social unconscious, I resort to a set of concepts that are more than a century and a half old and are seldom mentioned in the recent literature on the subject.

My use of the concepts of historical materialism and my advocacy of their continued application are because both psychoanalysis and historical materialism attempt their logical and historical reconstruction of their respective domains by means of categories that relate to their present structure (see Zepf and Hartmann 1989).

For instance, Marx (1857/58) writes:

> Bourgeois society is the most developed and the most complex historic organization of production. The categories which express its relations, the comprehension of its structure, thereby also allow insights into the structure and the relations of production of all the vanished social formations out of whose ruins and elements it built itself up, whose partly still unconquered remnants are carried along with it, whose mere nuances have developed explicit significance within in it, etc. (p. 105).

This conception, which Marx sums up in the sentence "Human anatomy contains a key to the anatomy of the ape" (p. 105), can be translated without problems into the language of the domain of psychoanalysis. The translated terms appear in italics in the following:

> *The psychic structure of an adult* is the most developed and the most complex historic organization of *his mind*. The categories which express its relations, the comprehension of its structure, thereby also allows insights into the *structure* and the *psychic relations* of all the vanished *forms of personality* out of whose ruins and elements it built itself up, whose partly still unconquered remnants are carried along with it, whose mere nuances have developed explicit significance within in it, etc.

Again, I do not wish to base my argument on the fact that both disciplines assume that humanity has a material foundation - the instincts in the case of Freudian psychoanalysis; economic conditions in that of historical materialism - that their form is that of a critique, and that according to Fromm (1932) "historical materialism is that theory of society with which psychoanalysis seems to have ... the greatest affinity" (p. 114f.). Nor is it decisive that Freud himself softens the contrast between psychoanalysis and historical materialism. His objection that historical materialism disregards the powerful effect, which he conceptualized as the superego (Freud 1933a, p. 67; see also p. 178), of the past in molding the present is withdrawn in a little known passage of a letter to R. L. Worrall dated 10 September 1937:

> I know that my comments on Marxism are no evidence either of thorough knowledge or a correct understanding of the writings of Marx and Engels. I have since learned - rather to my satisfaction - that neither of them has denied the influence of ideas and super-ego factors. That invalidates the main contrast between Marxism and psychoanalysis which I had believed to exist (Jones 1957, p. 345).

In fact, it seems to me that the quality of a scientific contribution should not be judged by an inherent sell-by date as if it were a pot of yoghurt. Just because something is older, it is not necessarily obsolete. At all events, neither the methodology whereby the knowledge gained through historical materialism was obtained nor its content has so far been repudiated in a manner that would justify its abandonment and recourse to a better theory of society. This applies in particular to the Marxian logical and historical analysis of the genesis and working of capitalism.

Given that there is no sign of the emergence of a critical theory with the potential to delve in greater detail and depth into the underlying laws of capitalism than that of Marx, there cannot at present be any reason for me to relinquish it.

The conception of the social unconscious as comprising common mental experiences in individuals proves, in the light of the concepts presented above, to be a psychologistic mystification of contents that belong to the society of individuals. Since human beings live in the same society, it is true that they have the contents of the social unconscious in common - but these contents are not mental but social in nature and their point of reference is not individual but social consciousness.

As it were in parentheses, I should like to point out that Fromm misunderstands this definition of the unconscious in Marx. On the basis partly of a formulation by Marx and Engels (1846) containing the phrase "suppression [in German: *Verdrängung*] of the ordinary [natural] desire" (p. 263f.), he concludes that Marx too sees the unconscious as mental in nature, and that Freud and Marx alike "believe that most of what man thinks consciously is determined by forces which operate behind his back, that is, without man's knowledge" (Fromm 1962, p. 112). "The fundamental difference between Marx and Freud" in his view lies "in their respective concept of the nature of these forces determining man" (ibid.). Fromm is convinced that whereas Freud locates these forces in human nature, Marx accommodates them in man's socioeconomic development.

Fromm's conception is surely mistaken. It is true that Marx and Engels use the terms *Verdrängung* and *verdrängen*, and that they do so not only in relation to desires, but also in a wide variety of other contexts, the words incidentally being translated into English in an equally wide variety of ways - e.g., Engels (1878, p. 13, p. 19, p. 26, p. 146, p. 148, p. 149, p. 256, p. 261, p. 265; 1882, p. 425, p. 433, p. 448, p. 520; 1884, p. 111, p. 114, p. 137, p. 145, p. 171, p. 191, p. 193, p. 220), Marx (1867, p. 99, p. 106, p. 386, p. 387, p. 391, p. 393 p. 429, p. 438, pp. 442f., p. 454, p. 635, p. 715, p. 717, p. 762; 1894, p. 114, p. 225, p. 252, p. 542, p. 573, p. 659, p. 682, p. 725), Marx and Engels (1846, p. 67, p. 83, p. 146, p. 289). However, there is not a single passage in which the word *Verdrängung* is used in the Freudian sense of repression. In Marx and Engels, the term does not refer to an intrapsychic operation, but consistently denotes "replacing something real by something real" in the sense of "pushing something aside" or "supplanting something."

Social consciousness consists of ideas that differ in content, in which different spheres of society are reproduced. Accordingly, it can be broken down into, for example, a moral, a scientific, a legal, a political, a religious, and an economic consciousness. Based on the definition of the social unconscious used by Marx and Engels, economic social consciousness should be seen as its point of reference. For them, the internal structure of society or the laws of economic relations that essentially determine social processes are not contained in economic social consciousness. This structure and these processes are therefore socially unconscious.

This does not imply that an unconscious must be attributed to society itself. Society is not a subject but an object, of whose characteristics individuals can become to a greater or lesser extent conscious. "Socially unconscious" refers to those laws of economic relations that have effects but are not contained in the social consciousness. Since social consciousness forms the basis of individual consciousness, these laws remain also outside the consciousness of the majority of individuals.

The extent to which the social unconscious, defined in this way, can lay claim to this designation in psychoanalytic terms too depends on whether the relationship between the social unconscious and social consciousness corresponds structurally to that between the individual unconscious and individual consciousness.

The first points to be decided are therefore the meaning of "economic relations" and the character to be ascribed to social consciousness. "Economic relations*" which Freud (1933a, p. 178) too considered to exercise a "decisive influence" upon men's "intellectual, ethical and artistic attitude," refer to a society's relations of production. In a capitalist societal formation, these are characterized by the fact that a minority possesses the means of production and that the majority comprises those who are excluded from their possession.

This majority has only its labor to sell - labor that produces more value than the amount of its own market price. This "surplus value" is appropriated by the minority. The contradiction of this societal system to which Marx and Engels draw attention is between social production and private appropriation of the socially earned surplus value.

The existing economic social consciousness is understood by Marx and Engels as the "final pattern of the economic relations as seen on the surface" - a pattern which can be "very much different from, and indeed quite the reverse of, their inner but concealed essential pattern and the conception corresponding to it" (Marx 1894, p. 209). The reason for this discrepancy is that the "ideas of the ruling class ... which is the ruling material force of society ... are in every epoch the ruling ideas," that the "ruling ideas are nothing more than the ideal expression of the dominant material relations, the dominant relations grasped as ideas" (Marx and Engels 1846, p. 59), and that the owners of the means of production have no interest in allowing the "concealed essential pattern" to become visible in the social consciousness in the concepts that correspond to it.

The concealment of this core figure, whose concepts point both to its historical origins and always also beyond them, is demonstrated by Marcuse (1964) by the example of conceptual abridgement. The continuity of the past with what points beyond the present moment in history is abolished by stripping concepts of their intentional definitions and then defining them solely by the functions and operations that are currently performed with objects to which they relate. This can be explained by the example of the concept of labor. As we know, Marx (1867) defined labor as:

> The necessary condition for effecting exchange of matter between man and Nature; it is the everlasting Nature-imposed condition of human existence, and therefore is independent of every social phase of that existence, or rather is common to every such phase (p. 183f.).

- i.e., as a conscious, active, and goal-directed process whereby human individuals, using tools in the course of the cooperation that links them together socially, act on nature, produce their conditions of existence for themselves, and realize themselves in this production.

This concept of labor includes not only the past forms of human labor, but also all potential future forms. If labor is seen in these categorical terms, it is possible, while preserving their identity, to take account of the specific differences between different forms of labor, to reconstruct the historical development of these forms in their interaction with social relations, and to determine the forms that have become possible and necessary on the basis of the existing historically specific social relations.

* Translator's note: The German word is *Verhältnisse*, which is also translated in the *Standard Edition* as "conditions" or "circumstances."

Again, this view necessarily entails both a critique of these relations and action to change them qualitatively if what has become possible in them - for instance, a given degree of self-realization - can nevertheless not be achieved.

The situation is different if one's definition of "labor" disregards the fact that labor is a social relation which determines its essence and defines it only functionally - for instance, as a "conscious, goal- and purpose-directed application of human physical, intellectual, and mental powers that is embodied in the results of labor (goods, services, or works of the intellect or of art) that serve the purpose of satisfying material and ideational needs" (Digel and Kwiatkowski 1992, p. 84; translated), as an "activity in which intellectual and/or physical powers are applied with a specific purpose in view" (Enzyklopädie Encarta [Encarta Encyclopaedia, German edition] 98; translated), or as an "activity in which one exerts strength or faculties to do or perform something" (Encyclopaedia Britannica 99).

In these definitions, an extensional aspect of labor - one of its specific historical phenomenal forms - becomes its general defining element. The concept of "labor" now relates only to the form in which labor appears today, and no longer to what it once was in the past and what it could be in the future. If the noun in a sentence is equated with the predicate, "the functionalization of language expresses an abridgement of meaning," for "names of things are not only 'indicative of their manner of functioning,' but their (actual) manner of functioning also defines and 'closes' the meaning of the thing, excluding other manners of functioning" (Marcuse 1964, p. 79).

If the historically specific is elevated to the status of the general, the connection in thought between the contents of the specific phenomenal forms of the general is broken. A thought based on operational concepts always remains confined to the present, which it isolates both from the past social practice of humanity, from which it has arisen, and from its future practice, into which it could develop. Historical reconstruction of a factual situation which at the same time provides information about that situation's potential for further development is feasible only with concepts whose intensions have not been trimmed to suit operational requirements.

Of course, operational abridgement of the knowledge admitted to social consciousness does not mean that this knowledge no longer coincides with social reality in any respect. However, it penetrates into social phenomena only to such an extent that the insights obtained do not call into question the prevailing form of social organization.

The knowledge remains in line with the superficial configuration in which social relations present themselves. For example, "wages," "profit," or "interest-bearing capital" are taken as what they appear to be: wages as the remuneration for work actually done, profit as a special case of wages - the reward accruing to the owner of the means of production for his or her work of organization in the production process - and interest as being produced by capital.

However, these phenomenal forms, which can be experienced empirically, conceal the essential content, which appears in them at the same time in disguised form. In reality, profit is a real phenomenal form of surplus value, in which, "disguised as profit, surplus-value denies its origin, loses its character, and becomes unrecognisable" (Marx 1894, p. 167).

Similarly, interest-bearing capital is "a converted form of surplus-value, a form in which its origin and the secret of its existence is obscured" (p. 48), and categories such as the "'value of labour'" are "categories for the phenomenal forms of essential relations" (1867, p. 537), in which these are both concealed and presented. Moreover, this applies not only to this category.

"For the rest," Marx writes,

> In respect for the phenomenal form, "value and price of labour," or "wages," as contrasted with the essential relation manifested therein, viz., the value and price of labour-power, the same difference holds that holds in respect to all phenomena and their hidden substratum (p. 564).

These phenomenal forms are not a matter of chance, but are necessary for the continued existence of the societal formation. For instance, on "the surface of bourgeois society the wage of the labourer [appears] as the price of labour, a certain quantity of money that is paid for a certain quantity of labour" (p. 535), and Marx adds that precisely this "wage-form ... extinguishes every trace of the division of the working-day into necessary labour and surplus labour," so that "all labour appears as paid labour" (p. 539).

To ensure that the fundamental structure of the accumulation of surplus value can be reproduced and maintained, those on whose surplus labor the surplus value depends must act in conformity with this phenomenal form - with the "categories for the phenomenal forms of essential relations." If they did not believe that their entire labor was being remunerated, they would understand the essence of their exploitation, and might also be more prepared to change the conditions under which they work[6].

The Relationships of the Unconscious and Consciousness in the Individual and in Society

The structural homogeneity of the relationships between the individual unconscious and individual consciousness and that between the social unconscious and social consciousness here emerges with particular clarity. Whereas individual substitutive formations are necessary for the continued functioning of the mental apparatus and present the real state of affairs in a way that does not correspond to reality but only to its appearance, and individuals can gain information about themselves only through substitutive ideas, the economic categories present phenomenal forms that are necessary for the continued existence of the present organization of society, the real conditions in them are conceptualized in the way in which they appear in reality but which does not correspond to their reality, and the "bearers and agents" of the "economic relations" can only "seek to understand them" in these "conceptions" (Marx 1894, p. 209). In both instances, the true essence of the conscious phenomenal forms cannot be deduced from direct empirical experience, but can be established only by a logical and historical analysis.

Besides displacement - the appearance of the value and price of labor as value and wages as the remuneration for work actually done can be seen as a structural counterpart of the psychoanalytic concept of displacement - it is also possible to discern mechanisms such as the operation known as "reaction formation," in which the opposite of what is unconsciously

[6] Marx (1967) formulated this as follows: "Hence, we may understand the decisive importance of the transformation of value and price of labour-power into the form of wages, or into the value and price of labour itself. This phenomenal form, which makes the actual relation invisible, and, indeed shows the direct opposite of that relation, forms the basis of all the juridical notions of both labourer and capitalist, of all the mystifications of the capitalist mode of production, of all the illusions as to liberty ..." (p. 540).

meant appears in consciousness. For instance, in German the entrepreneur (employer) is called the *Arbeitgeber* [literally, giver of labor] and the employee the *Arbeitnehmer* [literally, taker of labor], whereas in reality the workers *give* their labor and it is the entrepreneurs who *take* their labor, which they acquire by purchasing it. Ulmann (1975) draws attention to the consequences of this redefinition:

> Since the word "giver" defines attributes to which the words "benefactor," "helper," and the like also refer, while the word "taker" tends rather to imply "recipient of alms" or even "thief" or "robber" ..., an employer ["giver of labor"] appears as a "special case" of ... "benefactor," ... but not as a robber; while an employee ["taker of labor"] can be seen not as a benefactor, but ... always only as a taker (in the sense of a recipient of alms, a robber, etc.) (p. 103, translated).

Similarly, the term "reform" signified a change in the existing situation for the better. But by now the "reform of the pension system," "reform of the labor market," and "reform of the healthcare system" actually entail a deterioration in the amounts received by pensioners and the unemployed, and in patient care, while the cost of health insurance goes up, so that what is in reality a deterioration is portrayed as an improvement.

If the economic ideas admitted into social consciousness in fact relate only to the superficial configuration of society and no longer permit anything else to be judged as knowledge, social consciousness acquires the characteristics of what psychoanalysis describes as rationalization. This term, which was introduced to psychoanalysis by Jones (1908), denotes attempts to keep unconscious instinctual impulses that motivated substitutive actions out of consciousness by means of logically coherent reasons consistent with socially approved explanations of behavior. Like psychic rationalizations, social knowledge too always means more than it actually says. Just as in the psychological field the motive warded off is covered up in rationalizations, so that which is not supposed to enter into social consciousness appears in this knowledge in mystified form. In seemingly rational guise, both perform the same function: the former conceals that which is essential in the mental life of the individual, while the latter hides that which is essential in social reality. Both are simultaneously true and false, depending on whether they are considered in terms of the phenomena, or in terms of the overall structure of the mind in the one case and of society in the other.

In both instances the content of knowledge is falsified to the same extent as it is narrowed down. In a rationalization of psychological phenomena, the reduction is due to the fact that unconscious material can only appear in consciousness in distorted form, and the individual can only act in conformity with the conscious phenomenal forms of his or her unconscious contents; in rationalizations of social phenomena, the reduction entails their remaining in accordance with the superficial phenomena of society, and their foundation lies in the objective necessity that stems from the internal organization of society itself and compels one to remain on the level of objective phenomena if its fundamental structure is to be preserved. In both instances, issues appear in consciousness while at the same time remaining outside the field of vision; in both instances these are held captive in rationalizations of the existing situation - of the subjective in the one case and of the social in the other - and in both instances objective and necessary phenomena are taken literally and mistaken for their essence.

The consequences that ensue from the mental unconscious for individual action and from the social unconscious for social action are likewise the same, as Dahmer (1973, p. 379f.) points out. Just as the light of consciousness illuminates only a part of an individual's psychic world, so an appreciable part of the social world of individuals is concealed by a blind spot. In their individual activity the mental unconscious compels individuals constantly to repeat the same relational patterns, which assert their demands behind their backs like a force of nature - psychoanalysis describes this process as the "repetition compulsion" -, while in their social activity the laws of their societal form too assert their demands like a force of nature as long as they remain outside consciousness. What is no longer directly accessible to the consciousness of individuals in a societal formation based on private ownership of the means of production is the social context in which they act and produce their products. Instead, their activities are determined by the principle that each acts for his or her own individual benefit, and the social context always arises only at a later stage, in the exchange of products.

The exchange of products becomes a blind compulsion to which each individual's activities are subjected - a process that operates in accordance with *seemingly* natural laws. As long as people do not know what they are doing, the results of their activities take on the appearance of a natural phenomenon. Although the conditions result solely from their own activities, individuals are in this way subject to the laws of their unconsciously generated societal form as if these were natural laws. The monopolization of capital, the economic cycles, the downward trend of the profit rate, and the periodic occurrence of crises and unemployment thus become just as predictable as the disconcerting behavior of an obsessional neurotic or a phobic patient.

The engine of the efficacy of the "natural law" underlying these phenomena is in both cases the "unconsciousness of the participants" (Engels 1844, p. 434). Dahmer (1973) summarizes the situation tellingly as follows:

> In its practice that which escapes consciousness achieves its ends like a force of nature … Individuals are subject to the laws of their unconsciously generated (psychic or social) second nature as if these were natural laws (p. 379f., translated).

At the end of this section, one can see that the social unconscious can manifestly lay thoroughly justified claim to this denotation. Whereas, in the individual, interests serving the avoidance of 'unpleasure' keep the dynamic individual unconscious below his or her horizon, in social reality it is the social forces resulting from economic partial interests that prevent the internal structure of society from entering into social consciousness. Again, just as an individual's unconscious life history appears, and is concealed, in individual consciousness, so too the social unconscious both appears and is masked in social consciousness.

Individual and Social Consciousness

It is clear from the foregoing that the economic laws which are kept out of the social consciousness by social interests could not be summoned into consciousness by a mere "cathexis of attention" (Freud 1900a, p. 616) by individuals whose consciousness is formed on the basis of social consciousness.

The social unconscious also remains mystified in the consciousness of the majority of individuals in the categories in conformity with which individuals must live and in which it appears in social consciousness, in the categorical "pattern of the economic relations as seen on the surface" (Marx 1894, p. 209).

A crucial reason why individuals adhere to these categorical definitions is that, in the formation of their individual consciousness, substitutive formations of their mental unconscious always also become components of the necessarily false social consciousness prevailing in them. In proportion to the false concepts of individual unconscious contents entering into the false concepts of the social, so the mental unconscious is rationalized into social consciousness, whose abridged concepts it cements into an impermeable barrier to knowledge. The socially produced unconscious of individuals becomes fused with the prevailing rationalizations of the existing situation in such a way that these rationalizations are no longer amenable to argument and modification because they have to be adhered to for unconscious reasons.

Freud (1927c) explains this by the example of religious ideas. Individuals connect these ideas with now unconscious "conflicts of childhood ... which [they have] never wholly overcome," bring them "to a solution which is universally accepted" (p. 30), spare themselves "the task of constructing a personal ... neurosis" (p. 44), and instead join together in a "usual group formation" [*habituelle Massenbildung*] (1921c, p. 142). This process irrationally underpins the religious convictions that guarantee cohesion, with the consequence that these can no longer be seriously called into question by any arguments or even by reality.

This conception of religion can easily be applied to the prevailing social forms of intercourse. In the light of this, the prevailing social forms of intercourse come into view as socially approved offers for ways in which the individuals' specific unconscious contents may be manifested.

As with religious convictions, here too individuals join together in a "usual group formation," and, with the fusion of the individual unconscious and social consciousness, are pressed by way of their personality defects into the service of the prevailing social ideology and at the same time kept in a narrow-minded state in conformity with the system. All that can still arise in their consciousness are keloids of thought, which seal individuals off from the social suffering concealed in their psychic structures in the same way as they distort their vision of the contradictions inherent in society.

As a result, individuals hold fast to the social forms of production and exchange even though the contradictions of these forms and the associated problems become ever more manifest - distorted, so to speak, to the point of 'recognizability.' After all, the incorporation of the unconscious into the prevailing social forms of intercourse - this rationalization of the irrational - is necessarily accompanied by an irrationality. What is objectively irrational - say, ensuring the persistence of the existing organizational form of society, in which, as climate change is unmistakably demonstrating to us, we are even prepared to sacrifice the natural conditions on which our very existence depends to the interests of the valorization of capital - appears subjectively to be rational; whereas what would be objectively rational - the substitution of a more rational form of organization for the present one, which has become "irrational as a whole" (Marcuse 1964, p. 9) - appears irrational to individuals. Owing to the intimate association of social and subjective irrationality, rationality becomes a rationalization of both, or, in Adorno's (1955) inimitable and telling formulation, "scars of reason in a state of unreason" (p. 82).

THE DOMAIN OF ANALYTIC SOCIAL PSYCHOLOGY

The domain of an analytic social psychology is defined precisely by this situation. Its task, in relation to these rationalizations, is to "establish both their falsehood and their necessity and to bring what was hidden to light" (Adorno 1955, p. 82). Whereas psychoanalytic therapy illuminates the problematic relationship between the individual and society by taking as its starting point the "mental frontiers [*Seelenende*] of this world" (Freud 1985c, p. 273), and attempts to restore the 'subjecthood' of the individual so far as is feasible under the prevailing social conditions, analytic social psychology addresses the matter from the social standpoint and considers these conditions by opposing but interlocking approaches. It enquires into the ways in which, in a given society, unconscious contents are generated in individuals, and into the function performed by these unconscious contents in the establishment, preservation, and modification of the social organization and its institutions.

In its investigation of the social function of the individuals' unconscious, analytic social psychology can rely with its approach on both the Freudian and the Marxian critiques of religion. For Freud (1927c) "the effect of religious consolidations may be likened to that of narcotics" (p. 49), paralyzing human beings in their social action. He advises the individuals to cast off their "childish helplessness" (p. 24) vis-à-vis reality, and not to trust that the world to come will "compensate them for the sufferings and privations which a civilized life in common has imposed on them" (p. 18). Instead, they should withdraw "their expectations from the other world and [concentrate] all their liberated energies into their life on earth," so that "life will become tolerable for everyone and civilization no longer oppressive to anyone" (p. 50). "Then," he adds, ironically quoting Heinrich Heine, "without regret we leave Heaven to the angels and the sparrows" (ibid.).

By this demand, Freud is drawing close to Marx's critical position. For Freud, religion is like a narcotic, for Marx (1843) it is "the *opium* of the people"; for him, furthermore, to "abolish religion as the *illusionary* happiness of the people is to demand their *real* happiness" (p. 175f.). Whereas Freud (1927c) is concerned only with the substitution of a rational, scientifically based superstructure for the religious one - he pleads for the ascribing of "purely rational reasons to the precepts of civilization; that is to say, for deriving them from social necessity" (p. 41), and for replacement of "the effects of repression by the results of the rational opinion of the intellect" (p. 44) - Marx calls upon man to change the material foundations of society. This is because the "demand to give up illusions about the existing state of affairs is the *demand to give up a state of affairs which needs illusions*" (Marx 1843, p. 176). By laying bare the irrational "libidinal … 'cement'" (Fromm 1932, p. 130) that holds society together, and paralyzes any action that might bring about change in this "state of affairs," analytic social psychology is at the same time a critique of the social situation that needs illusions in order to survive[7]. As a "'science of the irrational'" (1970, p. 26), psychoanalysis in the guise of analytic social psychology is an "indispensable auxiliary science" to sociology (Horkheimer 1932, p. 119).

[7] This notion might also underlie a comment by Freud on child-raising which Anna Freud (quoted in Sandler 1983, p. 35) recalled in a conversation with Sandler: "I am reminded of something my father said … when he spoke of how we bring up our children. He said we supply them with a map of the Italian lakes and send them to the North Pole." At all events, if the family is the psychological agency of society, the map of the Italian lakes allows the children, when grown up, to survive in the frozen waters of the North Pole by imagining them to be Italian lakes.

Whereas sociology can answer the question *why* the irrational precipitates in individuals and *why* they must live in conformity with a false consciousness, analytic social psychology can provide information on *how* the irrational "libidinal cement" comes into being and *how* the false consciousness sets hard.

No matter whether psychoanalysis, in its therapeutic method, detects the unconscious in individuals and makes the unconscious system of conflicts that are blindly acted out accessible again to self-experience, restoring self-disposal by way of critical self-enlightenment, or whether, as an analytic social psychology, it explores the unconscious in social phenomena that are maintained by the unconscious life practice of individuals, in both cases it is criticizing individuals with the aim of enabling them to cast off their self-produced pseudo-natural living conditions, and of helping them to achieve the capacity to organize their lives in society, and hence also their personal lives, more consciously.

Evidently, then, the addressees of psychoanalytic insights and of those of analytic social psychology are different. Whereas, in the therapeutic process, insights are directed to the patient and the individual's irrational attachments to the existing situation are loosened by raising them out of the darkness into his or her individual consciousness, the knowledge accruing from investigative studies of analytic social psychology can be admitted into social consciousness. However, this does not eliminate the irrational attachment of individuals to the prevailing forms of production and exchange. It is true that society is thereby enabled:

> To learn something about itself, and moreover something for which it otherwise has no organ of perception, something of which it is not yet able, in the present state of its consciousness, to gain an overview, and which is therefore not yet in a position to correct (Mitscherlich 1966, p. 34; translated).

However, consciousness of this situation does not yet suffice to eliminate the irrational attachment of individuals to the prevailing forms of production and exchange. Even if people were to come to realize that they cling to these forms of their society for internal reasons that are concealed from them, their irrational attachment to the existing situation could not be corrected or inactivated by virtue of this insight alone.

Such a change would call for a change in society itself. Because this change can come about only in the arena of social conflict, only political groups can be the addressees of the knowledge ensuing from analytic social psychology.

Conclusion

I conclude with a brief summary of this chapter.

- Whether in the form of therapy or of analytic social psychology, the matter addressed by psychoanalysis with critical intent is suffering, the reasons for which it attempts to discover. As therapy, it focuses on the suffering of the individual resulting from his or her individual practice, and aims, with therapeutic intent, to bring about a change in this practice by way of a change in individual consciousness. As analytic social psychology, it concentrates on the suffering occasioned by society, and aims, with political and emancipatory intent, to achieve a change in social practice by way of a change in social consciousness.

- Knowledge gained in the process of therapy is directed to the patient. Knowledge accruing from analytic social psychology is addressed to political groups.
- Since, as Freud (1923b) correctly notes, "all our knowledge is invariably bound up with consciousness" (p. 19), it follows that in psychoanalytic therapy we "can come to know even the *Ucs* only by making it conscious" (ibid.). In psychoanalytic therapy, therefore, the change in the subject of the knowledge - of the unconscious - therefore precedes the gaining of the knowledge itself. In the investigative approach of analytic social psychology, on the other hand, the acquisition of knowledge about the subject - the unconscious attachment of individuals to society - precedes change. In the practice of analytic social psychology, Freud's (1927a) "inseparable bond between *cure* and research" (p. 256, my italics) is transformed into an "inseparable bond between *research* and cure."

Chapter translated by Philip Slotkin, MA Cantab. MITI.

REFERENCES

Adams, M. V. (2002). African American dreaming and the beast of racism. *Psychoanalytic Psychology*, 19, 182-198.

Adorno, Th. W. (1955). Sociology and psychology (Part 2). *New Left Review*, 47, 79-97, 1968.

Becker, E. (1973). *The denial of death*. New York, NY: Free Press.

Braun, K. H. (1979). *Kritik des Freudo-Marxismus*. Cologne: Pahl-Rugenstein.

Brenner, Ch. (1957). The nature and development of the concept of repression in Freud's writings. *The Psychoanalytic Study of the Child*, 12, 19-46.

Busch, H. J. (2001). Gibt es gesellschaftliches Unbewusstes? *Psyche - Zeitschrift für Psychoanalyse und ihre Anwendungen*, 55, 392-421.

Dahmer, H. (1973). *Libido und Gesellschaft*. Frankfurt/M: Suhrkamp.

Delgado, J. M. (1969). *Physical control of the mind*. New York, NY: Harper and Row.

Devereux, G. (1956). Normal and abnormal. In: G. Devereux (ed.), *Basic problems of ethnopsychiatry* (3-71). Chicago, IL: Chicago University Press, 1980.

Digel, W. and Kwiatkowski, G. (Eds.) (1992). *Meyers Grosses Taschenlexikon*, Bd. 2. Mannheim: Bibliographisches Institut.

Elias, N. (1939). The society of individuals. In: N. Elias (ed.), *The society of individuals* (pp. 1-66). New York, NY: Continuum, 1991.

Engels, F. (1844). Outlines of a critique of political economy. *Karl Marx and Friedrich Engels collected works*, Vol. 3, 418-443.

Engels, F. (1878). Anti-Dühring. *Karl Marx and Friedrich Engels collected works*, Vol. 25, 5-309.

Engels, F. (1882). Dialectics of nature. *Karl Marx and Friedrich Engels collected works*, Vol. 25, 311-588.

Engels, F. (1884). *The origin of the family, private property, and the state*. New York, NY: International Publishers, 2001.

Engels, F. (1886). *Ludwig Feuerbach and the outcome of classical German philosophy*. New York, NY: International Publishers, 1941.

Encyclopaedia Britannica CD 99. CD-ROM. *Merriam Webster's collegiate dictionary*, 10th Edition. Merriam Webster Inc.

Enzyklopädie Encarta 98. CD-ROM. 0797 Artikel-Nr. 88787. Microsoft Corporation.

Erdheim, M. (1982). *Die gesellschaftliche Produktion von Unbewusstheit*. Frankfurt/M: Suhrkamp.

Fenichel, O. (1945). *The psychoanalytic theory of neurosis*. New York, NY: Norton and Company.

Ferenczi, S. (1908). Psycho-Analysis and education. In: S. Ferenczi (Ed.), *Final contributions to the problems and methods of psycho-analysis* (pp. 280-290). New York, NY: Brunner/ Mazel, 1980.

Freeman, D. (1967). Totem and Taboo: A reappraisal. In: W. Münsterberger (Ed.), *Man and his Culture: Psychoanalytic anthropology after totem and taboo* (pp. 53-78). New York, NY: Taplinger.

Freud, S. (1896b). Further remarks on the neuro-psychoses of defence. In: J. Strachey (Ed.), *The standard edition of the complete psychological works of Sigmund Freud*, Volume, 3 (pp. 156-185). London: Hogarth Press.

Freud, S. (1900a). The interpretation of dreams. In: J. Strachey (Ed.), *The standard edition of the complete psychological works of Sigmund Freud*, Volume 4/5. London: Hogarth Press.

Freud, S. (1905e). Fragment of an analysis of a case of hysteria. In: J. Strachey (Ed.), *The standard edition of the complete psychological works of Sigmund Freud*, Volume 7 (pp. 7-122). London: Hogarth Press.

Freud, S. (1910a). Five lectures on psycho-analysis. In: J. Strachey (Ed.), *The standard edition of the complete psychological works of Sigmund Freud*, Volume 11 (pp. 1-56). London: Hogarth Press.

Freud, S. (1915d). Repression. In: J. Strachey (Ed.), *The standard edition of the complete psychological works of Sigmund Freud*, Volume 14 (pp. 141-158). London: Hogarth Press.

Freud, S. (1915e). The unconscious. In: J. Strachey (Ed.), *The standard edition of the complete psychological works of Sigmund Freud*, Volume 14 (pp. 159-204). London: Hogarth Press.

Freud, S. (1916-17a). Introductory lectures on psycho-analysis. In: J. Strachey (Ed.), *The standard edition of the complete psychological works of Sigmund Freud*, Volume 15 (pp. 1-463). London: Hogarth Press.

Freud, S. (1920g). Beyond the pleasure principle. In: J. Strachey (Ed.), *The standard edition of the complete psychological works of Sigmund Freud*, Volume 18 (pp. 1-64). London: Hogarth Press.

Freud, S. (1921c). Group psychology and the analysis of the ego. In: J. Strachey (Ed.), *The standard edition of the complete psychological works of Sigmund Freud*, Volume 18 (pp. 65-143). London: Hogarth Press.

Freud, S. (1923b). The ego and the id. In: J. Strachey (Ed.), *The standard edition of the complete psychological works of Sigmund Freud*, Volume 19 (pp. 1-66). London: Hogarth Press.

Freud, S. (1926d). Inhibitions, symptoms and anxiety. In: J. Strachey (Ed.), *The standard edition of the complete psychological works of Sigmund Freud*, Volume 20 (pp. 75-174). London: Hogarth Press.

Freud, S. (1927a). The question of lay analysis. Postscript. In: J. Strachey (Ed.), *The standard edition of the complete psychological works of Sigmund Freud*, Volume 20 (pp. 177-258). London: Hogarth Press.

Freud, S. (1927c). The future of an illusion. In: J. Strachey (Ed.), *The standard edition of the complete psychological works of Sigmund Freud*, Volume 21 (pp. 1-56). London: Hogarth Press.

Freud, S. (1933a). New introductory letters on psycho-analysis. In: J. Strachey (Ed.), *The standard edition of the complete psychological works of Sigmund Freud*, Volume 22 (pp. 1-182). London: Hogarth Press.

Freud, S. (1937c). Analysis terminable and interminable. In: J. Strachey (Ed.), *The standard edition of the complete psychological works of Sigmund Freud*, Volume 23 (pp. 209-253). London: Hogarth Press.

Freud, S. (1939a) Moses and monotheism. In: J. Strachey (Ed.), *The standard edition of the complete psychological works of Sigmund Freud*, Volume 23 (pp. 1-137). London: Hogarth Press.

Freud, S. (1940a). An outline of psycho-analysis. In: J. Strachey (Ed.), *The standard edition of the complete psychological works of Sigmund Freud*, Volume 23 (pp. 139-207). London: Hogarth Press.

Freud, S. (1968a). *The letters of Sigmund Freud and Arnold Zweig*. Freud, E. L. (Ed.). New York, NY: Harcourt and Brace.

Freud, S. (1985a). Overview of the transference neuroses. In: I Grubrich-Simitis (Ed.), *A phylogenetic fantasy* (pp. 5-20). Cambridge, MA: Harvard University Press, 1987.

Freud, S. (1985c). *The complete letters of Sigmund Freud to Wilhelm Flies 1887-1904*. Masson, J. M. (Ed.). Cambridge, MA: Harvard University Press, 1986.

Fromm, E. (1932). The method and function of an analytic social psychology. In: *The crisis of psychoanalysis* (pp. 110-134). New York, NY: Holt, Rinehart and Winston, 1970.

Fromm, E. (1962). *Beyond the chains of illusion. My encounter with Marx and Freud*. New York, NY: Simon and Schuster, 1985.

Fromm, E. (1970). The crisis of psychoanalysis. In: *The crisis of psychoanalysis* (pp. 1-29). New York, NY: Holt, Rinehart and Winston.

Fromm, E. (2000). The social determinants of psychoanalytical therapy. *International Forum of Psychoanalysis*, 9, 149-165.

Herron, W. G. (1995). Development of the ethnic unconscious. *Psychoanalytic Psychology*, 12, 521-532.

Horkheimer, M. (1932). History and psychology. In: M. Horkheimer, Between philosophy and social science. *Selected early writings* (pp. 111-128). Cambridge, MA: MIT Press, 1993.

Jones, E. (1908). Rationalisation in everyday life. *Journal of Abnormal Psychology*, 3, 161-169.

Jones, E. (1916). The theory of symbolism. In: E. Jones (Ed.), *Papers on psychoanalysis* (pp. 87-144). Boston, MA: Beacon Press, 1961.

Jones, E. (1957). *The life and work of Sigmund Freud*, Vol. 3. New York; NY: Basic Books.

Jung, C. G. (1928). *Contributions to analytical psychology*. New York, NY: Harcourt and Brace.

Lektorskii, V. A. (1965). *Problema sub'yekta i ob'yekta v klassicheskoy i sovremennoy burzhuaznoy filosofii. Moscow: Vysshaiya Shkola* [German translation: Lektorskii, W. A. (1968). *Das Subjekt-Objekt-Problem in der klassischen und modernen bürgerlichen Philosophie.* Berlin: Deutscher Verlag der Wissenschaften].

Leontyev, A. N. (1959). *Problems of the development of the mind*. Moscow: Progress Publishers, 1981.

Marcuse, H. (1964). *One dimensional man*. London: Routledge and Kegan.

Marx, K. (1843). Contribution to the critique of Hegel's philosophy of law. *Karl Marx and Friedrich Engels collected works*, Vol. 3, 175-187.

Marx, K. (1857/58). *Grundrisse: Foundation of the critique of political economy*. Harmondsworth: Penguin Books, 1973.

Marx, K. (1867). *Capital*, Vol. I. New York, NY: International Publishers, 1967.

Marx, K. (1894). *Capital*, Vol. III. New York, NY: International Publishers, 1976.

Marx, K. and Engels, F. (1846). The German ideology. *Karl Marx and Friedrich Engels collected works*, Vol. 5, 19-539.

Mitchell, J. (1982). Introduction I. In: J. Mitchell and J. Rose (Eds.), *Feminine sexuality: Jacques Lacan and the école Freudienne* (pp. 1-26). New York, NY: Norton.

Mitscherlich, A. (1966). *Studien zur psychosomatischen Medizin. Krankheit als Konflikt I.* Frankfurt/M: Suhrkamp, 1969.

Moore, B. E. and Fine, B. D. (Eds.) (1990). *Psychoanalytic terms and concepts*. New Haven, CT: American Psychoanalytic Association.

Nunberg, H. and Federn, E. (Eds.) (1974). *Minutes of the Vienna Psychoanalytic Society*, Vol. III: 1910-1911. New York, NY: International Universities Press.

Ogden, T. H. (1997). Some thoughts on the use of language in psychoanalysis. *Psychoanalytic Dialogue*, 7, 1-21.

Rustin, M. (1991). *The good society and the inner world, politics and culture*. London: Verso.

Sandler, J. (1983). Reflections on some relations between psychoanalytic concepts and psychoanalytic practice. *International Journal of Psycho-Analysis*, 64, 35-44.

Sandler, J. (1993). Fantasy, defence and the representational world. *Bulletin Anna Freud Centre*, 16: 337-347.

Sandler, J. and Rosenblatt, B. (1962). The concept of the representational world. *The Psychoanalytic Study of the Child*, 17, 128-145.

Schur, M. (1972). *Freud: Living and dying*. New York, NY: International Universities Press.

Smith, A. (1776). *An inquiry into the nature and causes of the wealth of nations*. New York, NY: Modern Library, 1937.

Ulmann, G. (1975). *Sprache und Wahrnehmung*. Frankfurt/M: Campus.

Wittich, D., Gössler, K. and Wagner, K. (1978). *Marxistisch-leninistische Erkenntnistheorie*. Berlin: Deutscher Verlag der Wissenschaften, 1980.

Yerushalmi, J. H. (1989). Freud on the "Historical Novel": From the manuscript draft (1934) of Moses and monotheism. *International Journal of Psycho-Analysis*, 70, 375-394.

Zepf, S. (2006). *Allgemeine psychoanalytische Neurosenlehre, Psychosomatik und Sozialpsychologie*, Bd. I. Gießen: Psychosozial-Verlag.

Zepf, S. (2012). Repression and substitutive formation - The relationship between Freud's concepts reconsidered. *Psychoanalytic Review*, 99, 397-420.

Zepf, S. and Hartmann, S. (1989). *Psychoanalytische Praxis und Erkenntnisbildung: Verstehen und Begreifen*. Heidelberg: Springer Verlag.

In: Psychoanalysis
Editor: Zelda Gillian Knight
ISBN: 978-1-63483-858-0

Chapter 6

THE USE OF ATTACHMENT THEORY AND THE CONCEPT OF THE CORRECTIVE EMOTIONAL EXPERIENCE IN THE REAL RELATIONSHIP IN PSYCHOANALYTIC SUPERVISION

Zelda G. Knight**, PhD
Professor of Psychology, Department of Psychology,
University of Johannesburg, Johannesburg, South Africa

ABSTRACT

Attachment theory has been used to understand the real relationship in psychoanalytic psychotherapy but it has not been used to understand the real relationship in supervision. This chapter aims to explore the real relationship in supervision but unlike previous research in the area, I propose that Attachment theory can also be used in supervision in relation to the real relationship. I also suggest that the concept of the corrective emotional experience, as first suggested by Alexander and French (1946) can be linked to the real relationship in supervision. In order to present my ideas I first briefly outline the emergence of the real relationship in psychoanalysis and supervision. Later, I link Attachment theory to the real relationship in supervision and include the concept of the corrective emotional experience which adds a new theoretical dimension to the understanding of the real relationship in supervision. I present a brief case vignette of a supervisee that I worked with to illustrate my thoughts.

Keywords: the real relationship, attachment theory, supervision, psychotherapy, corrective emotional experience, psychoanalysis

* Corresponding author: Zelda G. Knight, PhD. Department of Psychology, Faculty of Humanities, Auckland Park Kingsway Campus, Auckland Park, University of Johannesburg, Johannesburg, South Africa. E-mail: zknight @uj.ac.za.

INTRODUCTION

After a century of supervision, just as the constructs of the working alliance, transference, countertransference, and the real relationship have been considered in psychoanalysis, these same constructs have also been investigated in psychoanalytic supervision as well as other therapies. For example, the working alliance in supervision has been studied by various researchers (Bordin 1983, Gill 2001, Inman and Ladany 2008, Ladany 2004) and the concept of transference-countertransference and parallel processes in supervision has also been examined (Bernard and Goodyear 2009, Frawley-O'Dea and Sarnat 2001, Gill 2001, Gordan 1996, Lane 1990). Investigations however, into the real relationship in supervision have surprisingly lagged behind those of the real relationship in analysis, and it seems that it is only in recent years that the phenomenon has emerged.

Attachment theory has recently been used to understand the real relationship in psychoanalytic psychotherapy (Gelso, Palma and Bhatia 2013) but it has not been used to understand the real relationship in supervision. This chapter aims to explore the real relationship in supervision but unlike previous research in the area, I propose that Attachment theory can also be used in psychotherapy supervision in relation to the real relationship. I also suggest that the concept of the corrective emotional experience, as first suggested by Alexander and French (1946) can be linked to the real relationship in supervision. In order to present my ideas I first briefly outline the emergence of the real relationship in psychoanalysis and supervision. This is followed by the presentation of the main principles of Attachment theory and the innovative research by Gelso and colleagues (2013) that used Attachment theory to link to the concept of the real relationship in psychoanalysis. Later, I link Attachment theory to the real relationship in supervision and include the concept of the corrective emotional experience which adds a new theoretical dimension to the understanding of the real relationship in supervision. I present a brief case vignette of a supervisee that I worked with to illustrate my thoughts.

THE REAL RELATIONSHIP

The concept of the real relationship was first identified by Freud (1919, 1937) as those aspects of the analytic engagement that was beyond the normal transference-countertransference constellation. He emphasised that "not every relation between an analyst and his subject during and after analysis was to be regarded as transference; there were also friendly relations which were based on reality and proved to be viable" (Freud 1937, p. 222). The idea of a real relationship in analysis as being 'based on reality' is linked to Anna Freud's (1954) similar observation some years later when she said that "I still feel that somewhere we should leave room for the realization that patient and analyst are two real people, of equal status, in a real relationship to each other" (p. 372).

Charles Gelso (2002, 2003, 2004, 2006, 2009a, 2009b, 2011) together with his colleagues (Gelso and Bhatia 2012, Gelso, Palma and Bhatia 2013) has studied the real relationship extensively and has viewed it as an essential and pivotal underpinning of the process of the therapeutic relationship. The real relationship in psychotherapy has been defined as "the personal relationship existing between two or more persons as reflected in the degree to which each is genuine with the other and perceives the other in ways that befit the other" (Gelso 2011, p. 12). As psychological treatment has changed and core concepts have been developed over time, the concept of real relationship has not only upheld its place in psychoanalysis, but it also has been conveyed to other kinds of psychotherapy orientations (see summaries by Gelso 2011). In this regard, research has shown that all kinds of psychotherapies involve a real relationship and that it exists from the beginning to the end of the encounter (Gelso 2009a, 2009b, 2011) and that it remains a major contributor to the process of therapy, perhaps is equal in significance to the working alliance and it consists of at least two dimensions - realism and genuineness, (Gelso 2002, 2009a, 2011). Research in the area of the real relationship in therapy is burgeoning (Duquette 2010, Frank 2005, Gelso 2011, Gelso and Bhatia 2012, Gelso, Palma and Bhatia 2013) and there is an increasing focus on this same concept in psychotherapy supervision (Bordin 1983, Gill 2001, Inman and Ladany 2008, Ladany 2004, Watkins 2012, 2013a, 2013b, 2013c).

The concept of the real relationship in therapy has its early roots in the seminal work of Ralph Greenson (1965, 1967, 1972, 1974, 1978) and his colleague (Greenson and Wexler 1969). Greenson first introduced the terms 'realism' and 'genuineness' in reference to the real relationship in analysis. He defined realism as the transference-free and thus undistorted aspect of the analyst-patient relationship; he defined genuineness as the intimate and personal and thus authentic relatedness between analyst and patient. Gelso (2002, 2003, 2004, 2009a, 2009b, 2011) used the terms realism and genuineness in his own work on the real relationship in analysis and psychotherapy and indicated that they were vital in understanding the real relationship.

Despite its widespread nature, it seems that the real relationship is often a silent part of the relationship, existing in the periphery and only coming into the forefront at certain times, e.g., the beginning and termination phase of treatment, or when it is suddenly needed as a buffer of some kind against negative transferences (Gelso, Palma and Bhatia 2013). Moreover, they point out that it is helpful to make a distinction between the salience and the strength of the real relationship (Gelso, Palma and Bhatia 2013). They explain that a salient real relationship is one in which the personal relationship is explicit and overt or upfront and the therapist shares a great deal of what he or she may think or feel (Gelso, Palma and Bhatia 2013). They would not resist in agreeing that salience is an important factor in therapeutic success but they would also argue that strength of the real relationship is such a factor (Gelso, Palma and Bhatia 2013) and have presented possible ways in which strength can be developed in a real relationship without too much self-disclosure and other behaviours that create salience (Gelso 2011).

The Real Relationship in Supervision

With regards specifically to the construct of the real relationship in supervision, Watkins (2011a, 2011b, 2011c, 2011d, 2012, 2013a, 2013b, 2013c) seems to be the leading theorist in this area of investigation and has largely borrowed from and used the same understanding of the real relationship in psychoanalysis as in supervision. Based closely and almost mirroring the research previously done by such theorists as Greenson and Gelso on the real relationship in therapy, theorist Watkins (2011c) subsequently transfers this work on the real relationship to the supervision context and proposes that the real relationship in supervision is: 1) a central aspect of the supervision relationship that has trans-theoretical implications; 2) exists from the moment supervision starts until its end and thus is always existing in the supervision process and encounter; 3) is a silent but essential contributor to supervisory process and outcome; 4) has a significant impact on a) the development of the supervisory working alliance and b) the development of the transference-countertransference in the supervisory situation; 5) consists of at least two dimensions in supervision - realism and genuineness, and 6) should be given the same significance and importance as the working alliance and transference-countertransference.

If the real relationship implies a personal interaction that is beyond the working alliance and transference-countertransference configuration, it also implies that the experience of self or self-presentations are somehow different in that moment. Innovatively using Karen Horney's (1950) construct of the 'real self,' Watkins (2012) suggests that the real relationship in supervision is the expression of the real self. In this context, he recommends that in terms of the realism aspect of the real relationship, the real relationship can be viewed as those processes that give rise to the experience of the real self.

To this end, Watkins (2012) concludes that "When manifested in supervision, the real self can also be seen as the source of authentic, genuine experiencing, action, and interaction between supervisor and supervisee. Constructive, vital and vitalizing in effect, it can be considered to provide the very heart or core that makes supervisory real relationship phenomena possible" (p. 253). Moreover, Watkins is contending that "all real relationship considerations - to be most meaningfully and concretely understood and explicated - would be best anchored within a real self context" (p. 253).

In this next section, with the real relationship as foreground, I outline the main principles of Attachment theory and the research by Gelso and colleagues (2013) that used this theory to understand the real relationship in psychoanalysis. Later I link Attachment theory to the real relationship in supervision and include the concept of the corrective emotional experience, as first proposed by Alexander and French (1946), which adds a new perspective to the understanding of the real relationship in supervision. I later present a short case vignette to illustrate these thoughts of mine.

ATTACHMENT THEORY

Attachment theory was first developed by psychoanalyst John Bowlby (1969, 1973, 1980, 1988) but at that time the fraternity of psychoanalysis was not open to his theory because it dangerously veered away from a focus on the intrapsychic towards a focus on the interpersonal (Eagle 2013) as well as its emphasis on what the parents actually did with their children and how they actually engaged with them leading to a focus on psychological health and psychopathology as rooted in the interpersonal as well as the intrapersonal; and its de-emphasis on the role of sexual and aggressive drives in psycho-sexual development, which went against the classical psychoanalytic understanding of the motivation for behaviour (Eagle 2013).

However, with the ushering in of the relational tilt in the 1980s into mainstream psychoanalysis, spearheaded by innovative and pioneering theorists, Steven Mitchel (1988) and Lewis Aron (1996) Attachment theory has been increasingly accepted in psychoanalysis.

Moreover, long before psychoanalysis as a body of theory and technique gained an interest in the use of Attachment theory in therapy, it must be noted that there has been generations of practitioners of so-called brief or time-limited dynamic psychotherapy, rooted in the work of both Bowlby and Sullivan (1953, 1954) who have extensively used Attachment theory in therapy. Some of these intergenerational therapists are Davanloo (1978, 1986), Malan (1963, 1976, 1980), Sifneos (1987) and more recently, with more than 20 years' experience with using attachment-informed theory, internationally renowned Hannah Levenson (1995, 2010) and Levinson and Strupp (1999, 2007). Attachment theory has been extensively employed in these therapies to formulate therapy cases and make sense of clients relational patterns or styles of attachment that have become dysfunctional and cyclical giving rise to relational problems in living.

Psychoanalyst John Bowlby's (1969, 1973, 1980, 1988) presentation of Attachment theory was unique at the time as it proposed that the primal and instinctual need in human beings was to seek out and connect to others. This person-seeking was the primary motivating force of behaviour rather than in contrary to the prevailing understanding that behaviour was motivated by sexual and aggressive instincts, as propounded by Freud. Bowlby's Attachment theory included an explanatory psycho-developmental framework to suggest that people create or form certain patterns of attachment as a way to emotionally connect to and sustain a meaningful relationship (Bowlby 1973). While Attachment theory originally referred to infants behaviour in seeking closeness or proximity with the mother, Bowlby later thought that such attachment patterns that originated in early infancy continued throughout life. In his book, *A Secure Base* (1988), he noted that the need to attach to another was fundamentally an instinctual behaviour of all human beings, and that humans are biologically hardwired to gravitate towards another and form close, emotional bonds. Bowlby, in asserting the infant sought close proximity to the mother, indicated that these early attachment patterns were originally framed as patterns of 'dependency and over-dependency' (1988).

Bowlby (1988) also considered attachment behaviour as applied to the patient-therapist relationship in psychoanalysis and psychotherapy. The implication was that attachment patterns were played out in the therapy process.

The Main Principles of Attachment Theory

The main principles of Attachment theory are that attachment patterns that originated in infancy in order to secure a 'secure base' and 'safe haven' in the form of the mother who, it was hoped, would adequately supply the physical and emotional needs of the infant and so participate in the psychological development of the infant, were later echoed in adulthood and termed adult attachment patterns (Bowlby 1988).

Bowlby (1988) asserted that securely attached children would have had caregivers who responded in helpful and caring ways and thus were good enough in their emotional sensitivity or attunement and responsiveness to their children. Such children would have developed a sense of self as being valued, worthy and cared for, and that others also valued them. These children are described as having a 'secure attachment,' a safe haven, and that all that happens to them, whether negative or positive, means that they will have developed a sufficiently stable sense of trust in their own ability to manage as a result of the good enough care they received earlier.

The securely attached child would have had an attachment figure who provided a 'safe haven' because he or she would have been a source of comfort and security, and this person would have provided a 'secure base' from which the child could explore the world safely, take risks, and be secure in knowing that there was a secure base from which to return.

On the other hand, Bowlby (1988) noted that children who do not have a secure base, and thus have insecure attachment patterns, come from an emotional developmental background where the caregivers did not respond or responded inconsistently or inadequately. These children would have learned that when they are under threat, distressed or unhappy, they cannot manage and thus cannot trust in their own abilities and they have learned to not reply on others to assist them. From this analysis, there were two types of attachment patterns - the secure and the insecure or insecurely attachment patterns.

A contemporary of Bowlby, Ainsworth (1969) and later with her colleagues (Ainsworth, Blehar, Waters and Wall 1978) further developed this notion of secure versus insecure attachment patterns in infancy. She presented three main classifications related to the kinds of early childhood care, or lack of, given by the caretakers leading to three kinds of attachment patterns: the secure attachment pattern, similar to Bowlby's conceptualization, and two sub-types of insecure attachment patterns - anxious resistant pattern or an anxious avoidant pattern.

Attachment theory extends to adult living and adult attachment patterns are the direct result of childhood experiences of patterns of attempting to get close to the original caregiver. Adult attachment patterns give rise to cognitive beliefs about self-other, and are what Bowlby (1973) termed Internal Working Models (IWMs).

The significance of these IWMs is that they are powerful internal maps to how we navigate the world, and thus they act as guides to not only thoughts and feelings but also how we view self and other. In addition, Bowlby remarked that they function as internal rules that determine how we process information related to attachment. They form a lens through which we see ourselves and see others and how to behave towards ourselves and others.

Through the IWMs that we have created, we develop self-other representations, and we treat ourselves in a way that reflects how we were actually treated by our caregivers from infancy onward. Such IWMs are built up over a period of time through a series of relational experiences and, as a lens through which to see and relate to the world, they often become stuck and rigid, and ossify over time.

As a result, in this rigid and unyielding nature they become dysfunctional because although they were functional at the time when we were children, the reality is that as adults, things are now different. For example, an IWM may be something like this: "I am not worthy to be loved" (self-representation) and "Others will not love me" (self-other presentations).

It is not difficult to notice how useful Attachment theory can be used in therapy to conceptualise clients or patients problems that are rooted in their IWMs. The IWMs may be expressed through 'cyclical maladaptive patterns' (CMPs) (Levenson 2010) and comprised of four psychological categories around which a theme or narrative story is held together. They serve as an organising function for the IWMs (Levenson 2010).

These four inter-linked categories of CMPs, described below, under the auspices of Attachment theory, are explored in psychodynamic therapy and time-limited dynamic therapy (Levenson 2010) so that a wider menu of ways of relating and being may be selected. In this way, the goals of attachment-based therapy are to encounter a new experience and a new understanding.

Attachment Theory in Psychotherapy

As indicated, Attachment theory in therapy or attachment-informed therapy has been used for several decades in brief or time-limited dynamic therapies, but the use of Attachment theory in psychoanalysis has not always been valued. However, it is steadily increasing in prominence. Adult patients present with various attachment patterns and the concomitant dysfunctional IWMs or CMPs).

In psychotherapy, Attachment theory is used to identify these dysfunctional relational patterns in IWMs and how they manifest in patients CMPs. They are important in assisting with the development of case formulations which include assessment, conceptualisation and interventions. The basic tracking procedure for the emergent themes or attachment patterns, as Levenson (2010) points out can be as follows: 1) Acts of the self, 2) Expectations of others behaviours, 3) Acts of others, 4) Acts of self towards self, and 5) counter-transference.

Bowlby (1988) presented five therapeutic tasks which centred on the role of the therapist in providing "conditions in which his patient can explore his representational models of himself and his attachment figures with a view to reappraising and restructuring them in the light of the new understanding he acquires and the new experiences he has in the therapeutic relationship" (p. 138). In terms of this, Bowlby stated that the therapist must provide a secure base (trusted companion) from which patients could begin to explore their false or dysfunctional view of self-world, or cyclical maladaptive patterns of relating. This secure base would present patients with the possibility of attempting to understand and change the IWMs or cyclical maladaptive patterns (CMPs). The provision of a new experience and a new understanding are one of the principle goals of modern relational or psychodynamic psychotherapies, including, as noted by Levenson (2010) time-limited (psycho) dynamic therapies. For decades, as indicated earlier, many clinicians have used this concept of a new experience and a new understanding as the major goal of time-limited dynamic therapy (Levenson 2010). Bowlby's understanding of this innovative technique in psychoanalysis - a new experience and a new understanding - is arguably essentially the same principle as the corrective emotional experience, first proposed by Alexander and French (1946). In their seminal book, *Psychoanalytic Therapy: Principles and Applications*, (1946) Alexander and French challenged the prevailing assumption that the way to bring about change in therapy was for the analyst to uncover painful childhood repressed memories through the use of free association and interpretation.

The corrective emotional experience on the other hand, that they were proposing as the main agent of change was defined as the offering by the therapist of an emotional experience that was in contrary to or corrective for what patients had come to expect. Thus in the engagement with the patient, the therapist would identify the dysfunctional IWMs and present a contrary experience and thus begin to halt the continued maladaptive relational patterns. Years previously in a joint book, *The Development of Psychoanalysis*, in 1925, psychoanalysts and once close friends and colleagues of Freud, Ferenczi and Rank had been advocating a similar issue with regards to emphasizing the patient's new emotional experience in therapy with the analyst. When referring to a patient case study, Alexander and French emphasized the following in terms of a new experience:

> The patient had to experience a new father-son relationship before he could release the old one. This cannot be done as an intellectual exercise: it has to be lived through, i.e.,

> felt, by the patient and thus become an integral part of his emotional life. Only then can he change his attitudes (Alexander and French p. 63).

The use of the corrective emotional experience in psychoanalysis implied that the therapist was active, engaged and participating with the patient in terms of attempting to provide a corrective emotional experience that would halt the cyclical maladaptive patterns or IWMs and new ways of relating and experiencing could be adopted.

It is noted that within the psychoanalytic community, the concept of a corrective emotional experience was, and to some extent still is, controversial. At that time it instigated a major upheaval in terms of theory and technique and shifted the underlying ideology of the agent of change in therapy to something the therapist *does to* the patient.

The concept met with such strong resistance that the work of Alexander and French (1946) was ignored for many years. It is however, not the scope of this chapter to argue for its inclusion in mainstream psychoanalysis but in therapies that understand the concept of the real relationship, it can be useful and used.

Attachment Theory and the Real Relationship in Psychotherapy

As indicated earlier, Charles Gelso (2002, 2003, 2004, 2009a, 2013) is a major theorist in terms of the real relationship in psychotherapy. Recently he and his colleagues have used Attachment theory as a guide to understanding and working with transference and the real relationship in psychotherapy (Gelso, Palma and Bhatia 2013).

In his paper, Gelso and his colleagues have paid attention to the role of the therapist as a secure base within the real relationship, and to the patient's IWMs as it relates to transference. This was achieved by documenting the essential features of attachment theory, transference, and the real relationship. In order to illustrate these three inter-related dimensions, the journal article written by these authors presented a detailed case study of long-term psychodynamic psychotherapy case and which ultimately demonstrated the usefulness of Attachment theory in terms of understanding the transference and the real relationship in psychotherapy. They stressed that it is a false assumption to conclude that transference and the real relationship as two constructs are on the opposite sides of a dimension. They instead argued that both might exist to some extent in any given treatment, segment of treatment, or even in any relational communication.

This means that they are of the view that any statement by a patient may partly reflect transference and partly reflect the real relationship. They concluded that there are real relationship elements in all transferences, and vice versus, meaning that transference elements may also occur in all real relationships (Gelso, Palma and Bhatia 2013).

Moreover, in terms of Attachment theory and the real relationship Gelso (Gelso, Palma and Bhatia 2013) asserted that in the real relationship, Attachment theory relates to it in terms of the therapist's stance toward the patient. The therapist, as a real person, seeks to offer the patient a secure base and thus provide a safe haven (Gelso, Palma and Bhatia 2013).

In this way, the therapist attempts to not take sides in the therapy and through his or her 'genuineness' makes an effort to create an 'empathic relationship.' This sets up a process for the patient in which "this strong, attachment-informed real relationship is likely curative in and of itself" (p. 1166).

He stops short however, of transferring the use of Attachment theory in understanding the real relationship in psychotherapy to the use of Attachment theory in understanding the real relationship in supervision. He also does not use the corrective emotional experience in the context of the real relationship in either psychotherapy or supervision.

In this next section, Attachment theory and the concept of the corrective emotion experience as a guide to understanding and working with the real relationship in supervision is explored.

ATTACHMENT THEORY AND THE CORRECTIVE EMOTIONAL EXPERIENCE AS A GUIDE TO UNDERSTANDING THE REAL RELATIONSHIP IN SUPERVISION

To my knowledge the use of Attachment theory and the corrective emotional experience in understanding the real relationship in supervision has not been explored before. If Attachment theory relates to the real relationship in terms of the therapist's *stance toward the patient*, (my emphasis) and that the therapist, as a real person, seeks to *offer the patient* (my emphasis) a secure base and thus provide a safe haven (Gelso, Palma and Bhatia 2013) this is effectively the offering of a corrective emotional experience, as outlined by Alexander and French (1946). The therapist as a real person presents something to the patient that will be curative in nature.

Likewise, Attachment theory relates to the real relationship in terms of the supervisor's stance toward the supervisee. I am suggesting that the supervisor, as a real person in the real relationship in supervision, may also offer the supervisee a secure base and thus provide a safe haven – which is the offering of a corrective emotional experience within the attachment-informed real relationship. In this way, the supervisor, through his or her genuineness and realism makes an effort to create a supervisory relationship in which the real person of the supervisor is responsive to the supervisee and this is likely curative in and of itself. This implies that by exploring the supervisee's IWMs of self and other, the supervisor will be able to identity what kinds of relationship or attachment patterns are evoked in relationships outside supervision and also within supervision.

I shall present a case vignette of an attachment-informed real relationship in supervision to illustrate this point. In order to protect the identity of the supervisee, names have been changed and certain aspects of the history and case have been altered but the essence of the encounter remains the same.

Attachment Theory in Supervision: The Case of Joslyn[1]

Joslyn was a mature woman in her 50s, married with two grown-up children. She had returned to university once the children had left home. When we met for psychoanalytic psychotherapy supervision she presented as a warm and intelligent woman, well-dressed,

[1] Not her real name. In addition, all identifying data has been disguised to protect her identity.

polite and anxious to be seen to be doing well as a therapist. All her process notes were neatly typed up and each patient file was colour-coded and kept in strict order.

I liked her immediately and found myself smiling at her compulsive need to be neat and well prepared something I recognized in me.

At the time of writing up this case, Joslyn had just begun her clinical internship and was anxious to do the right thing with all her patients. She filled my office with an energy and vitality that I found refreshing, and she spoke about her patients with care and sensitivity. We often shared my office couch together and she would spread out her books and papers between us and talk excitedly about her cases and what she had done in their sessions. She would have a bottle of water with her and often drink thirstily with little time to put the bottle down, and this meant that her one hand was usually holding the bottle as if somehow she was afraid to lose it. In talking about her patients, she included large amounts of information and would quickly go through the work, with dramatic swings of the water bottle in her hand.

I wondered about her presence in therapy as I wondered about her presence with me. Week after week Joslyn worked hard with her patients and she presented some very interesting cases and her case formulations were always insightful and intelligent. However, I began to feel that there was something missing, that there was a level of engagement between us that was walled off and hidden. I also began to note her increased anxiety about her role as therapist and she had a fear that her patients would reject her and leave therapy prematurely.

This was also extended to her fear that I would find her inadequate as a therapist and also reject her. She began to feel more anxious as the therapies continued and the patients wanted to know more about her and attempt to get closer. As her self-doubts and lack of confidence about helping her patients increased she also began to feel shameful in wanting my help and yet pushing me away. In the ensuring weeks, she also started to ask me if I felt she was 'doing okay' and would look at me with almost an unrealistic terror that I may say she is not doing okay and is basically messing up the therapy. I tentatively began to explore her background in between the careful and considered presentations of her patients. I used Attachment theory to make sense of Joslyn presentation style and the ways she related to me and her patients.

Background

Joslyn grew up in a small middle-class family of two biological and educated parents and one older brother, Harry. Her parents were married young and the birth of her brother was a much celebrated event. When she was born, it seems that her birth was unplanned and from the beginning Joslyn felt an outsider to the 'holy trinity' of the original three as she referred them to. She spoke with a longing and sadness rather than a sarcastic or malignant tone when referring to her family and the sense of being left out. Her brother Harry was five years older and it seemed he was the favourite one. Her mother was quite absorbed in the son and appeared to largely abandon Joslyn. When it came to Joslyn, she reported that her mother was detached from her and could not remember her mother ever holding her or cradling her when she was distressed. Joslyn remembers trying to please her mother as a child, and trying to win her affection. She would work hard at school and play hard in the sporting events but it seemed her mother was devoid of any real care and responsiveness to her daughter. Joslyn has memories of coming home from sporting events at school with the first prize and showing her mother the trophy only to be told that she had brought dirt into the house and now that had to be cleaned up before Harry came back. In the midst of the sweeping and cleaning, the trophy was set aside as well as the excitement that Joslyn had when she came home.

Joslyn would spend time alone in her room and listen to all the cooing given to Harry. It was not that Joslyn was jealous of her brother but that she missed her mother's love and felt that she was unwanted. Interestingly, Joslyn never felt much about her own accomplishments from that day on and while she continued to do well at school and on the sports field, she did not give herself much merit in such achievements and would often downplay her outstanding academic marks, marks that would often be better than her brother's. Joslyn recalls falling out of a tree in the backyard one day and crying in pain as her arm broke. She remembers calling to her mother and could see her mother standing at the window but not coming out to her. Joslyn recalls lying down on the ground holding her broken arm and calling out but her mother did not come. Then she had to get up and go inside the house and find her mother, who seemed to be annoyed about being disturbed. It seemed to Joslyn that her mother took a while to get the car out of the garage and drive her to the emergency unit at the hospital. She also remembers that the mother was paying more attention to the Harry and asking him how he was and not asking her how she was. Sometime after that incident Joslyn learned to turn her attention away from a mother that she felt would never love her to find friendships and love elsewhere. In this context, the mother represented the antithesis of a secure base and a safe haven during times of stress. As a result of not finding such a secure base and safe haven, she focused her energies on others and became popular in school and had many friends. She liked to be liked by others but her friendships seemed shallow and lacked intimacy.

Her father on the other hand did pay some attention to her when she was a little girl. She remembers her father taking her to the local park and playing with her. She also recalls her father buying her a birthday cake and secretly eating it with only her and not including her mother and brother. It was as if her father knew that she was sidelined and wanted to make reparations for the mother's failings. Other times, however, Joslyn recalls her father as having a short-temper and he would shout at her and sometimes spank her. She recalls also being afraid of his temper and unsure when next he would explode. The relationship with her father could be described as a mixture of, on the one hand, attentive and caring, and on the other hand, one of sadness and fear and in which she felt angry and let down by him. This relationship was short-lived when he left home one day and never came back. She was eight years old at the time of his disappearance and she experienced this as a painful rejection. Years later when she was an adult, she found out from her father that he met another woman and had re-married. At the time of our supervision, Joslyn had little contact with her parents. In attachment pattern terms, the father provided some care but this was inconsistent, unpredictable and short-lived. It also came with a fear of being ridiculed and punished. In terms of attachment theory, the attachment pattern that would seem to fit Joslyn is described as the 'anxious resistant pattern.' Children with this attachment style or pattern exhibit a mixture of insecurity, including sadness and fear, and of intimacy alternating with anger. In some cases, the anxious resistant child may seem coy, "as though they were anticipating a negative response from the parent, they try to ingratiate themselves by showing off, perhaps being cute or especially charming" (Bowlby, 1988, p. 128).

Later when Joslyn left school and married, she oscillated between being popular and feeling a deep sense of inadequacy and hollowness. She did what she thought was socially expected of her, and had two children, the white house with the large double garage doors, the swimming pool and the big, flat screen TV. But she never felt happy and all the friends that came to the house for dinner parties never seemed to be able to fill up the emptiness she felt inside. She began to either anticipate that others would leave her, as her father did, and so protected herself by not getting too close, or that others did not really want or like her but were only using her for what she could provide for them by way of dinner parties.

Once the children left home she found herself alone and lonely in the house and decided to go back to school and study. She had the support of her family for this move and she found that she enjoyed the challenge of working and did well at her studies.

Personality Dynamics

In terms of Attachment theory, Joslyn has an insecure attachment pattern with a marked anxious-resistant pattern. She wants to make meaningful contact with others but becomes anxious about being used or exploited or that the other will find an unworthy self if she opens up and comes closer. She flits between self-doubts as a therapist, and wanting to have my approval on the one hand, and a terror that I may think she is not good enough even though her work with patients and her case formulations are good. She presents with narcissistic character traits with an underlying sense of unworthiness and shame, but an equal neediness to be liked and to have mirroring experiences that could fix her injured self-esteem. To get close would be to discover the unworthy self and therefore the defectiveness within her, so she keeps patients and others away, including me in supervision and I am left with a feeling that something is missing.

Attachment Theory in Supervision and the Provision of a Corrective Emotional Experience

As the months pass, Joslyn and I worked together well in supervision. I would describe our working alliance as conducive to good supervision and a good learning experience. I also believe we have had a strong real relationship that has served as a secure base and safe haven for exploration of her attachment patterns and IWMs or CMPs where anxiety and fear of closeness were heightened and an almost ingratiating manner with me separated us from each other and perhaps from her patients. The attachment patterns Joslyn had adopted to make connections with others and more importantly to her patients were transferred in the transference to me in the supervision. Sometimes the real relationship has aspects of the transference dynamics – this links to Gelso and colleagues (Gelso, Palma and Bhatia 2013) who remark that any statement by a patient may partly reflect transference and partly reflect the real relationship. They maintain that in all real relationship elements there are aspects of transferences, and vice versus, meaning that transference elements may also occur in all real relationships. This same applies to supervision – in the real relationship, there will be elements of the transference situation. As a real person in the real relationship in supervision, I could provide a corrective emotional experience and safe haven for Joslyn's painful exploration of her attachment patterns that were dysfunctional, rigid and expressed in CMPs as outlined by Levenson (2010). It is suggested that an attachment-informed supervision is possible and the ways to work within such an attachment-informed supervision is similar to working in and with psychotherapy, is to track the CMPs in the supervisee.

This can be accomplished as follows: 1) Acts of the self, 2) Expectations of others behaviours, 3) Acts of others, 4) Acts of self towards self, and 5) counter-transference. In Joslyn's case, her attachment pattern in supervision was insecure with anxious resistant. Some of Joslyn's CMPs were along the lines of 1) "I am not worthy," 2) "Others will find me inadequate," 3) Others reject me," 4) I will keep others from getting close to me," and 5) my countertransference was that I felt as if I was missing something with her, that she pushed me away and kept herself walled off for fear of intimacy and possible rejection. The corrective emotional experience in supervision is in providing a *relational* experience that is contrary to what Joslyn has come to expect. This implies that my role in being a secure base and a safe haven within the real relationship gave her the opportunity to explore painful dimensions of her life and relationship. This exploration involved repeated emotional (not intellectual) challenges to her CPMs through my offering of repeated corrective emotional experiences. For example, in the real relationship as a real person relating to her, I presented Joslyn with an experience between us in the supervision in which she did not have to feel unworthy this time, in this relationship, and in which she also emotionally experienced my behaviour not as rejecting (her expectations based on her experiences with her mother and later father, i.e., transference) but as accepting (a contrary experience) and providing a secure attachment from which she could begin to take risks and explore.

Another important dimension to working with Attachment theory and the real relationship in supervision is that the supervisee may model new ways of being and relating that was experienced in supervision with their clients and patients. After a full year of supervision, Joslyn as a therapist began to use Attachment theory in therapy and offer herself as a safe haven and secure base from which her own patients could begin to explore their own dysfunctional CMPs. In the real relationship and the genuineness and realism that are the two key elements of this kind of relationship, mixed with some bits of transference, Joslyn's patients began to experience significant ways of relating to self and other that not just expanded their repertoire of relating but replaced the old ways of relating.

CONCLUSION

In this chapter, I have presented the basic elements of the real relationship in supervision and have linked this to Attachment theory, with a focus on how Attachment theory can be useful in understanding the real relationship in supervision. I have used the work of Gelso (Gelso, Palma and Bhatia 2013) in how they applied Attachment theory to therapy when the real relationship manifests. They asserted that in the real relationship, Attachment theory relates to it in terms of the therapist's stance toward the patient. The therapist, as a real person, seeks to offer the patient a secure base and thus provide a safe haven. I have presented the case of supervisee Joslyn in my supervision as a way of also exemplifying an attachment perspective on the real relationship not in therapy but in supervision.

I have also introduced the concept of the corrective emotional experience into supervision. I have linked this concept to Attachment theory and the maladaptive relational patterns that Joslyn presented while in supervision. Using the real relationship, meaning myself as a real person, I was able to work with Joslyn to provide her with a secure base and this provided the basis for a corrective emotional experience.

Joslyn's attachment to me was initially insecure, reflective of her transference history, but later became secure in that she allowed me to serve as a secure base and a safe haven within the context of a strong real relationship.

Thus the corrective emotional experience allowed for a shift from an insecure attachment to a secure attachment with me. This also exemplifies how Attachment theory can illuminate the roles of the real relationship and the corrective emotional experience.

While I presented a safe haven and a secure base within the real relationship, I was able to offer Joslyn the sense of safety in which she was able to explore difficult aspects of her painful past in terms of exploring her approach to and perceptions of self-others.

In this way, Joslyn was able to see what she transfers onto me and maybe onto her clients, and through the corrective emotional experience in supervision with me, she could also begin to understand what she creates in relationships with both her clients, her friends and others and in how she perceives them as being echoed in the relationship with me as supervisor.

This work is based upon research supported by the National Research Foundation, South Africa. Any opinion, findings and conclusions or recommendations expressed in this material are those of the author(s) and therefore the NRF do not accept any liability in regard thereto.

REFERENCES

Ainsworth, M. S., Blehar, M. C., Waters, E. and Wall, S. (1978). *Patterns of attachment: A psychological study of the strange situation*. Hillsdale, NJ: Erlbaum.

Alexander, F. and French, T. (1946). *Psychoanalytic therapy: Principles and applications.* New York, NY: Ronald Press.

Aron, L (1996). *A meeting of minds: Mutuality in psychoanalysis.* Hillsdale, NJ: Analytic Press.

Bowlby, J. (1969). *Attachment and loss, Volume I: Attachment*. New York, NY: Basic Books.

Bowlby, J. (1973). *Attachment and loss, Volume 2: Separation, anxiety and anger*. New York, NY: Basic Books.

Bowlby, J. (1980). *Attachment and loss, Volume 3: Loss, sadness and depression*. New York, NY: Basic Books.

Bowlby, J. (1988). A *secure base: Clinical applications of attachment theory*. London, England: Routledge.

Couch, A. S. (1999). Therapeutic functions of the real relationship in psychoanalysis. *The Psychoanalytic Study of the Child*, 54 (1), 130-168.

Davanloo, H. (Ed.). (1978). *Basic principles and techniques in short-term dynamic psychotherapy*. New York, NY: Spectrum.

Davanloo, H. (1986). Intensive short-term psychotherapy with highly resistant patients. *International Journal of Short-term Psychotherapy*, 1, 107-133.

Duquette, P. (1997). The role of the real relationship in long-term psychotherapy. *International Journal of Psychotherapy and Critical Thought*, 4 (1), 11-20.

Duquette, P. (2010). Reality matters: Attachment, the real relationship, and change in psychotherapy. *American Journal of Psychotherapy*, 64 (2), 127-151.

Eagle, M. N. (2013). *Attachment and psychoanalysis: Theory, research, and clinical implications*. New York, NY: Guilford Press.

Ferro, A. (2013). *Supervising psychoanalysis: The Sao Paulo clinical seminars*. London: Routledge.

Frank, K. A. (2005). Toward a conceptualization of the personal relationship in therapeutic action: Beyond the "real relationship." *Psychoanalytic Perspectives*, 3 (1), 15-56.

Freud, A. (1954). The widening scope of indications for psychoanalysis: Discussion. *Journal of the American Psychoanalytic Association*, 2 (4), 607-620.

Freud, S. (1919). Lines of advance in psychoanalytic therapy. In: J. Strachey (Ed.), *The standard edition of the complete works of Sigmund Freud*, Volume 17 (pp. 157-168). London: Hogarth Press.

Freud, S. (1937). Analysis terminable and interminable. In: J. Strachey (Ed.), *The standard edition of the complete works of Sigmund Freud*, Volume 23 (pp. 209-254). London: Hogarth Press.

Gelso, C. J. (2002). Real relationship: The "something more" of psychotherapy. *Journal of Contemporary Psychotherapy*, 32 (1), 35-40.

Gelso, C. J. (2003). Measuring the real relationship: Theoretical foundation. *Paper presented at the 111th annual convention of the American Psychological Association*, Toronto, Canada.

Gelso, C. J. (2004). A theory of real relationship in psychotherapy. *Paper presented at the annual meeting of the Society for Psychotherapy Research*, Rome, Italy.

Gelso, C. J. (2006). Emerging findings about the real relationship in psychotherapy: Introductory remarks. *Paper presented at the annual meeting of the Society for Psychotherapy Research*, Edinburgh, Scotland.

Gelso, C. J. (2009a). The real relationship in a postmodern world: Theoretical and empirical explorations. *Psychotherapy Research*, 19 (3), 253-264.

Gelso, C. J. (2009b). The time has come: The real relationship in psychotherapy research. *Psychotherapy Research*, 19 (3), 278-282.

Gelso, C. J. (2011). *The real relationship in psychotherapy: The hidden foundation of change*. Washington, DC: American Psychological Association.

Gelso, C. J. and Bhatia, A. (2012). Crossing theoretical lines: The role and effect of transference in nonanalytic psychotherapies. *Psychotherapy*, 49, 384-390. DOI:10.1037/a 0028802.

Gelso, C. J., Palma, B., and Bhatia, A. (2013). Attachment theory as a guide to understanding and working with transference and the real relationship in psychotherapy. *Journal of Clinical Psychology*, 69 (11), 1160-1171. DOI: 10.1002/jclp.22043.

Greenson, R. R. (1965). The working alliance and the transference neurosis. *The Psychoanalytic Quarterly*, 34 (2), 155-181.

Greenson, R. R. (1967). *The technique and practice of psychoanalysis* (Vol. 1). New York: International Universities Press.

Greenson, R. R. (1968). The "real" relationship between patient and psychoanalyst. In: M. Kanzer (Ed.), *The unconscious today* (pp. 213-232). New York: International Universities Press.

Greenson, R. R. (1972). Beyond transference and interpretations. *International Journal of Psychoanalysis*, 53 (2), 213-217.

Greenson, R. R. (1974). Loving, hating, and indifference towards the patient. *International Review of Psychoanalysis*, 1 (3), 259-266.

Greenson, R. R. (1978). *Explorations in psychoanalysis.* New York: International Universities Press.

Greenson, R. R. and Wexler, M. (1969). The non-transference relationship in the psychoanalytic situation. *International Journal of Psychoanalysis*, 50 (1), 27-39.

Horney, K. (1950). *Neurosis and human growth: The struggle toward self-realization.* New York: W.W. Norton.

Inman, A. G. and Ladany, N. (2008). Research: The state of the field. In: A. K. Hess, K. D. Hess and T. H. Hess (Eds.), *Psychotherapy supervision: Theory, research, and practice* (2nd ed., pp. 500-517). Hoboken, NJ: Wiley.

Jacobs, D., David, P. and Meyer, D. J. (1995). *The supervisory encounter: A guide for teachers of psychodynamic psychotherapy and analysis.* New Haven, CT: Yale University Press.

Ladany, N. (2004). Psychotherapy supervision: What lies beneath? *Psychotherapy Research*, 14, 1-19.

Levenson, H. (1995). *Time-limited dynamic psychotherapy: A guide to clinical practice.* New York, NY: Basic Books.

Levenson, H. and Strupp, H. H. (1999). Recommendations for the future of training in brief dynamic psychotherapy. *Journal of Clinical Psychology*, 55, 385-391.

Levenson, H. and Strupp, H. H. (2007). Cyclical maladaptive patterns: Case formulations in time-limited dynamic psychotherapy. In: T. D. Eells (Ed.), *Handbook of psychotherapy case formulation* (2nd ed.) (pp. 164-197). New York, NY: Guilford Press.

Levenson, H. (2010). *Brief dynamic therapy.* Washington, DC: American Psychological Association.

Malan, D. H. (1963). *A study of brief psychotherapy.* London, England: Tavistock.

Malan, D. H. (1976). *The frontier of brief psychotherapy.* New York, NY: Plenum.

Malan, D. H. (1980). The most important development in psychotherapy since the discovery of the unconscious. In: J. Davanloo (Ed.), *Short-term dynamic psychotherapy* (pp. 56-79). New York, NY: Aronson.

Mitchell, S. (1988). *Relational concepts in psychoanalysis: An integration.* Cambridge, MA: Harvard University Press.

Sifneos, P. E. (1987). *Short-term dynamic psychotherapy: Evaluation and technique.* New York, NY: Plenum.

Sullivan, H. S. (1953). *The interpersonal theory of psychiatry.* New York, NY: Norton.

Sullivan, H. S. (1954). *The psychiatric interview.* New York, NY: Norton.

Watkins, C. E. Jr. (2011a). Celebrating psychoanalytic supervision: Considering a century of seminal contribution. *The Psychoanalytic Review*, 98, 401-418.

Watkins, C. E. Jr. (2011b). Is psychoanalytic education effective? A comment on Damsa et al. (2010). *American Journal of Psychoanalysis*, 71, 290-292.

Watkins, C. E., Jr. (2011c). The real relationship in psychotherapy supervision. *American Journal of Psychotherapy*, 65, 99-116.

Watkins, C. E. Jr. (2011d). Toward a tripartite vision of supervision for psychoanalysis and psychoanalytic psychotherapies: Alliance, transference-countertransference configuration, and real relationship. *The Psychoanalytic Review*, 98, 557-590.

Watkins, C. E. Jr. (2012). Moments of real relationship in psychoanalytic supervision. *American Journal of Psychoanalysis*, 72, 251-268.

Watkins, C. E. Jr. (2013a). Psychotherapy supervision in the new millennium: On pressing needs and impressing possibilities. *International Forum of Psychoanalysis*, DOI: 10.1080 /0803706X.2013.779748.

Watkins, C. E. Jr. (2013b). The evolving nature of psychoanalytic supervision: From pedagogical to anagogical perspective. *International Forum of Psychoanalysis*, DOI: 10. 1080/0803706X.2013.847532.

Watkins, C. E. Jr. (2013c). The contemporary practice of effective psychoanalytic supervision. *Psychoanalytic Psychology*, 30, (2), 300-328.

In: Psychoanalysis
Editor: Zelda Gillian Knight
ISBN: 978-1-63483-858-0

Chapter 7

CUSHIONED PATIENT, TURMOILED THERAPIST: AWARENESS AND USE OF COUNTERTRANSFERENCE AND ENACTMENT AS PART OF THE THERAPEUTIC PROCESS

Melissa Card[1,*], MA, and Zelda G Knight[2], PhD
[1]University of Johannesburg, Johannesburg, South Africa
[2]University of Johannesburg, Faculty of Humanities, Johannesburg, South Africa

ABSTRACT

The therapeutic relationship can be difficult to navigate particularly when communication is projected through the *unsaid* or unconscious processes in the room. The therapist is tasked with being able to detect the unsaid through implicit or explicit countertransference. How the therapist deciphers the communication and works with the experienced countertransference impacts on the therapy. The therapy can either flourish or terminate prematurely. In presenting a case study of such an experience, I explore countertransference, enactment and the therapeutic relationship with a patient who struggled to engage with her own needs. I also explore my struggle of not being able to communicate my understanding of her need to her.

Keywords: therapy, therapeutic process, countertransference, enactment

INTRODUCTION

The purpose of psychotherapy[1] is to improve an individual's life functioning and satisfaction, and the value of psychotherapy is measured by this improvement (Norcross

* Corresponding author: Melissa Card, MA. Department of Psychology, Auckland Park Kingsway Campus, University of Johannesburg, Johannesburg, South Africa. E-mail: melissacard@me.com.

[1] The terms 'psychotherapy' and 'therapy' are used interchangeably, with the latter term used as a shortened version of the former.

2000). Psychotherapy can be effective in alleviating psychological symptoms and effecting character change (Fosshage 2011, Lipsey and Wilson 1993, Seligman 2003, Wampold 2000). The therapeutic relationship comprises of two parties—a therapist and a patient. For therapists to be effective agents of change, they must be both physically and mentally fit. To enable this, therapists engage in physical self-care (e.g., exercise and diet) and reflect on their patterns through journaling, attending supervision, consulting with other professionals and participating in personal therapy. These activities contribute to the maintenance of a healthy level of functioning (Fosshage 2011, Jennings and Skovholt 1999, Mahoney 1997, Norcross 2000, Seligman 2003). A healthy level of functioning enables less entanglement within the patient's story and also allows for change to occur (Fosshage 2011, Norcross 2000).

Research has explored the role of the therapist and the role of therapy in the personal transformation of the patient (Fosshage 2011, Lipsey and Wilson 1993, Seligman 2003, Wampold 2000), but less focus has been directed at exploring what happens in the exchange of the *unsaid* between the two parties and its contribution to the treatment process (Macran, Stiles and Smith 1999). Being aware of the *unsaid* or latent messages between patient and therapist takes skill—often a skill honed with experience—to understand what is being communicated through the therapeutic process (Orange 2002), thus making the therapeutic relationship itself essential to treatment. Given this, supportive practices such as supervision, personal therapy, peer supervision and/or peer discussions can assist therapists to be mindful of what is happening in the therapeutic process.

Personal therapy, that is, the intervention in which the psychotherapist is a patient, has a significant impact on therapists' *perceptions* of their own professional effectiveness (Skolveldt and Ronnestad 1995). Benefits of personal therapy include increased empathy, heightened self-awareness, increased understanding and tolerance of patients, and awareness of countertransference and transference processes (Fosshage 2011, MacDevitt 1987, Macran et al. 1999, Norcross, Strausser-Kirkland and Missar 1988, Wiseman and Shefler 2001, Zachrisson 2009).

The focus of this chapter is the treatment of a patient who was also a psychotherapist. The chapter tracks her process of negotiating life, love and work. I highlight the therapeutic process between us, the impact of the manifest and latent content on both of us, and the importance of boundaries, countertransference feelings and enactments in forging a strong enough therapeutic relationship. This was a relationship able to withstand a premature termination, a return to therapy, a physical illness, personal transformation and mutual influence. Withstanding the onslaught of transference expectations is a process with which many psychoanalytic psychotherapists engage. Having the knowledge of how to do this is attained with professional experience and is not necessarily taught. In presenting this case, I explore how uncertainty and ambivalence in both the patient and the therapist could have ruined the therapeutic relationship; I show how it created space for trust and connection. I argue for the use of countertransference feelings and experiences, particularly in the form of measured countertransference disclosure that facilitates greater relational engagement with the patient.

THE THERAPEUTIC RELATIONSHIP

Freud's focus on the relationship between therapist and patient peaked in the 1930s with the advent of ego-psychology (Hatcher 2010). The interest in relational processes in therapy led to the psychoanalytic therapist supporting the notion of a split in the ego to allow for the development of an observing, rational part of the ego and the irrational forces existing in the patient's transference (Hatcher 2010). In the 1950s the term 'therapeutic alliance' (Zetzel 1956) was coined, and it referred to the conscious, rational and collaborative agreement between patient and therapist (Walters 2009, Zachrisson 2009). The term also referred to the nature of the therapeutic work and how both patient and therapist could proceed with it (Gilbert and Orlans 2011). The 1960s brought shifts in thinking about therapeutic work. The therapeutic alliance was split into a tripartite model, which consisted of the working alliance, the transference-countertransference relationship and the real relationship (Gelso and Hayes 1998). These facets have a strong psychoanalytic conceptualisation; however, the alliance was not seen as curative in itself. Cure was the domain of therapeutic techniques or interventions, and the relationship was meant to facilitate the conditions for interventions to bring about the cure (Safran and Muran 2000).

The therapeutic alliance can be articulated as three dichotomies or conflicts (Kivlighan and Shaughnessy 2000, Stiles et al. 2004): (1) the conflict between the rational (reasonable) relationship and the irrational (transferential) relationship through which the therapeutic alliance aims for "an alignment" (MacKewn 1997, p. 87) between the rational (reasonable) sides of both therapist and patient; here, the therapeutic alliance provides an anchor for the patient when the work becomes overwhelming, such as during analysis of transference or in the surfacing of difficult emotions; (2) a conflict between relationship and technical factors, wherein work on the relationship is not understood as an intervention; and finally, (3) a conflict between facilitative and curative factors of therapy, where establishing the alliance between therapist and patient allows for techniques and interventions but is not necessarily therapeutic (Mitchell 1998, Safran and Muran 2000). The conflicts that arise in the therapeutic relationship can be negotiated and worked through depending on the quality of the alliance.

The quality of the therapeutic alliance depends on the interaction between the patient and therapist. Four emergent alliance patterns may be encountered (Stevens et al. 2007, Stiles et al. 2004). The first pattern is a stable alliance, characterised by little change in strength of the alliance throughout the therapy; the second is a linear growth pattern, where there is an increasing strength in the alliance (Campiao 2012); the third relates to a U-shaped alliance, in which a high-low-high pattern emerges, because a strong alliance exists at the beginning and end of therapy but is weak in the middle; the fourth is a V-shaped pattern wherein the middle of the therapy process is marred by ruptures and repairs that strain the alliance, yet enough of a connection still exists for repair (Campiao 2012, Kivlighan and Shaughnessy 2004, Stiles et al. 2004).

Therapist and patient negotiate the therapeutic alliance both consciously and unconsciously. This involves a process of understanding the conflicts that may be at play in the room and is achieved through deciphering whether the conflicts are based on the rational (real) or irrational (transferential) part of the relationship. Relational psychoanalytic theory maintains that therapeutic ruptures are co-created by both the therapist and patient; this implies that the therapist needs to understand her part in the relationship and in the rupture and repair process (Aron 1996, Mitchell 1997, Ringstrom 2010, Safran and Muran 2000, Stolorow, Atwood and Orange 2002). The therapeutic alliance is influenced by experiences of both past and present interactions with others, on the part of both therapist and patient. Past experiences are reignited in the therapy situation through transference on the patient's side; and, on the therapist's side, the therapist experiences countertransference reactions in relation to the patient, both in the room and/or in her personal and private spaces.

To understand the interactional process of what might occur between patient and therapist, elaboration of transference and countertransference is required because they feed into how the therapist and patient experience each other in the room (Gold and Stricker 2011, Haskayne et al. 2014, Kivlighan and Shaughnessy 2004, Safran and Muran 2000, Stiles et al. 2004).

Transference and Countertransference

The term transference was coined by Freud (1905, p. 116), when he spoke of and defined transference as:

> new editions of facsimiles of the impulses and fantasies which are aroused and made conscious during the progress of the analysis; but they have this peculiarity, which is characteristic for their species, that they replace some earlier person by the person of the physician. To put it another way: a whole series of psychological experiences are revived, not as belonging to the past, but as applying to the person of the physician at the present moment.

Freud (1912) believed that the goal of transference in therapy is for the patient to find the link between the current symptoms or behaviours and past experiences. Furthermore, in uncovering the link between symptoms and past experiences, the therapist analyses the emotional reactions evoked in the patient. Freud's idea of transference is linked to his idea of *transference neurosis*, where a patient's earlier or past experiences and relationships act as contributors that trigger the unconscious feelings and reactions associated with past figures that are then aimed at the therapist in the therapeutic setting. Moreover, Freud cautioned that the transference could turn the therapist-patient relationship into an emotional one, often marred by feelings linked to fantasies, particularly those from the first proper fantasised relationship of the patient's childhood (Sandler et al. 1992).

Others, like Alexander and French (1946), stress the irrational repetition of stereotyped reactions and patterns of behaviours that have not been adjusted to the current or present situation.

With varying definitions of transference having been formulated, an appropriate position to adopt is that transference is only a part of the relationship between therapist and patient and is not the 'total' relationship. It is the part of the relationship that is often irrational and not justifiable within the objective situation (Bateman and Holmes 1995, Osbourne 2011):

> Transference could therefore be defined as a specific illusion which develops in regard to the other person, one which, unbeknown to the subject, represents, in some of

its features, a repetition of a relationship towards an important figure in the person's past or an externalisation of an internal object relationship (Sandler et al. 1992, p. 58).

Freud (1910) used the term *countertransference* to denote the therapist's transference of unconscious past experiences onto the patient. Freud did not write much about countertransference, but other theorists (Gabbard 2009, Lemma 2003, Osbourne 2011) have interpreted his work and provided a more comprehensive understanding of the concept. Seemingly, Freud argued that *countertransference* occurred when the patient triggers unresolved conflicts within the therapist, and these conflicts surface when the therapist is unable to properly deal with those characteristics of the patient that represent a problematic figure from her own past, implying that the therapist needed more therapy (Osbourne 2011). Freud elaborated on how the 'counter' of countertransference represented both transference of emotions onto the patient, as well as a reaction to the patient's transference (Osbourne 2011).

The concept of countertransference, like transference, has evolved over the last century. The classical view of countertransference dominated psychoanalytic circles until psychoanalysts questioned Freud's conceptualisation.

In 1946, Klein introduced the concept of projective identification – an intrapsychic process and defence mechanism, wherein unacceptable parts of the self are split off and projected onto the object in an attempt to get control over and dominate the object (Klein 1946/1975, Segal 1986). In its original form, the concept was unrelated to countertransference. Later, however, the concept was given a central role in the understanding of the analytic relationship (elaborated on in patient-induced countertransference).

The contemporary definition of countertransference includes all the therapists' feelings and reactions to the patient (Heimann 1950, Kernberg 1965). This definition is broader than the classical definition and includes realistic, as well as distorted and conflict-based reactions to the patient. In addition, this definition considers countertransference to be both beneficial and harmful, whereas the classical definition considers it essentially negative.

Heimann (1950) argued that countertransference reactions can be used to better understand the patient, in so far as therapists are aware of their countertransference feelings. From this viewpoint, countertransference provides a unique opportunity to investigate the patient's unconscious conflicts and defences (Heimann 1950). The therapist's emotional reactions towards the patient were considered an important tool in analytic work (Heimann 1950). To echo Heimann's work, Little (1951) wrote, "If we can make the right use of countertransference may we not find that we have yet another extremely valuable, if not indispensable tool?" (p. 33). Sullivan (1953) recognised that the key to using countertransference beneficially is for therapists to be aware of their own reactions and then use them judiciously. These positions extended Freud's idea that all individuals, by means of their unconscious, have a tool for the interpretation of others' unconscious expressions (Falchi and Nawal 2009).

Contemporary thinking of countertransference differs from Freud's classical model in that it puts forward a direct connection between countertransference and its use as a tool or technique in therapy. Heimann (1950) extended Freud's concept of the therapist's evenly suspended or hovering attention to include not only the patient's experiences, but also the therapist's own experiences and reactions. The argument is that therapists, through experiencing their own reactions with a patient, are more able to follow the patient's affective shifts, unconscious fantasies and somatic movements, thus gaining insight into the unconscious latent material and unspoken messages (Falchi and Nawal 2009, Gelso and Carter 1985, 1994; Ivey 1999; Safran and Muran 2000). This broad view conceptualises countertransference predominantly as a reaction to the patient's unconscious conflicts as they unfold in the process and is less about the internal unprocessed conflicts and personality traits of the therapist.

In this way, countertransference is 'created' by the patient and is part of the patient's personality. Given that the patient is creating 'something' in the room with the therapist, a warning to therapists is that they should not become co-actors in the patient's drama and should also avoid exploiting the relationship for their own needs at the expense of the patient (Heimann 1950, Little 1951, Racker 2007). Ivey (1999) clarifies this:

> Although transference and countertransference are conceptually distinct, in reality they are fused components of an intersubjective field in which patients unconsciously dramatise their transference illusions and compel therapists to relive elements of the patients' childhood histories and internal object relations by means of countertransference evocations (p. 63).

The broad view of countertransference is used in most contemporary theories and analytic settings because many therapists seem to accept that countertransference is a complex unconscious phenomenon, a joint creation, co-constructed by therapist and patient in the communicative field of the therapy process (Falchi and Nawal 2009, Hoffman 2006, Racker 2007, Walters 2009).

An Integrated Experience of Countertransference

A third definition of countertransference has evolved too. This seems to be a combination of the classical and broad views. The third definition, which I would like to term an *integrated experience*, is conceptualised as the "internal and external reactions in which unresolved conflicts of the therapist, usually but not always unconscious, are implicated" (Gelso and Hayes 2002, p. 269). Also, these reactions can be used beneficially "if the therapist successfully understands his or her reactions and uses them to help understand the patient" (Gelso and Hayes 2002, p. 269). This definition is similar to the classical view in that countertransference consists of therapist reactions that are irrational rather than reality-based (Gelso and Carter 1985, 1994; Gelso and Hayes 1998, Safran and Muran 2000). However, it differs in terms from the classical definition by being similar to the broad view that countertransference reactions can be used beneficially as a tool in therapy.

Therapists inevitably will experience their own personal challenges and changes. In the therapeutic profession, as they develop, they would be required to take these experiences to their own therapy, but those concerns remain private and should not be shared with their patients. When blurred lines exist between the origins of patient-induced and therapist-based countertransference, more damage than good may occur. Thus, to assist therapists on their developmental journey in the field, various theorists (Gelso and Hayes 1998, Hayes 1995, Ivey 1999, Racker 2007, Reich 1951) have attempted to categorise or organise countertransference reactions.

Annie Reich (1951) was one of the first analysts to attempt to distinguish between countertransference responses. She argued for the need to distinguish between two types of responses: (1) where the therapist acts out some unconscious need or fantasy with a patient (which Heimann and Freud warned against), and (2) where the therapist defends against some unconscious need or fantasy (Ivey 1999, Reich 1951).

Types of Countertransference

Therapist-Induced Countertransference

Countertransference can be as present as transference in a psychoanalytic psychotherapy process. An essential differentiation is to understand whether the countertransference is predominantly patient-induced or therapist-based. Subjective or therapist-induced countertransference refers to the therapist's own unresolved neurotic difficulties, (re)activated in the therapeutic setting, which could influence or disrupt the analytic attitude and effectiveness of the therapy, either temporarily or chronically (Falchi and Nawal 2009). This can give rise to resistances or 'blind spots' (Freud 1910), or an unconscious need to use a patient for the gratification of the therapist's own neurotic needs (Heimann 1950, Little 1951, Racker 2007, Reich 1951).

Within therapist-induced countertransference, two broad categories may be further distinguished: situational countertransference and characterological (personality) countertransference. Situational countertransference refers to the event of the therapist being unusually vulnerable to respond to a patient in atypical ways because of transient life situations, which impacts on the ability to listen and intervene effectively (Brandchaft 1991, Heimann 1950, Little 1951, Racker 2007, Waska 2008). Characterological countertransference occurs when the therapist *persistently* responds to patients in a manner determined by personality characteristics disproportionate with the therapeutic attitude, irrespective of situational factors. Therapist-induced countertransference derives from situational factors, personality factors or some combination of these (Brandchaft 1991, Brandchaft and Stolorow 1990, Busch 2006, Ivey 1999, Racker 2007, Waska 2008).

Patient-Induced Countertransference

Objective or patient-induced countertransference refers to the countertransference of the therapist that is based primarily on the unconscious identification with some projected part of the patient's internal world, and it occurs after some unconscious interactional pressure from the patient in the form of subtle (or gross) verbal or behavioural cues (Busch 2006, Gabbard 1995, Ivey 1999, Racker 2007, Waska 2008). This includes projective identification and role-responsiveness.

Projective Identification

Projective identification, a concept first proposed by Melanie Klein (1946), was conceptualised as separate from countertransference; more recently, however, it has found its place in relation to countertransference experiences (Segal 1986). According to Klein (1946), projective identification involves an intrapsychic fantasy through which the projector rids herself of an anxiety-provoking part of the self (a self or object-representation) by depositing it onto the projectee, and this occurs together with an interpersonal process in which the projector induces emotional reactions in the projectee that correspond to the projected component (Klein 1946, Segal 1986, Waska 2008).

The concept of projective identification has been used and adjusted by many Kleinian theorists or object relational theorists (Busch 2006, Racker 2007, Sandler 1976). Racker (2007) distinguishes between two forms of identification, depending on whether the projected component comprises an internal self-representation, in which case it is called a *concordant identification*, or whether it comprises an internal object-representation, in which case it is referred to as a *complementary identification*. Projective identification seems to be a mechanism used by a patient to communicate unconscious material non-verbally by inducing a certain kind of affect shift, somatic feeling or thought in the therapist (Bateman and Holmes 1995, Busch 2006, Racker 2007, Sandler et al. 1992, Waska 2008). It is considered to be a patient-induced countertransference because it stems from the patient's internal representations of objects, which is projected onto the therapist who then enacts (countertransference) in a particular way specific to the patient, induced by the patient's projections.

Role-Responsiveness

Another form of patient-induced countertransference is what Sandler (1976) termed role-responsiveness. In this case, transference is not simply a fantasy or perception of the therapist; it also involves an attempt by the patient to manipulate the therapist into actualising a relationship based on complementary roles derived from the patient's experience in her family of origin (Racker 2007, Sandler 1976).

The two forms of patient-induced countertransference are useful when applied to dynamics of transference with patients. One question to consider is: Are therapists in the room with patients more prone to experience some form of projective identification, and/or are they designated a particular role by the patient, thus being compelled to behave in the way the patient needs them to behave? Furthermore, therapists may have their own personal experiences to contend with and this may cloud their judgment in managing the co-constructed communication in the web of countertransference experiences. Notably, countertransference is a compromise formation between personal tendencies and the role unconsciously imposed upon therapists by their patients. Thus, the therapeutic setting is an interactional field of mutual influence wherein both participants unconsciously affect each other while discovering idiomatic aspects of their intrapsychic lives (Stolorow et al. 2002, Racker 2007, Busch 2006). Ivey (1999) succinctly summarises this: "Transference and countertransference refers not simply to internal states or intrapsychic configurations, but also to relational transactions carrying unconscious contributions, from both patient and therapist" (p. 350).

Countertransference in Psychoanalytic Psychotherapy

Countertransference is not to be understood in isolation from transference, therapeutic interventions and other psychoanalytic processes as all of these are considered important in the therapeutic process or relationship between therapist and patient (Hill and Knox 2009). The psychoanalytic framework in therapeutic treatment is the space to explore countertransference (Safran and Muran 2000). Countertransference can therefore be "something [that] takes place in the analyst threatening to bring him or her out of analytic position" (Zachrisson 2009, p. 178). The "something" could refer to a feeling of irritation, anxiety or loneliness. It may also refer to tendencies to be too pleasing toward a patient or not sticking to the frame or agreements as expected (Campiao 2012).

The therapist-as-person has to meet the patient with a particular mentality and way of behaving—this is the analytic attitude (Zachrisson 2009). Zachrisson (2009) argues that therapists need to give attention to what happens to themselves in the therapy process. Countertransference reactions will allow them to recognise when they fall out of the analytic position or when they deviate from the frame. To maintain the frame, the analytic attitude accompanies the therapy process and includes skills such as emotional neutrality, empathic listening and evenly suspended attention (Bion 1962, Haskayne et al. 2014, Hoffman 2006, Reich 1951, Wachtel 2008). This requires a balanced presence wherein the distance/closeness and emotional temperature has been negotiated in relation to the patient.

Therapists also find their own personal style within the analytic frame. The personal style allows the therapy situation to work. Zachrisson (2009, p. 179) provides a list of dimensions or conditions for therapists to heed:

- Maintaining respectful distance: not too distant, or reserved and arrogant; not too close, making it [too] intimate;
- Keeping an open mind for everything that is there, whatever it may be;
- Avoiding moralistic judgments, avoiding 'knowing better,' avoiding fussiness;
- Using tact, responsibility and politeness combined with seriousness, impartiality and sobriety;
- Focussing on both or all sides of the patient's internal and external conflicts, as well as considering their own influence on the patient;
- Avoiding either/or thinking.

When a therapist bears these conditions in mind, a sense of being a therapist and a personal style of working with patients may be developed. Therapists need to develop and discipline their own way of working to form their own personal styles.

Further, questions may arise about behaviours, thoughts, fantasies or pictures that can unexpectedly appear to therapists (Ivey 1999, Lemma 2003, Racker 2007, Zachrisson 2009). Also, subtle or overt mood shifts may occur; therapists may be more or less alert, bored or drowsy, and these may be signs of possible unconscious reactions, either as a reaction to the patient or because of their own issues (Wampold 2012).

Thus, many behaviours, mood shifts, thoughts, experiences and emotions can be classified as countertransference reactions, but these all occur in relation to the patient.

Zachrisson (2009) argues that focus should not be on the overt countertransference reactions on which the therapist stumbles but rather on the more subtle unnoticeable deviations in method and attitude. These deviations can be easily explained in one instance, yet in the next, inadequate or unfortunate analytic action may end up compromising the treatment (Walters 2009, Zachrisson 2009).

Signs of exaggerated countertransference reactions toward patients can be identified in the therapist worrying about a patient and the session long after it has ended, being preoccupied with the patient between sessions, engaging in arguments with the patient, or feeling hurt by criticism or contempt (Hill and Knox 2009, Ivey 1999, Zacchrison 2009). Outside awareness, these countertransference experiences can be detrimental.

Lack of awareness of personal issues and 'blind spots' can result in a host of reactions, both internal and behavioural, that adversely impacts the therapist-patient relationship, but also determines the likelihood that the patient will benefit from therapy (Safran and Muran 2000, Wachtel 2008). Therapists, who might be blocked in their empathic ability, may filter out relevant patient material that is too painful to hear, or they might inadvertently minimise patients' struggles in an attempt to avoid their own pain (Greenson 1967, Wachtel 2008).

Generally, countertransference reactions, namely, mistakes, dreams, unclear emotions and slips of tongue, appear as signs of unconscious feelings and conflicts within the therapist. Therapists could also find themselves being uncertain of the patient's feelings, struggling to feel empathic with the patient, and overidentifying with the patient. Therefore, therapists should know themselves well enough to easily recognise changes in their ways of being with patients. This would make therapists more aware of countertransference reactions and (re)enactments.

COUNTERTRANSFERENCE AWARENESS AND ENACTMENT

Maroda (1998) describes a countertransference enactment as:

> an affectively driven repetition of converging emotional scenarios from the patient's and the analyst's lives. It is not merely an affectively driven set of behaviours, it is necessarily a repetition of past events that have been buried in the unconscious due to associated unmanageable or unwanted emotion. Enactment thus involves mutual stimulations of repressed affective experience, ideally with the patient taking the lead (p. 124).

As with transference enactments, the therapist needs to be aware of the transference in order to notice the enactment. The same is true for countertransference, as it also becomes conscious only after an unconscious acting-out (enactment) with patients (Shumsky and Orange 2007). Renik (1993) explains this theoretical position:

> As it stands, our theory of technique indicates that an analyst should strive to minimize his *[sic]* countertransference enactments in order to maximize his countertransference awareness. However, if countertransference enactment is a prerequisite for countertransference awareness, then elimination of countertransference

enactment is not only unattainable as a practical technical goal, but it is misconceived even as a technical ideal toward which the analyst should strive (p. 139).

As these extracts illustrate, therapists need to engage in enactments in order to become aware of the countertransference experience. Therapists need to be aware of what is being stirred up in them when they are working with a patient. The literature indicates that countertransference enactments are not always negative for they could have a positive effect on the therapy, but only if the therapist makes correct use of it. Countertransference enactments occur when "an attempt to actualise a transference fantasy elicits a countertransference reaction" (Gabbard 1995, p. 479). Therapists are tasked with the responsibility of understanding the contents of the transference fantasy and how they need to respond to it. In being able to understand this, enactments could be avoided. If it is not possible for the therapist to understand what the transference need is, the countertransference enactment serves as the key to provide clarity on the situation.

Because sparse literature exists on countertransference *awareness* and its centrality within the therapeutic context or the 'in-the-room' experience, I will try to add to this body of knowledge by delving into my countertransference experience with a particular patient. This involves how I experienced, made sense of and managed the countertransference reactions in relation to this patient. The discussion hereafter will focus on these understandings of countertransference, with the aim being to present countertransference awareness as a tangible process. In other words, I aim to illustrate how the unsaid of countertransference can be explored and articulated with therapeutic goals in mind. The case material thereby provides insights that can enable discussion and classification of countertransference within the project of advancing understanding of this highly complex construct (Gelo and Hayes 1995, Ivey 1999, Kasper, Hill and Kivlighan 2008, Lambert 2007, Racker 2007).

The case is of Gina who I had treated for about two years. This was a complex process because the therapy process began when I was still finding my feet as a therapist and I had not clearly and maturely developed my therapeutic style within the psychoanalytic framework. The initial phase with Gina was filled with transference expectations, which I struggled to meet; and this resulted in a process difficult for Gina to negotiate with me, leading to a premature termination.

Case Material: The Case of Gina

Gina[2] is a 29 year old, single, unmarried female psychologist in Johannesburg, South Africa. She works at a government (public) hospital. She originates from a coastal South African town where she resided with her family. After completing her internship, she relocated to Johannesburg to complete a compulsory community service year to meet the requirements for registration as a clinical psychologist with the country's professional body. She originally attended therapy while completing the community service year. Her reason for initiating therapy was reported to be "*like the right thing to do*" while she worked with her assigned hospital patients.

[2] Gina is a pseudonym used to protect the identity of the patient.

Gina's history is that of a typically parentified child. She is the second oldest of four children. She reported having sensed the family's expectation that she would keep the household going, while her siblings "*could live their lives.*" She considered her eldest brother not to have any obligations to the family, perceiving him to do whatever he wanted to. The two younger siblings were sent to a boarding school, thus she was the only child at the parental home and was expected to continue living with her parents. She was provided with the funds to begin her studies at university, but her parents could not afford to sustain her through the years. She therefore had to work, saving enough funds to pay the university fees. She worked as an au pair in the United States and the Netherlands. She seemed to forge relationships with her host families while working for them and had fond memories of her time overseas. When she returned to South Africa, she completed her studies in psychology and reported that she always felt her relationships were never 'normal.' She felt that the way she related to people was "off" and that she found herself becoming more and more annoyed with her hospital patients. During the initial therapy process, which lasted about 7 months, Gina struggled to connect to her own intimacy and dependency needs. The therapy was initially difficult because every caring intervention I made was met with suspicion and guilt. She explained she did not need someone to feel 'sorry' for her, and when I showed concern and understanding, she felt as though I was mocking her. Nevertheless, I experienced moments when she allowed me access to her vulnerabilities and she accepted my care. These moments, however, were few, and she felt terribly ashamed afterwards, resorting to cancelling the subsequent sessions as a means of preserving her sense of self and dignity.

Gina's account of her life revealed she experienced her mother as very punitive and harsh, as well as non-responsive to her needs. She described her mother as not being able to respond to her when she tried to engage her; instead her mother told her to go to church or pray about her difficulties because that was where Gina was told she could find the answers. Her father was described as caring, soft and "a bit of a walk over" as her mother dominated him "completely". This was Gina's expectation of me: I would dominate her. When I did not play into the punitive role, I was met with suspicion and hostility, being told that I was behaving like her father and that that was not "okay" because, as a woman, I should behave as her mother would. Gina admitted that she had struggled to relate to women and found interactions with men far easier. Interactions with women were strained as she felt that she needed to always take responsibility for the interaction, as she had done with her mother.

Given that Gina was trained as a psychologist, she knew much about therapeutic processes and often commented on or identified the interventions I used. Often, she countered my reflections by telling me that she thought the textbook would have provided a different response to mine but she can accept my attempt. I suspected that this was her way of trying to help me understand the inferior feelings she had about herself. Another difficulty in the initial therapy process was that I struggled to connect with her. I often felt frustrated and rejected by her, as though she did not need me but still came to therapy, perhaps out of obligation, because it was 'the right thing to do.' When I tried to use my countertransference feelings in the room, Gina felt as though I was taking up her space with my feelings and rejected my attempts at understanding her. Eventually, Gina decided that, after her community service year, she would not continue with therapy with me as she would not be treating patients, and therefore did not consider the need for her own therapy. I reflected to her that it must be very difficult for her to feel as though she always had to be the responsible one. I added that I could imagine the amount of strain she takes in making sure that she meets the needs of others but I wonder who takes care of her needs and provides her with the support she needs. This led to Gina becoming teary, and for the first time since I had been treating her, she cried in therapy. She thereafter spoke of all the times she felt misunderstood and unheard in her familial and intimate relationships. Although I felt the relief that came with the emotional release, I wondered what the consequences would be for our relationship as she was not comfortable with showing any vulnerability.

The following week, she cancelled the session, due to her family visiting her. Two weeks later, in the next session, she told me she thought she was ready to terminate therapy as she felt that she had dealt with her issues. She reasoned that her parents had come to visit her, and she found herself dealing with her mother in a much better way in the previous week. I believed that she was not ready for termination so I was able to say to her that I did not think that this was the most appropriate time to end. I also expressed that I wondered if her wish to terminate therapy was related to dynamics in the previous session. She denied that the decision to terminate was linked to feeling vulnerable and feeling resentment toward me for bringing out her emotional and tearful response. I offered my thoughts on the matter again: I did not think that she should terminate but it was her decision. I also pointed out that leaving therapy would mean she is playing into her patterns of leaving a situation when things are tough or when they do not work in her favour. She responded by saying that she will take her chances but she thinks she is fine. At the end of the session, which turned out to be our termination session, while she was leaving, she asked if the door was open, should she wish, to return in the future. I responded affirmatively and assured her that I would not hold her decisions against her and that she could return at any time. After the session, I felt confused by what had happened but also angered by the premature termination. I felt as though she left without any discussion or explanation. I was also angered by the position she allocated to me, that is, to either 'force' for her to stay in therapy (mother's position) or to let her go and live her life (father's position). Over the next few months, I often remembered Gina, wondering about how she could be fairing. I wondered if she would return to therapy, and if we would ever have the opportunity to discuss what happened between us.

Exactly one year later, I received a call from Gina, enquiring if she could return to therapy. I responded that a time slot had become available that week but I had relocated my practice to my home. She expressed surprise, but she agreed to attend the session. Our second attempt at therapy started well. She spoke of our past sessions and about how she remembered me, stating that she had had conversations with me in her mind. I experienced a sense that she needed to make sure that the space was safe to return to and that she needed to reassure me of my influence on her. Gina admitted that perhaps she was angry at me for making her feel things that she was not ready to feel or admit to, and she needed to "*get out, so leaving you was the only thing I could think to do*". We were able to speak about the abrupt ending and she wondered if it affected me in the way it did her. She hoped she had not disappointed me but she took a chance in returning because she saw how different I was in comparison to her mother and that she had been unfairly painting me with the brush of past experiences.

I was very happy to see Gina again and relieved that we had the chance to close the previous chapter and start a new one. The second bout of therapy with Gina started when she was working at a local tertiary institution and was unhappy there. We spent the first few months trying to establish what the unhappiness was about. Gina had a history of trying out new experiences but not necessarily committing to them. Often, the challenge in starting something new motivated her, but once it became routine, she fought against it or escaped.

This was a concern given our first therapy process. I raised this, and she responded, "*You're not a shiny new toy or challenge, so I don't feel like this is going to be something I run from again.*" Gina reported that she was still struggling to rely on people and she experienced difficulties with expressing her needs to anyone. Even though therapy focused on her career choices and questioning about what she would like to do going forwards, Gina also spoke of having a lump in her groin that first appeared in 2007, to which she did not pay attention. The lump appeared and then disappeared; this concerned her but she was too afraid to have it examined because she did not want to find out if it was cancerous. About two months into our second therapy process, the lump reappeared and it was still there two months thereafter. When the lump reappeared we discussed at length her options and fears around the lump. She eventually went to a physician and was referred to an oncologist who diagnosed her with lymphoma, and he required her to go for stage testing. She was uncertain of what to expect. She did, however, do what was needed and succeeded in navigating the initial phases of the diagnosis and treatment without telling anyone other than me. She could not fathom having anyone else involved in the process of attending chemotherapy sessions. As an attempt to reach out to someone, she said very solemnly: "*I need someone who would be impartial and objective, would you be able to accompany me to my first chemo session?*" This raised a remarkable thought process for me after the session; but in the moment when she asked this, my whole being gave a resounding "*yes, of course, I will be there for you.*" Even though I knew she would not have me attend the session with her, her asking this of me meant a lot to both of us. The meaning was that she was able to ask the question and admit to needing someone to accompany her through the process.

The next 9 months felt like a rebirthing process for both of us. She was navigating various processes of being diagnosed with cancer and needing treatment every 21 days. She started to reflect on her life, trying to find a reason for why this was happening. This included thoughts of her past behaviours having brought on the cancer as a punishment for those deeds. There was no family history of cancer; she was only 31 years old; she could not understand why this was happening to her. Gina disclosed her illness to her brother, who arranged for one of his friends to attend the first chemotherapy session with her. She wanted me there too, but she also did not want to hold me to accompanying her because she expected me to be working and therefore did not want to disturb me. So, she had her brother's friend attend the session with her as he was emotionally removed from her. She explained that having someone emotionally close to her at her treatment would have been too difficult for her to handle as she is not used to being vulnerable in the presence of people close to her. Still, she displayed an inherent need to present a brave face for her family and not let on to anyone how severely the diagnosis had affected her. She tried to be strong for her siblings because she did not want them to feel pity for her. She often said, "I don't want them to look at me with those eyes, the cancer pity eyes." Eventually, she softened and opened up to me about her experiences and what it was like to attend chemotherapy. She recalled this: "*the chemo smell, the loss of taste, following a particular diet and not being able to drink alcohol, I feel like I'm sick, like there is something wrong with me and I'm not the same.*" I felt more connected to Gina through this process, to the point where it felt as though we had been going through the treatment together.

Gina could not find any joy or feeling in the world; everything was difficult and was too much effort. If people tried to interact with her, they were met with skepticism and negativity. She tried to isolate herself but those friends who knew about the illness did not allow this. She eventually disclosed to her mother, who reacted as Gina expected. Her mother told her to go to church and pray for help. Gina was angry with herself for hoping for a different response from her mother and started to rely on her siblings, friends and therapy for support.

One day, she had heard on the news that a local television presenter had died in a car accident. This seemed to upset Gina tremendously because "*he chose to die*", she said. She could not understand "*why he had chosen to die when he had such a nice life from what we could see.*" I reflected to her how angry she seemed about him choosing to die, yet she, who is alive, is choosing not to live. She was able to hear this reflection and thought about it for a while. She said she could see how she has chosen to "die" in the way that the actor did. This seemed to spark something for Gina, because from that point, she used that experience to measure her level of engagement with life.

While Gina was gaining a new lease on life, I was experiencing my own personal turmoil of loss and grief, with periods of anger, depression and acceptance. I struggled to understand why she had been diagnosed with cancer, and why I was incredibly angry about the diagnosis and the treatment process. When she arrived, once, feeling as though she wanted to stop the treatment, I said, "*We've been through so much with this diagnosis, and we only have two more chemo sessions to get through.*" For Gina, these words made her feel that I was accompanying her through the process. Consequently, she said, "*I have never felt this held and supported, as though I've had a pillow under my head, because you've held me through this process. I don't think I would have gotten through it if it wasn't for this space and for you being you. It's like you are with me.*"

I considered this to be a beautiful and profound acknowledgement. Little did she know that over the preceding 3 months, I experienced repeated periods of questioning whether or not I had cancer or an undetectable illness. I submitted myself to many medical and blood tests to rule out any illness; I also changed my diet and exercise routine, all in an attempt to remain healthy and to (irrationally) prevent cancer in some way. While I carried much of the anxiety of being diagnosed with cancer and enacted this outside of the therapy room, I was able to connect to the scared part in her. The enactment allowed us to connect to each other because I allowed myself to feel her very fears and she concurrently allowed herself to feel my care. Gina completed her chemotherapy and felt relieved at the prospect of not returning to the medical center where she was receiving treatment and "inhumanely treated by the doctor and nurses who forced me to accept the diagnosis". Gina was able to look back on her experience and find some solace in her ability to have survived the treatment process and ask her friends and siblings for assistance when she needed it. The rest of her time in her therapy focused on her finding meaning in her life post cancer diagnosis and treatment.

Making Sense of Experiences

In recalling Gina's case, I am reminded about the importance for a therapist to be aware of the latent messages being exchanged between patient and therapist. To understand what is being communicated through the therapeutic relationship and process, I needed to be mindful of the parts of both therapist and patient being played out in the process (Orange 2002). Winnicott (1974) refers to a truly transformative therapeutic process only being possible when the focus goes beyond just the transference and countertransference in the room. The therapy process should allow for the both patient and therapist to push boundaries in each other, so that the patient can feel that the therapist is able to survive the attempt at therapeutic destruction (Winnicott 1974).

At first, Gina and I did not have a strong therapeutic alliance because neither of us felt a rhythm or strong connection to each other. The first attempt at therapy with Gina was a struggle for both of us; I tried to reach her in a particular manner and perhaps she was not ready for that kind of intervention. Every attempt I made to show care and concern was met with hostility and anger, which could be seen as her attempt at destruction (Winnicott 1974). Working through the initial transference situation with Gina, where I was expected to be just like her mother, was difficult for me because she strongly expected me to behave in a manner that was not me. She wanted me to be emotionally cold, distant and unaware of her emotional needs. Attempts by the patient to evoke specific responses from the therapist often indicates the patient's need to allocate a specific transference identity or role to the therapist, resulting in the unconsciously reliving of the disturbed object relationship from the past (Sandler 1976). The transference was clear in my interaction with Gina, yet difficult for me to analyse. When exploring patient-induced countertransference, the therapist must apply the experience to the dynamics of transference with the patient.

In the situation of a strong compulsion to behave in a manner that is inconsistent with the self of the therapist, a process of complimentary identification is considered to be occurring (Racker 2007). This is a process that can be explored and discussed with the patient, but the patient's reaction to this material is unpredictable and something a therapist may wish to avoid as a means of protecting the relationship. However, it can then result in some form of an enactment. With Gina, however, towards the end of our first therapeutic interaction, I started to rebel against the complimentary identification process and tried to interpret her transference. She was not ready to hear or engage with the interpretation; this process in and of itself could be considered as an enactment on my part. I may have been actively trying to show her or provide her with a new experience but she rejected this different approach. She could not accept being vulnerable at the time and could not see my concern for her for what it was, that is, genuine concern and care, so she terminated the therapy. Possibly, my letting go of her was a form of complimentary identification enactment, where I did behave like the internal object representation she needed me to be—distant, but appreciative of her feelings, as her father had been. Further, given that I consider therapy as a co-constructed process, I needed to take into account my own personal process at that time. I was not feeling heard in my own personal life and with Gina not hearing me in the sessions, I added to the co-constructed communication in the web of countertransference experiences. I was forceful in trying to get my point across and less intent on her staying and working with me.

Of note is that countertransference is a compromise between personal tendencies and the unconscious role imposed upon therapists by patients. Therefore, therapists must always bear in mind that therapy is an interactional field with mutual influence, where both the patient and the therapist unconsciously affect each other while discovering aspects of their intrapsychic lives (Busch 2006, Racker 2007, Stolorow et al. 2002). It took Gina a year to recover from the initial process with me and then to become more aware of her own needs. She returned to therapy and was able to work through her needs and accept vulnerability. There was a different interaction the second time around. I felt she was able to trust me with more of her self and her needs. She was able to become vulnerable and form a healthy dependence on me, without viewing her dependence as a problematic way of being in the world. While Gina was struggling with her diagnosis of cancer, she became concerned with herself and her progress, sidelining the pattern in which she needed to be concerned about me and how I was dealing with her diagnosis.

In the dominant pattern as shown in her process with her mother, she was always concerned about how her mother would deal with information thus Gina could not explore her own feelings about the situation. I interpreted this as a sign of progression in our process, where she could separate me out from the internal object representation and see me for who I was and what I meant to her. She was no longer painting me with the same brush of past experiences.

I was, however, struck by my behaviours in the first 3 months following her diagnosis. I submitted myself to physical check-ups and blood tests, changed my diet and adjusted my physical exercise routine, all in an attempt to detect or prevent cancer. In relating these behaviours to my supervisor and therapist, I realised I was holding on to a part of Gina that she was not ready to cope with just yet: the part of her *self* that was struggling to accept the diagnosis of cancer. A form of concordant identification (Racker 2007) occurred, where Gina was projecting a part of her self onto me. When I realised what was happening in our process, I held on to that part of her, despite nudges from my supervisor to feed back to Gina her difficulty in accepting the diagnosis. I held that off and engaged in an enactment process through colluding with her in those moments of utter disbelief, anger and sadness around the diagnosis. Perhaps, I did not feel that I could put her through facing the cancer as the doctors and nurses did at the treatment centre. I wanted to create a space for her to explore what she wanted without having her choice to engage being removed. By the time we could both deal with the diagnosis, name it eventually, talk about its appearance in her life and examine its impact, she had already received four chemotherapy sessions and she was able to access the feelings of anger, sadness and disappointment about the cancer.

Countertransference enactments become conscious only after an unconscious acting-out has occurred (Shumsky and Orange 2007). Contemporary thinking around enactments argue that therapists have to engage in enactments to be aware of what the countertransference is about. Therapists need to be aware of what is being stirred up in them when they are present with a patient (Maroda 1998l, Shumsky and Orange 2007).

Although classical psychoanalytic theory argues for the negative influence of enactments on the therapy process (Renik 1993), contemporary literature argues against the negative influence (Maroda 1998, Ehrenberg 1992). Countertransference reactions and enactments are not always negative; they can impact positively on the therapy if utilised correctly. When therapists understand that countertransference enactments are "an attempt to actualise a transference fantasy" (Gabbard 1995, p. 479) and when therapists take the responsibility of understanding the transference fantasy and the need of the patient, the negative impact of an enactment becomes demystified.

Conclusion

Therapists' awareness of themselves and their own needs is as important as that of the patient and the patient's needs. Therapists need to be aware of physical, emotional and cognitive changes in themselves as these changes could form part of a countertransference experience that impacts on the therapy in positive or negative ways. It has long been thought that countertransference and countertransference enactments are unnecessary evils in a therapy process and that they should be banished and taken care of by the therapist. However, contemporary writings argue for an integration of countertransference as a useful tool in therapy, with enactments often serving as necessary evils that provide insights after the fact. Being aware of countertransference reactions allows therapists to better recognise when they deviate from the therapeutic frame or their usual ways of engaging with patients. Being able to hold onto the therapeutic frame and sense of self facilitates therapy as it allows for emotional neutrality, empathic listening and evenly suspended attention (Bion 1962, Haskayne et al. 2014, Hoffman 2006, Reich 1951, Wachtel 2008).

References

Alexander, F. and French, T. (1946). *Psychoanalytic therapy: principles and applications.* New York, NY: Ronald Press.

Aron, L. (1996). *A meeting of mind: Mutuality in psychoanalysis.* Hillsdale, NJ: Analytic Press.

Bateman, A., Holmes, J. (1995). *Introduction to psychoanalysis.* London: Routledge.

Bion, W. R. (1962). *Learning from experience.* London: Karnac.

Brandchaft, B. (1991). Countertransference in the analytic process. *Progress in Self Psychology*, 9, 209-230.

Busch, F. (2006). Countertransference in defense enactments. *Journal of American Psychoanalytic Association*, 54(1), 67-85. doi: 10.1177/ 00030651060540010501.

Campiao, P. (2012). The alliance the relational turn and rupture and repair processes in the therapeutic relationship: *The CAPA Quarterly*. 1, 12-35.

Ehrenberg, D. B. (1992). *The intimate edge: Extending the reach of psychoanalytic interaction.* New York, NY: Norton.

Falchi, V. and Nawal, R. (2009). Transference, countertransference and interpretation: The current debate. *European Journal of Clinical Hypnosis*, 9 (1), 11-18. Retrieved from http://www.ejch.com.

Fosshage, J. L. (2011). How do we "know?" what we "know?" and change what we "know?." *Psychoanalytic Dialogues*, 21, 55-74. DOI: 10.1080/ 10481885. 2011.545328.

Freud, S. (1910). The future prospects of psycho-analytic therapy. *Collected Papers*, 2, 289. London: Hogarth Press.

Freud, S. (1912). The dynamics of transference. *Collected Papers*, 2, 314-322. London: Hogarth Press.

Gabbard, G. (1995). Countertransference: The emerging common ground. *International Journal of Psychoanalysis*, 76, 475-485.

Gabbard, G. (2009). Transference and countertransference: Developments in the treatment of narcissistic personality disorder. *Psychiatric Annals*, 39 (3), 129-136. doi: 10.3928/00485713-20090301-03.

Gelso, C. J. and Carter, J. A. (1985). The relationship in counselling and psychotherapy: Components, consequences, and theoretical antecedents. *The Counselling Psychologist*, 13, 1 55-243.

Gelso, C. J. and Carter, J. A. (1994). Components of the psychotherapy relationship: Their interaction and unfolding during treatment. *Journal of Counselling Psychology*, 41, 296-306. doi: 10.1037/0022-0167.41.3.296.

Gelso, C. J. and Hayes, J. A. (1998). *The psychotherapy relationship: Theory, research, and practice*. New York, NY: John Wiley and Sons, Inc.

Gelso, C. J. and Hayes, J. A. (2002). The management of countertransference. In: J. Norcross (Ed.), *Psychotherapy relationships that work* (pp. 267-284). New York, NY: Oxford University Press.

Gilbert, M. and Orlans, V. (2011). *Integrative therapy: 100 key points and techniques*. London: Routledge.

Gold, J. and Stricker, G. (2011). Failures in psychodynamic psychotherapy. *Journal of Clinical Psychology*, 67, 1096-1105. doi: 10.1002/jclp.20847.

Greenson, R. R. (1965). The working alliance and the transference neuroses. *Psychoanalysis Quarterly*, 34, 155-181.

Haskayne, D., Larkin, M. and Hirschfeld, R. (2014). What are the experiences of therapeutic rupture and repair for clients and therapists within long-term psychodynamic therapy? *British Journal of Psychotherapy*, 30, 68-86. doi: 10.1111/bjp.12061.

Hatcher, L. R. (2010). Alliance theory and measurement. In: J. C. Muran and J. P. Barber (Eds.), *The therapeutic alliance: An evidence-based guide to practice* (pp. 5-25). New York, NY: Guildford Press.

Hayes, J. A. (1995). Countertransference in group psychotherapy: Waking a sleeping dog. *International Journal of Group Psychotherapy*, 45, 521-535.

Heimann, P. (1950). On countertransference. *International Journal* of *Psychoanalysis*, 31, 81-84.

Hill, C. E. and Knox, S. (2009). Processing the therapeutic relationship. *Psychotherapy Research*, 19 (1), 13-29. doi: 10.1080/ 10503300802621206.

Hoffman, I. Z. (2006). The myths of association and the potentials of the analytic relationship. *International Journal of Psychoanalysis*, 87, 43-61.

Ivey, G. (1999). Transference-countertransference constellations and enactments in the psychotherapy of destructive narcissism. *British Journal of Medical Psychology*, 72, 63-74.

Jennings, L. and Skovholt, T. M. (1999). The cognitive, emotional, and relational characteristics of master therapists. *Journal of Counseling Psychology*, 46 (1), 3-11.

Kasper, L., Hill, C. E. and Kivlighan, D. (2008). Therapist immediacy in brief psychotherapy therapy: Case study I. *Psychotherapy: Theory, Research, Practice, Training*, 45, 281-287.

Kernberg, O. (1965). *Countertransference in borderline conditions and pathological narcissism*. North Vale, NJ: Jason Aronson.

Kivilghan, D. M. and Shaughnessy, P. (2000). Patterns of working alliance development: A typology of client's working alliance ratings. *Journal of Counseling Psychology*, 47, 362-71.

Klein, M. (1946). Notes on some schizoid mechanisms. In: D. E. Scharff (Ed.), *Object relations theory and practice* (pp. 136-155). North Vale, NJ: Jason Aronson.

Lambert, M. J. (2007). Presidential address: What have we learned from a decade of research aiming at improving psychotherapy outcome in routine clinical care. *Psychotherapy Research*, 17, 1-14.

Lemma, A. (2003). *Introduction of the practice of psychoanalytic psychotherapy*. England: John Wiley and Sons.

Lipsey, M. W. and Wilson, D. B. (1993). The efficacy of psychological, educational, and behavioural treatment: Confirmation from meta-analysis. *American Psychologist*, 48 (12), 1181-1209.

Little, M. (1951). Countertransference and the patient's responses to it. *International Journal of Psychoanalysis*, 32, 32-40.

MacDevitt, J. W. (1987). Therapists' personal therapy and professional self-awareness. *Journal of Psychotherapy*, 24 (4), 693-703.

Mackewn, J. (1997). *Developing gestalt counselling*. London: Sage.

Macran, S., Stiles, W. B. and Smith, J. A. (1999). How does personal therapy affect therapists' practice? *Journal of Counseling Psychology*, 46 (4), 419-431.

Mahoney, M. J. (1997). Psychotherapists' personal problems and self-care patterns. *Professional Psychology: Research and Practice*, 28 (1), 14-16.

Maroda, K. (2004). *The power of countertransference*. Hillsdale, NJ: The Analytic Press.

Mitchell, S. A. (1988). *Relational concepts in psychoanalysis: An integration*. Cambridge, MA: Harvard University Press.

Mitchell, S. A. (1997). *Influence and autonomy in psychoanalysis*. Hillsdale, NJ: Analytic Press.

Norcross, J. C. (2000). Psychotherapist self-care: Practitioner-tested, research-informed strategies. *Professional Psychology: Research and Practice*, 31 (6), 710-713.

Norcross, J. C., Strausser-Kirkland, D. and Missar, C. D. (1988). The processes and outcomes of psychotherapists' personal treatment experiences. *Journal of Psychotherapy, Theory, Research, Practice, Training*, 25 (1), 36-43.

Orange, D. M. (2002). There is no outside: Empathy and authenticity in psychoanalytic process. *Psychoanalytic Psychology*, 19, 686-700.

Osborne, S. (2011). What do psychoanalysts mean by 'transference' and 'countertransference' and 'how do they contribute to the process of psychoanalysis? Retrieved from: https://www.essex.ac.uk/sociology/ documents/pdf/ug_journal/vol5/ 2011SC213_SamuelOsborne.pdf.

Racker, H. (2007). The meanings and uses of countertransference. *Psychoanalytic Quarterly*, 76, 725-777.

Reich, A. R. (1951). On counter-transference. *The International Journal of Psychoanalysis*, 32(1), 25-31. Retrieved from http://www.pepweb.org/.

Renik, O. (1993) Analytic interaction: Conceptualizing technique in light of the analyst's irreducible subjectivity. *Psychoanalytic Quarterly*, 62, 553-71.

Ringstrom, P. (1998). Therapeutic impasses in contemporary psychoanalytic treatment: Revisiting the double bind hypothesis. *Psychoanalytic Dialogues*, 8, 297-316.

Ronnestad, M. H. and Skovholt, T. M. (2003). The journey of the counselor and therapist: Research findings and perspectives on professional development. *Journal of Career Development*, 30, 5-44.

Safran, J. D. and Muran, J. C. (2000). *Negotiating the therapeutic alliance: A relational treatment guide*. New York, NY: Guilford Press.

Sandler, J., Dare, C. and Holder, A. (1992). *The patient and the analyst: The basis of the psychoanalytic process*. London: Karnac.

Sandler, J. (1976). Countertransference and role responsiveness. *International Review of Psychoanalysis*, 3, 43-47.

Satir, D. A., Thompson-Brenner, H., Boisseau, C. L. and Crisafulli, M. A. (2009). Countertransference reactions to adolescents with eating disorders: Relationships to clinician and patient factors. *International Journal of Eating Disorders*, 42, 511-521. doi: 10.1002/eat.20650.

Schaverien, J. (2007), Countertransference as active imagination: Imaginative experiences of the analyst. *Journal of Analytical Psychology*, 52, 413-431. doi: 10.1111/j.1468-5922.2007.00674.x.

Segal, H. (1986). *Delusion and artistic creativity and other psycho-analytic essays*. Free Association Books. New York, NY: Norton.

Seligman, S. (2003). The developmental perspective in relational psychoanalysis. *Contemporary Psychoanalysis*, 39, 477-508.

Shumsky, E. and Orange, D. (2007). Our first fight: Reflections on the psychoanalytic concept of enactment. In: P. Buirski and A. Kottler (Eds.), *New developments in Self Psychology practice* (pp. 181-192). Jason Aronson (an imprint of Rowman and Littlefield Publications).

Skolveldt, T. M. and Ronnestad, M. H. (1995). *The evolving professional self: Stages and themes in therapist and counselor development*. Chichester, England: Wiley.

Stevens, C., Muran, C., Safran, J., Gorman, B. and Winston, A., (2007). Levels and patterns of the therapeutic alliance in brief psychotherapy. *American Journal of Psychotherapy*, 61, 2.

Stiles, W. Glick, M. Osatuke, K. Hardy, G. Shapiro, D. Agnew-Davies, R. Rees, A. and Barkham, M. (2004). Patterns of alliance development and the rupture-repair hypotheses: Are productive relationships U-shaped or V-shaped? *Journal of Counselling Psychology*, 51 (1), 81-92.

Stolorow, R. D., Atwood, G. E. and Orange, D. M. (2002). *Worlds of experience: interweaving philosophical and clinical dimensions in psychoanalysis*. New York, NY: Basic Books.

Sullivan, H. (1953). *The interpersonal theory of psychiatry*. New York, NY: Norton.

Wiseman, H. and Shefler, G. (2001). Experienced psychoanalytically oriented therapists' narrative accounts of their personal therapy: Impacts on professional and personal development. *Psychotherapy*, 38 (2), 129-141.

Wampold, B. (2000). Outcomes of individual counselling and psychotherapy: Empirical evidence addressing two fundamental questions. In: S. D. Brown and R. W. Lent (Eds.), *Handbook of counselling psychology* (3rd ed.) (pp. 711-739). New York, NY: John Wiley and Sons.

Wachtel, P. L. (2008). *Relational theory and the practice of psychotherapy*. New York, NY: Guilford Press.

Walters, D. (2009). Transference and countertransference as existential themes in the psychoanalytic theory of W. R. Bion. *Psychodynamic Practice*, 15 (2), 161-172. doi: 10.1080/14753630902811367.

Waska, R. (2008). Using the counter-transference: Analytic contact, projective identification, and transference phantasy states. *American Journal of Psychotherapy*, 62 (4), 1-19.

Winnicott, D. W. (1974). Fear of breakdown. *International Review of Psychoanalysis*, 1, 103-107.

Zachrisson, A. (2009). Countertransference and changes in the conception of the psychoanalytic relationship. *International Forum of Psychoanalysis*, 18 (3), 177-188. doi: 10.1080/08037060902727761.

Zetzel, E. R. (1956). Current concepts of transference. *International Journal of Psychoanalysis*, 37, 369-378.

In: Psychoanalysis
Editor: Zelda Gillian Knight

ISBN: 978-1-63483-858-0

Chapter 8

SOME ARTICULATIONS BETWEEN THE SYMBOLIC EXCHANGE IN ARCHAIC SOCIETIES AND THE DONATION OF BIOLOGICAL MATERIAL IN CONTEMPORARY SOCIETIES: THE PSYCHOANALYTIC VIEW

Simone Perelson[1,*], PhD, and Maria Isabel Fortes[2], PhD
[1]Universidade Federal do Rio de Janeiro, Rio de Janeiro-RJ, Brazil
[2]Universidade Católica do Rio de Janeiro, Rio de Janeiro-RJ, Brazil

ABSTRACT

In this chapter, we will seek to articulate the logic implied in the donations of engenderment material (semen, eggs and embryos), practiced in the field of the new reproductive technologies (NRT), with the system of exchanges of some archaic societies described by Marcel Mauss in his famous essay *The gift: forms and functions of exchange in archaic societies* (1924/1967). This articulation will also be elaborated in the light of three important interpreters of this essay – Lévi-Strauss, Maurice Godelier and George Bataille – so as to present some consequences that the NRT pose to psychoanalysis and vice versa.

Keywords: new reproductive technologies, exchange system, gift, excess

* Corresponding author: Simone Perelson. Professor of the Graduate Program in Psychoanalytic Theory and of the Undergraduate Communication's Course at Universidade Federal do Rio de Janeiro, Brazil. E-mail: simoneperelson@oi.com.br.

INTRODUCTION

From the middle of the last century onwards, with the development and practice of the so-called new reproductive technologies (NRT), a new way of making children and, consequently, building families, began to take place. Today, this development is already well advanced and this practice has become not only widespread but also quite familiar. While anthropology has greatly examined in recent years the elements put into play by these technologies, psychoanalysis has shown a rather timid approach regarding this topic. A major contribution to this arid field is the articulation suggested by the psychoanalyst Geneviève Delaisi de Parseval between the logic implied in the donation [*don*] of engendering material – semens, eggs and embryos – and the one described by Marcel Mauss, concerning the forms of exchange he unveiled in the archaic societies, in his famous *The gift: forms and functions of exchange in archaic societies* (1924/1967)[1]. In this chapter we intend to explore the articulation suggested by the psychoanalyst, not only in Mauss formulations on the *gift*, but also in three interpreters of his essay – Lévi-Strauss, Maurice Godelier and George Bataille –, in order to extract some consequences and therefrom explicit some questions that NRT pose to psychoanalysis and vice versa.

Before going any further, it is necessary, however, to observe that in this first paragraph, there already subtly appear a series of issues that would each require a full explanation. Firstly, what are the so-called NRT and to what extent can we assure their novelty over previous reproductive practices? Given the scope of this issue, it would not be possible to deal with it properly here. For our purposes, we will just focus on the so-called new reproductive technologies, involving breeding practices in which a technical act replaces the sexual act in the origin of life (artificial insemination and *in vitro* fertilization) and the material of its engendering (eggs, semens or embryos) is made available (manipulated, stored, frozen, discarded, donated or sold) out of the body (considered until recently its natural receptacle).

Secondly, it must be clarified that, since the success rates of the most sophisticated treatments barely reach 40% today, the advancement of NRT to which we refer concerns less the result and the effectiveness of the treatments than the diversification and complexity of their techniques.

Thirdly, it is worth noting that, while we argue that NRT have become familiar nowadays, we deem relevant to highlight the double meaning of the term "familiar" (common or banal but also pertaining to a family), as we are aware of the serious risk implied in using such a term. In other words, to eclipse its uncanny (*unheimlich*) character, the fact that, in such practices, the family appears in the guise of the new and the new appears in a familiar way. Claiming that they have become familiar, however, does not mean denying that the new reproductive practices cause estrangement, bewilderment and amazement.

Having made these three points, we can now enter our field of research.

The new reproductive (and family-building) practices include, as mentioned above, the provision of engendering material out of the body, which, in turn, becomes liable to circulation, marketing (allowed only in very few countries, including the United States) or donation, among other purposes. It is precisely the circulation of this material, now increasingly present both in the making of children and in the creation of social ties (between donors, recipients and human beings generated by donations), that seems to demand serious

[1] In French the same word - "Don" - means both donation and gift.

thought. How to understand this *uncanny* circulation of an equally *uncanny* material, increasingly present in the formation of new families and societies?

The medical and legal devices moved swiftly, in all countries where the engendering material circulation was put into play, to impose norms that might regulate this circulation properly. Although there is great diversity in the regulation in different countries, and these have been promoting in recent years major changes to their norms, they are basically reduced to five elements: absence of payment, anonymity, medical confidentiality, phenotypic similarity and selection criteria for donors and recipients. The first two norms seek, respectively, to support the ideas that the foundation for the circulation is altruism, which should not give rise to any form of family tie between the adults themselves, i.e., recipients and donors, or between them and the donation's fruit, i.e., the children. Maybe owing to risks that remain dormant, announcing somewhat insistently that things might not happen as expected, the last three rules could be useful if it proves necessary to refuse the return of the repressed, either the disclaimed reality or the foreclosed real: in other words, the presence of some kind of tie (not exactly kinship as we understand it nowadays) and other affects other than altruism.

Of course, medical and legal rules (in Brazil, more medical than legal) do not homogenize the meanings (conscious and unconscious) nor the absence of meaning, that the exchange system of the engendering material imposes on the singular subjects that are part of it. It is not our intention to approach them here, as it could only be done on a case by case basis and would not admit generalizations. The goal of our investigation is more precisely to seek some theoretical tools that would enable us, however partially, to bring light, or even half-light to the uncanny (*unheimlich*) character of this new form of circulation that today underlies family and social ties. A character that is alarmingly present, yet clearly avoided by repression, denial or foreclosure.

The approach to this character, simultaneously *founding* and *uncanny*, of the circulation of engendering material inherent to the NRT will be introduced here by means of the important reading undertaken by Lévi-Strauss of the *The gift: forms and functions of exchange in archaic societies* (1924/1967) by Mauss. Then, we will explore the articulation proposed by Geneviève Delaisi de Parseval (1994) between the logic regulating the donation and the logic that, in her view, should regulate the gifts of gametes and embryos. Then, we will present the distinction proposed by Godelier between the three categories of objects – those to be sold (goods), those to be given (the objects of gift and counter-gift) and those not to be sold or given, but kept to be transmitted (sacred things). Finally, we will discuss three forms of exchange identified by Maurice Godelier – the exchange of women, the *kula* and the *potlatch* – the last, in particular, will raise the interest of Bataille, a philosopher who will lead us to the questions and formulations which will conclude this chapter.

Mauss and Lévi-Strauss: The Gift and the Structural Logic of the Exchange of Women

In the introduction to *The gift: forms and functions of exchange in archaic societies* (1924/1967), Marcel Mauss exposes briefly his program: the description of the exchanges carried out in various civilizations around us or immediately before us, in the form of gifts, in theory voluntary and free, but actually interested or, more precisely, compulsorily given and retributed. Not only useful things would be exchanged but, first of all, "pleasantries, banquets, rites, military, women, children, dances, festivals, fairs."

Anyway, it still surprises the anthropologist that most of these exchanges are marked by the principle of rivalry and antagonism, so that the aim of the donation is largely to defy the donee (the head of the rival tribe), placing him in a position of inability to retribute in a similarly high standard.

The type of exchange that takes this logic to the extreme is the *potlatch*. We will return to this particular type of exchange later. For now, it must be pointed out that, according to Mauss, the morality and economy implied in this necessary form of exchange, which makes us suppose that there is, in the thing given, a force that causes the donee to be obliged to repay it and of which the market is only one of the moments. Such force is still steadily at work in our societies, even underlying them. For this reason, the anthropologist believes to have found in it one of the human rocks on which our societies are built.

These formulations will be fundamental to lead Lévi-Strauss, in his *Introduction to the work of Marcel Mauss* (1924/1987), to point out that, for the first time in the history of ethnological thought, the social becomes a system. In other words, he reveals that the seemingly random events of social life (such as birth, marriage and death) can be reduced to a limited number of logical combinations among an equally limited number of determined symbolic elements. The careful reader of Mauss can thus formulate his own conception: every culture can be considered as a set of symbolic systems, at the fore of which lie language, matrimonial rules, economic relations, art, science and religion.

But it is not in any symbolic system that Mauss will find the foundation of society, but in the one which is adequate to 'the gift,' an act that comprises a threefold need – giving, receiving, retributing – creating debts and establishing a relation of proximity and distance between donor and donee.

Based on the influence of Mauss, one of the main Lévi-Strauss projects is defined: to clarify the logic of the various gifts and counter-gifts of women present in different societies, while laying out their differences and their common point, as well as underscoring the fact that it is always a particular update in a general structure of women exchange that underlies the place of the social foundation. Thus, as different as the numerous societies – archaic or modern – may be, they always result from different, however limited, logical combinations of certain symbolic elements that constitute a single structure. In conclusion: the exchange of women lies at the foundation of every society; different, though limited, forms of exchange of women lie at the foundation of various societies in their own times and places.

However different thousands of human societies may seem, they cannot help but refer to a common logical structure. That is why the structuralist interpretation is, according to the anthropologist, an operation of the same kind that, in psychoanalysis, enables us to reconquer our uncanniest self and in the ethnological research, makes us reach the uncanniest of others, as if it were another self of ours (Lévi-Strauss 1924/1987).

The reading Lévi-Strauss undertakes of Mauss serves, firstly, as an important gateway to support the idea that the gifts circulating today in NRT do not have as a consequence only the possibility to enable infertile people or couples to have children. Its consequences and meaning may have a much wider range: they can, in fact, involve major changes with regard to the foundations of contemporary sociability, i.e., the logic governing the social ties that lie at its base.

Secondly, his reading indicates how the structuralist interpretation favors the recognition of the uncanny (*unheimlich*) character of the particular logic of exchange specific to each society. Here, the author could not be more Freudian: the uncanny is the same in the form of the alterity or the alterity in the form of the same. So, thinking about the uncanny specific to the engendering material circulation in NRT implies articulating this circulation to other forms of circulation that occurred, or occur, in other societies, or in our own, in order to reveal how the well-known appears, today, under new forms and how the new appears under an old form. It means realizing that our bewilderment regarding the NRT does not derive from its absolutely new and unknown character, but rather from the relation they put into play between the traditional and the new, the known and the unknown. In fact, as mentioned above, the legal and medical devices seek to transform the new forms of reproduction and filiation into a copy of the old well-known "natural reproduction" (establishing itself as a simulacrum of that), and in some countries, such as France, for example, into a copy of the traditional *heterosexual monogamous family*. This is the first form under which the *uncanny* appears. On the other hand, Mauss, as we have seen, when listing things exchanged in the building of our societies, mentions children and women. We know the circulation of children has always happened and continues to happen in all societies, according to a logic specific to each of them. As for women, we saw that Lévi-Strauss raises them to the rank of the most precious object of exchange lying at the origin of society, the very explicitation of the structure governing their exchange being thus crucial to understanding them.

Today, however, a new object of exchange, the engendering biological material, and its new logic, or rather, new forms of logic, seem to impose themselves replacing the circulation of children and women, emerging as the foundation of new forms of social ties.

What relation can be established between these three forms of circulation? Is it possible to think in terms of a displacement (or exchange) of precious objects of exchange that lie at the foundation of our society: no more children or women, but gametes and embryos?

It is possible to think that the logic shown by Lévi-Strauss to be present in the exchange of women appears updated in a new way, in the circulation of engendering material?

Is it possible then to see on the latter the presence of a known logic in an unknown way?

Before seeking to answer these questions, giving meaning to the eventual displacement at issue, for the time being it concerns us, above all, to support its coming onto the stage, pointing out that there are no few limits to the formulation of a meaning or response both to this possible displacement and to these necessary inquiries.

Indeed, the formulation of these issues relates to our effort not to explain, but at least to get around the uncanny character of the circulation of engendering material. For this purpose, the articulation suggested by Geneviève Delaisi de Parseval between the gift and the circulation of engendering material in NRT will be invaluable.

Mauss and Geneviève Delaisi De Parseval: The Gift and the Donation of Engendering Material

Geneviève Delaisi de Parseval is a psychoanalyst who has devoted many years to a research on parenting and new reproductive technologies, having collaborated on numerous bioethics committees. She is quite vehement in her criticism of the French medical and legal logic governing the donations of engendering material, and proposes, instead, what she calls a *relational ethics* (1994). The formulation of this ethic will build largely on her reflection on the meaning of the *gift* as revealed by Mauss. It is, in fact, sustained by her reading of Mauss that the psychoanalyst notes, firstly, that every gesture of gamete donation – and, we may add, of embryos – "is inscribed, like any gift, in a logic of exchange and counter-gift" (Delaisi de Parseval and Verdier 1994, p. 148), so that "the medical institutions should favor the expression of these counter-gifts" (ibid p. 153). It is as the favoring of this expression that relational ethics will be understood and supported by the psychoanalyst. That implies, of course, putting into question the guiding idea of the logic governing the device of engendering material donations: the *disinterested and altruistic gift*. As Geneviève Delaisi de Parseval (1994) observes:

> "The supposedly disinterested gift is a fiction that gives too much importance to the intention of the giver (…). By refusing any possibility of reciprocity, we cut the fact of giving from its social context and deprive it of all its relational significance. But no one is fooled by these allegations on the grounds of principles and as we see the perverse effects induced by the affectation of disinterested generosity, (we realize) it would have been better that the gift had never existed." (Delaisi de Parseval and Verdier 1994, p. 156-57)

Secondly, the author argues that it is necessary to understand that what is given, under the guise of simple biological substances, "is life" (ibid p. 148). It is also given "fantasms that will feed the family romance of the children who will be born thanks to donors" (ibid). It is given, ultimately, *fils* – a term that in French has the double meaning of *children* and *ties*. It is shown here not only that what is given is not of the order of the economically useful things, but also that the gift in question produces social ties.

Thirdly, based on etymology, ethnology and on psychoanalysis itself, Parseval highlights the ambivalent aspect of the *Gift* donated. Note that, in classic German, the term has a double meaning: *present* and *poison*. Ethnology, in turn, shows that all parts and detachable substances (waste) from the body (semen, blood, milk, hair, etc.) are, in all traditional societies, perceived as linked to *magic*, with all the ambivalence it entails. They are furthermore considered *impure* objects, and, from a cultural as well as a fantasmatic point of view, impurity is bound to the anal area. It is Freud, in turn, who, revealing the unconscious chain of symbolic equivalences (excrement – gift – child – money), will allow the psychoanalyst to impart a metapsychological sense (including the economic sense) to the engendering material (in this case, more particularly, to the semen), to these *body wastes*, which, before being donated, are stocked in institutions or banks that "treat them, retain them, transform them into samples, finally, act in the manner of bankers in their dealings with money" (ibid). In addition, the *secret ties* are also donated. In other words, the secret acts as a knowledge that is experienced by the protagonists in the way of anal *retention* and *domination*. To complete the elements that update the symbolic chain, the psychoanalyst refers us to the etymological relationship between *secret* (secret) and *excrement* (feces).

Finally, as shown in ethnology, the separation and circulation of such body waste always give way to purification rites. Hence, it becomes possible to understand the role played by the institutions that store the engendering material, which involves purifying (desexualizing) this material and allowing its circulation.

According to the psychoanalyst, this is a very important role, either in the psychoanalytic point of view, as a phobic and obsessive ritual, or in the ethnological point of view, as a rite of passage and separation.

The parallel suggested here between phobic and obsessive rituals on the one hand, and transit and separation on the other is provocative and stimulating. Certainly, the approach to this complex approximation would require an extensive analysis, a task that cannot be considered unimportant. Nevertheless, we will stick here just to the indication that the phobic and obsessive rituals may allow, in some way, the separation between the subject and the deadly enjoyment, which is what Lacan, in fact, maintains, when he addresses the symptom by the perspective of the *sinthome* (Lacan 1975-76/2005). He also does not miss that the symptom is, in its nature, enjoyment (Lacan 1962-63/2014). As a matter of fact, this paradoxical relationship between symptom and enjoyment underlined by Lacan is nevertheless indicated in the equivalence, revealed by Freud, between gift, child, feces and money. It is revealed here, in fact, the relationship between the precious currency market exchange – the so helpful money – and feces, a useless waste product of the body.

Banks and institutions where substances of enjoyment (sperm) and useless body waste (eggs and supernumerary embryos) are stored not only purify these materials, allowing them to become objects of exchange (exchanges that are neither purely altruistic nor clearly mercantile). They are, in fact, the locus where countless complex *transmutation* reactions between *altruism*, *mercantilism* and *eroticism* are produced; as well as between *separation* and *alienation*; between *utility* and *futility*; between *lack* and *excess*. Maybe it is not for nothing that one of the main difficulties posed both to bioethicists and to subjects entangled in NRT, is the ominous passage that they operate from the *representation* of a *lack* of children to the *non-representable* one, of an excess of embryos (Corrêa 2001).

From their reading of Mauss' essay, Maurice Godelier and George Bataille provide us with major elements to think *that*, described insistently by Mauss as an *unthinkable excess* at the very core of a logic understood by many authors (against which our reflection is addressed) as grounded in the *mere objective donation of biological material*, either in the *absolute purity of the altruistic and desinterested gift of life*, or, in short, in the *complete perverse mercantilization of man*. In addition, they provide us with important tools to reflect on the merits and limits of the relational ethics proposed by Parseval.

Aiming at approaching this unthinkable excess, ignored by the understandings referred to herein, as well as developing a reflection on the relational ethics, we will examine next the contributions of these two authors.

Godelier and Bataille: The Exchange of Women, the Kula and the Potlatch

The efforts made by Godelier, in his reading of *The gift: forms and functions of exchange in archaic societies*, will be directed, mainly, to the distinction between objects circulating in the donation, movement whose logic of circulation is revealed by Mauss, and objects that escape this logic, either because they are put, as a commodity for sale, or because, due to their sacred character, they are not put into circulation, but saved to be transmitted. The French anthropologist proposes to explore the distinctions that exist between the things that are sold, the ones that are given and, finally, those that should not be either sold or given, but kept to be transmitted. The same object can successively be purchased as a commodity, circulate as a gift and counter-gift and finally, remain hidden in a clan hoard as a sacred thing, therefore escaping for a while any form of circulation, mercantile or not (Godelier 2007).

In this chapter, we address only the objects that circulate in the donation. We deem it interesting, however, to explicit the distinction formulated by the author, not only because it provides an important insight into the particularity of these objects, but also because it leads us to launch a question. Would the circulation of engendering material be operating nowadays a mix of these three types of objects? And would this happen by means of the mercantilization of gametes and embryos, or through the inclusion of the embryos in the gift circuit, as these are objects heavily invested, imaginarily, with a sacred character? Regarding the latter possibility, it is worth reminding that, today, it is no longer God, but our genetic code that supposedly underlies the guidelines of our destiny.

Before seeking to answer this question, which does not seem possible yet, let us analyze the three examples of exchange described by Godelier. We will observe that each of them gives us important clues to examine different elements present in the engendering material circulation.

The first example comes from his own observation: it is the *exchange of women* in Baruya society. In the situation, the author points out that, contrary to what one might think, reciprocal counter-gifts do not cancel the debts that each clan engendered with its gift, what indicates that "give back" (*redonner*) is not "return" (*rendre*). What happens as a result of reciprocal gifts is that each clan "is at the same time superior to the other as a donor, but inferior to the other as a donee" (Godelier 2007, p. 75). Thus, what is produced is not the mutual cancellation of debts, but its *balance*. "On account of this logic, observes the anthropologist, gift and counter-gift permanently feed obligations and debts, that generate flows of services and reciprocal solidarity" (ibid.). Here the difference is clear between the commercial exchanges that, when complete, delete any link between donor and recipient, and the exchanges of gifts, which, even when compensated with counter-gifts, leave an underlying link among those who participated in the prestations: a ballast of a double and contradictory relationship of power, though somewhat inclined toward balance.

We have indicated above the possibility to be faced today with an important and intriguing displacement: if Lévi-Strauss saw in the exchanges of women and more particularly in the logic governing them, the basis for the rules of kinship and social organization, the present times offer us new forms of gifts – gametes and embryos – which may eventually lie at the foundation of new forms of kinship and social ties. Contrary arguments about the relevance of speaking of effective transformations in this field divide many researchers from various fields such as anthropology, sociology, law, psychoanalysis and bioethics, but what is undeniable is that we can no longer escape from this issue.

Instead of taking sides for or against the conception of the emergence of new ties, we deem relevant to ask, from this first example approached by Godelier, some questions. Would not the logic that mostly governs NRT be contradictory, inasmuch as it seeks at the same time to oppose any form of mercantilization of donations and refuses the establishment of any form of bond between donor and donee?

As we have seen, Delaisi de Parseval criticizes this logic. In her view, preventing the donee from returning the gift puts him in an extremely vulnerable situation, due to the eternal debt to which he becomes subject.

This is why she proposes a relational ethics, which would favor the gift restitution. But according to Godelier (1996/1999), as we have also seen, the restitution does not cancel the debt, it only allows the establishing of a double and *balanced* power relationship between donor and donee. Is it then worth questioning in what form, or forms – either socially instituted or uniquely invented – could the donee could return an engendering gift so as to establish a balance in power relations? And how to understand this balance? Would there be, then, any real possibility of achieving it? Or does relational logic propose something impossible? Those are some of the questions that Godelier's comments regarding the exchange of women he observed led us to formulate.

We will leave these questions open in order to approach now the second example of exchange commented by Godelier (1996/1999). It is the *kula*, a practice observed by Malinovsky among the Trobriand Islanders, and referred to by Mauss as the most solemn of a vast system of prestations and counter-prestations. In the *kula*, a *precious object* is put into circulation by its owner to receive another object instead. What is intriguing here is that this precious object, when released, continues, even after given, to be a the possession of the donor. His donee owns it on a temporary basis (the donor may at any time ask for its restitution) and has no right of ownership over it, but only of use – exclusive use to make other gifts. As Godelier notes, the *kula* highlights the fact that the donated objects are *alienated* in the circulation of gifts, while remaining, at the same time, inalienable property of the originary donor.

Here, the similarities between the *kula* objects and the engenderment material, as well as the questions that these similarities lead us to, seem to creep into the scene more clearly. Both are transmissible property that may be circulated in the form of gifts, but nevertheless remain the inalienable property of the originary donor. This specter haunts, in fact, all technological reproduction devices. It is not enough to state that filiation is always a social and psychological construction and never a mere genetic fact: the fantasm remains. And what if it is not simply, as several authors argue, the hegemony of biologizing speech or the genetics empire that lie at the base of the persistence of this persistent fantasm, but the unconscious knowledge – social and unique – that, in the donations of engendering material, what is donated does not separate from his donor?

If we take seriously Mauss and Godelier, we must not reduce the fantasies related to the power of donors – fantasies quite frequently posing donees in fragile situations to sustain the integrity of their maternity or paternity – only to generate confusion among genitors and parents. We must consider that between these two terms, a third arises: the donated engendering material. Hence, a greater complexity appears, demanding new approaches, which cannot be reduced to that plain old opposition between what is *constitutively genetic*, on the one hand, and what is *culturally or subjectively produced*, on the other.

The third example approached by Godelier, which we will focus on, because of its importance to our reflection, is the *potlatch*, a practice present in some indigenous tribes of the American Northwest, which expresses the apex of the antagonist gift. What is put into circulation in the *potlatch*, with the purpose of conquering or retaining titles, status, or power, are ostentatious – *excessive* – donations of wealth during festivals or competitions by the chiefs of tribes, in order to humiliate, challenge or subjugate a rival.

As the anthropologist points out, in the *potlatch* "we are no longer in the logic of non-agonistic gifts and counter-gifts, that culminate in a relatively equal distribution of resources necessary for the reproduction of social groups" (Godelier 2007, p. 77).

On the contrary, the real potlatch is the one that makes it impossible to retribute. Thus, this social practice achieves its best performance when the gift acquires such a force it makes impossible any retribution on the part of the opponent. In the *potlatch* something is given to 'crush' the other with this gift. This is why one gives more than (what one thinks) the other could give or retributes much more than what he gave. As with non-agonistic gifts and counter-gifts, the gift-potlatch indebts and obliges the one who receives it, but the intended goal is explicitly to make it very difficult, if not impossible, to retribution with an equivalent gift; it is to put the other almost permanently in debt, to cause him to lose his prestige publicly and so to affirm, as long as possible, one's own superiority.

Thus, rather than the formation of social ties marked by balance, such as in the case of the *kula*, the ties produced by the *potlatch* are necessarily marked by the *imbalance of power*.

But donations here do not happen exclusively through excessive gifts: there may also occur spectacular *destruction* of wealth itself. There are examples of sumptuary destruction of slaves, dogs, village fires and sinking of canoes. Thus, it is also specific to this form of gift the fact that it is marked, rather than by the principle of ownership, by the principle of loss. In *potlatch*, in fact, the greatest power for a chief refers to his ability to lose. Material goods must be dilapidated so that it immaterial gains occur, that is, the honor and the glory are an acquisition parallel to the economic loss.

The wealth appears as an acquisition, as power is purchased by the rich man, but it is entirely directed to the loss, in the sense that this power is characterized as the power of losing. It is only through the loss that the glory and the honor are bound to him.

We can state, then, that the object circulating in the *potlatch* is approximately a *cumulative surplus* for *dilapidation*. If we follow the reflection of Caillé (1998), there is in this form of gift the statement of an anti-utilitarianism par excellence; the pointing to the realm of what in human societies escapes the domain of utilitarian reason or servicing of goods. However, according to the author, the uniqueness of Marcel Mauss's theory is not only the statement that social order is irreducible to utilitarian economic order. This postulate is hardly a novelty, because we find it in classical sociology in authors such as Weber, Simmel and Tocqueville. The novelty of the gift paradigm would be the fact that it proposes a "positive anti-utilitarianism" (Caillé 1998), which appears as the foundation of another social order. Regarding the readings about the *potlatch*, the fact that it is governed by the principle of loss led the philosopher Georges Bataille to elaborate the notion of *waste* to think of a form of economy that would govern both individuals and social systems. Bataille highlighted the *potlatch* as a social order that necessarily demands the dilapidation of assets.

The understanding of the dilapidation of goods has been elaborated by Bataille in an essay called "The notion of expenditure" (1933), in which he claimed there existed within social groups, in permanent endemic state, an excess energy that needed to be spent. The central ideas of this essay were much later reworked in his book *The accursed share: an essay on general economy* (1949/1991).

Thus, Bataille (1933/1985; 1949/1991) proposes that the notion of unproductive expenditure would indicate an economic activity opposed to the principle of classical utility. If to utility the important thing is the acquisition and preservation of its assets, reproduction and preservation of life, conversely it appears that there is a domain of human society which aims at the loss and wastage of goods. It does not seem possible for the domain of utility to conceive that a human society may have an interest in considerable losses in disasters that cause, according to defined needs, tumultuous depression, anxiety attacks and, ultimately, a certain orgiastic state. Therefore, there is a contradiction between the classical social conceptions and the real needs of society, in which the demand for dilapidation lies.

Thus, the principle of loss claims that consumption can be either for the use of the energy needed for the preservation of life and the species, or for unproductive expenditure, the first motor power of economic institutions. This form of dilapidation appears in parties, in luxury, war, games, funerals, spectacles and various other social activities.

The French philosopher points out that classical economics would not suppose that the exchange had as cause not the need to purchase, but rather, the demand for destruction and loss. The economic concepts developed by Bataille are therefore a kind of reversal of the common economic thought, since the dimension of excess is necessarily included in the exchange system.

CONCLUSION

If the *kula* puts into play the fundamental question of the inalienable character – be it imaginary, symbolic or real – of engendering material, the *potlatch* takes us precisely to the presence of what remains in the new reproductive technologies as excess, and more precisely, as *excess* purposedly produced to be *dilapidated*. We refer to what constitutes the main theme of the current bioethical discussions: the so-called supernumerary embryos. In fact, the new forms of people making, supposedly governed by rational management, instrumental reason or calculating logic, suppose, at least thus far, the production of an *uncanny remainder*, an *unwanted leftover* or a *inconvenient surplus*.

It is essential, however, to observe, as did Caillé about the *potlatch*, that the production of this excess – which will remain frozen until a destination (transfer, donation or disposal) is given – is not merely an occasional deviation of management, reason and logic as mentioned above. On the contrary, it lies at its core, as an *enabling condition*. Without the production of a greater number of embryos than the ones to be transferred to the woman, there would be meager chances of successful results in the treatment. Hence, the new forms of people making depend not only on the circulation of the engendering material (in its supposedly rational management), but also on the production of an excess that, given the difficulties of its representation and the subjective difficulties to give it a destination, put into play the folly and the vulnerability both of the techniques and of the subjects involved in them.

It should be noted that if, in the *potlatch*, the voluntary dilapidation of the goods is a way for the subject to assert his power, the so-called disposal of embryos – or, conversely, the excess discard ban (which occurs, for example, in Brazil) – brings to scene rather the *denial of power*, the *bewilderment* and *helplessness* of the subjects, that have to deal with a remainder, with which they do not know what to do, nor how to represent or call it, either.

It is worth pointing out some of the issues philosophically formulated by bioethicists or imaginarily raised by donors and donees, about the surplus embryo status. Would it be a living being or a dead thing? A simple biological material or a child waiting for parents to adopt it by a transfer to an uterus? A mere disposable and marketable thing or a potential person whose dignity should be protected? The double impossibility – either to avoid the formulation of these questions or to provide them with an answer – outlines the contours of the traumatic or even catastrophic nature of the surplus embryos universe.

This difference does not cancel, however, the fact we are keen to point out: at the foundation of the alleged utilitarian reason governing the new forms of reproduction lies the necessary production of excess marked by the impossibility of representation and bound to dilapidation. Life production and expenditure, reproduction and disposal, get entangled here to such an extent that we cannot help thinking that the leading NRT motive power may not be directed to enable the rational management of reproduction by autonomous individuals but, conversely, to foster the excessive production of life to be disposed by thunderstruck subjects.

Bataille was puzzled with the odd relationship established in *potlatch* between, on the one hand, the social production of considerable, distressing or even catastrophic losses and, on the other hand, a certain orgiastic condition. Bringing this relationship to the context of NRT, we are led to seek to make explicit what we understand as a latent and powerful relationship between utilitarian reason – which seeks to control, in a calculating way, the reproduction of man and society – and anti-utilitarian reason, which constitutes the driving power of an excessive production of life potentiality intended for orgiastic dilapidation.

References

Bataille, G. (1933/1985). The notion of expenditure. In: A. Stoekl, C. R. Lovitt and D. M. Leslie, Jr. (Eds.), *Visions of excess: Selected writings, 1927-1939* (pp. 116-129). Minnesota: University of Minnesota Press.

Bataille, G. (1949/1991). *The accursed share: An essay on general economy, volume 1.* New York, NY: Zone Books.

Caillé, A. (1998). Neither holism nor methodological individualism. Marcel Mauss and the paradigm of the gift. *Journal of Social Sciences*, 13 (38), 5-38.

Corrêa, M. (2001). *New reproductive technologies. Limits of biology or biology without limits?* Rio de Janeiro: Eduerj.

Delaisi de Parseval, G. and Verdier, P. (1994). *No one's child.* Paris, France: Odile Jacob.

Godelier, M. (1996/1999). *The enigma of the gift.* Chicago: Chicago University Press.

Godelier, M. (2007). *The foundations of human societies: What we learn from Anthropology.* Paris, France: Albin Michel.

Lacan, J. (1962-63/2014). *Anxiety: Book 10, The seminar of Jacques Lacan.* Malden: Polity Press.

Lacan, J. (1975-76/2005). *The symptom: Book XXIII, The Seminar of Jacques Lacan.* Rio de Janeiro: Jorge Zahar.

Lévi-Strauss, C. (1924/1987). *Introduction to the work of Marcel Mauss.* London, UK: Routledge and Kegan Paul.

Mauss, M. (1924/1967). *The gift: Forms and functions of exchange in archaic societies.* New York, NY: Norton Library.

INDEX

A

B

C

I

J

K

L

M

N

O

P

T

U

V

W

Y